THE
ABANDONED GOSPEL

THE
ABANDONED GOSPEL

*Confronting Neo-Pentecostalism
and the Prosperity Gospel
in Sub-Saharan Africa*

editors

Philip W. Barnes,
Bazil Bhasera,
Matthews A. Ojo,
Jack Rantho,
Trevor Yoakum,
Misheck Zulu

The Abandoned Gospel

Copyright © 2021 by Philip W. Barnes

All rights reserved.

ISBN: 978-9-9661-2144-8

Dewey Decimal Classification: 276
Subject Heading: AFRICA--RELIGION / NEO-PENTECOSTALISM /
CHRISTIAN HERESIES

Cover design and digital collage illustration by Emily Keafer Lambright. Cover images © NiseriN, Kendal Swart, HuntImages, shilh, and NNehring / iStockphoto; DigitalMagus, neung_pongsak, JeremyWhat / shutterstock.

Printed in Africa

1 2 3 4 5 6 7 8 9 10 • 25 24 23 22 21

CONTENTS

PART 3: CHURCH PLANTING AND CHURCH DEVELOPMENT

Foreword

Chuck Lawless

As I write this foreword, the world is reeling with the spread of the novel coronavirus. Nations have been locked down. Borders have closed. Travel has come to a halt. Business owners have been required to close their businesses. No matter where we live, this virus has somehow affected all of us.

In some ways, this crisis has reminded us just how connected we are with each other. From one sick person in East Asia has spread a virus that has touched the majority of countries around the world. The world is so interconnected that a crisis in one city has become a crisis in many cities.

Scientists around the world are seeking cures and developing vaccines we trust will help return life to some sense of "normal." Somebody somewhere will eventually find an answer, and word will spread quickly. Herd immunity that protects the masses may develop at the same time. In either case, prevention will be a primary means to halt the spread of infection.

The Abandoned Gospel is about preventing another kind of virus—a theological virus—that is spreading around the world. The growth of

Neo-Pentecostalism and the prosperity gospel has influenced much of the world. Even in the most conservative churches at times, the promise of health and wealth has diverted the attention of leaders and congregations from the true gospel. Instead, they have turned to a false one that focuses more on the temporary than on the eternal. The enemy's forces of deception are at work, and they are winning far too often.

This book, however, reminds church leaders to cling to the true gospel. It aims for a clear gospel focus that prevents the spread of false teachings. It is a continuation of the work my friend and colleague Dr. Randy Arnett began years ago with his work, *Pentecostalization: The Evolution of Baptists in Africa*. Randy and his wife, Kathy, loved Africa. Walking with them through West Africa was a lesson in African history, cultural awareness, worldview discipleship, and healthy missiology. Randy was particularly concerned about the spread of the prosperity gospel, and he committed his life to addressing this issue and raising up leaders to combat it. This volume—prayerfully the first of several tools to accomplish this task—fittingly honors Randy and Kathy, who tragically died in an automobile accident in Africa in 2018.

All the authors of this book live in Africa, just like Randy and Kathy did. They are not just theoreticians speaking into culture; they are African church leaders and missionaries, all scholar practitioners living in the crucible of the spread of Neo-Pentecostalism. They have seen its negative effects. They know its powerful pull, even on believers. They grieve its influence on individual lives and local churches. For some, even friends and family members have gone astray under its sway.

At the same time, though, they love their peoples, and they speak with a uniquely African voice into this conversation. They know God's call on their lives to stand for the truth of the gospel on the magnificent continent of Africa. From that continent will rise a new generation of African pastors, theologians, and missionaries—all who will have opportunity to touch the nations with the gospel. I trust this book will encourage church leaders to focus so strongly on the true gospel that their teaching will help prevent the continued spread of false teachings around the world.

Chuck Lawless
Dean of Doctoral Studies and Vice-President for Spiritual Formation
Southeastern Seminary
Team Leader, Theological Education Strategists
The International Mission Board

Introduction

Philip W. Barnes, PhD, Malawi

Mangoes and bananas are both fruit, but a mango would never be confused for a banana. They look different, they smell different, they taste different, and they grow on different kinds of trees. Even though these two types of fruit are very different, it is possible that someone could inadvertently eat the wrong one. Doing so, however, would not result in any major negative consequences, since most people find them both quite tasty and both are good for your health. Meanwhile, different forms of pills may look similar while having completely different chemical properties. One small white pill might treat a headache while another small white pill is rat poison. Knowing how to spot the difference in this case is a life-and-death ability. Although different formations and presentations of the gospel may look similar to many people, one is healthy, and one is deadly. The aim of this book is to help readers see thoughtful and conviction-based discernment is of supreme and eternal value when applied to the Christian faith in Africa.

The authors hope that after reading this volume you will be able to see and understand the difference between a gospel-preaching, Bible-believing church and a Neo-Pentecostal and prosperity gospel group in the same way that you can tell the difference between a life-giving medicine and life-taking poison. While both a banana and a mango are sweet and useful for replenishing one's strength and energy, Neo-Pentecostalism and the prosperity gospel are both poisonous pills that are deadly to the life of individuals and churches, slanderous to the purity of Christ's bride, and dishonouring to our Creator God and Christ.

In this introduction, I will help to answer some questions that the reader is sure to have. I will look at why we are undertaking this project. I will discuss to whom this project is targeted. I will talk about questions regarding the where and who of the project. Finally, I will look at the what and how of the volume you hold in your hands.

WHY?

Why are we concerned with false teaching and bad doctrine? There are at least two main reasons. First, both Jesus and Paul warned us that false teachers would come. In Matt 7:13–23, Jesus warned about false teaching using several different images. In the first image, Jesus taught that the road to hell is broad and that the way to life is narrow and difficult. In contrast, Neo-Pentecostal teachers tend to describe the road to eternal life as one of ease and leisure. In the second image, Jesus warned against false prophets by describing them as ones who look like innocuous sheep but are actually rancorous wolves. Prosperity gospel teachers use language that is familiar to Christian audiences and even quote Scripture, but they twist and pervert the Word of God to make it appear to mean whatever their depraved minds have conceived.

Jesus took His third image from agriculture. Good trees produce good fruit. Bad trees produce bad fruit. By watching the fruit of the labours of Neo-Pentecostal preachers and teachers, one will be able to see that they are simply bad trees. Greed, manipulation, a lack of integrity, and an overall dishonest approach to ministry are the hallmarks of many of these self-proclaimed prophets, apostles, and shepherds. Although we may not know the hearts of different individuals, Jesus does call us here to examine fruit. After these three images, Jesus gave a stark and dire warning: "Not everyone who says to me, 'Lord, Lord,' will enter the kingdom of heaven."[1] We should not be deceived into thinking that everyone who utters the words "Jesus is Lord" is a true gospel teacher.

In Acts 20:28–31, Paul warned the Ephesian elders that false teachers would arise from both within and without. These false teachers would not bring a message of truth and salvation that leads to the glory of Christ but of falsehood and deceit that leads to the glory of the teacher. These false teachers will be motivated by a desire to gather followers for themselves and not to make disciples of Jesus. The result of following these false teachers will be worse than death—it will lead to eternal damnation. The church elders (i.e., the shepherds) are commanded by the apostle to guard both themselves and their flocks against these wolves.[2]

As we have seen from both Paul and Jesus, the first reason that we wrote this book is because ignoring false teachers is direct disobedience to Scripture. Likewise, in considering the claims of prosperity teachers, the heart of the gospel and, by extension, the lost world are at stake. The lost world needs a witness. Romans 10:9–13 teaches that believing in and confessing Jesus as Lord is the irreducible requirement for salvation.

---

[1] Matt 7:21.

[2] Notice, of course, that Paul uses the same imagery as Jesus. The false teachers are wolves, and the elders are shepherds armed for protecting their sheep from these predatorial heretics.

Paul follows the logic of this truth by declaring that since the confession of Jesus's saving work is necessary, so must proclamation of the gospel be necessary. If what the church professes and shares with the world is not the true gospel but a false distortion of it, then the world will not hear the true message of the Scriptures. If the gospel is not heard, then people will not be saved. Since the lost world's ability to hear and believe the gospel is at stake, we must seek to guard the gospel from these various forms of false teaching.

Additionally, the bride of Christ must be pure. In Eph 5:22–33, we learn that in His death Jesus was motivated by His love for the church and His desire to keep her pure. His desire to keep the bride of Christ holy and blameless led Him to make the sacrifice that He made. The concept of purity is multifaceted. While many associate the concept of purity only with moral spotlessness, the biblical concept of purity includes the idea of theological purity. From the condemnation of idolatry throughout the Old Testament to the New Testament commands to hold fast to truth (Titus 1), theological purity is a theme of Scripture. Sharing Christ's desire to keep His bride holy should be normative for all those who seek to shepherd the church. Let us have the same passion for the church's purity.

Finally, God deserves the glory of the nations. In Psalm 96, the psalmist connects the glory of God among the nations to the declaration of His power, sovereignty, righteousness, and faithfulness. When we abandon the gospel for a false message of temporal prosperity and earthly blessings, we rob the Creator of the glory that is due from His creation. In the end, of course, this robbery will not be complete, and in God's providence, He will gather worshipers from every tribe, tongue, people, and nation.[3]

---

[3] Rev 7:9.

Nonetheless, when we abandon the gospel for a heretically false teaching, we stand in opposition to God's plan to be glorified by all peoples.

There are many types of false teachings in the world, and specifically in Africa, today. I regularly see Mormons and Jehovah's Witnesses in the town in which I live—Lilongwe, Malawi. These groups represent a dangerous trend that also must be addressed. However, we believe that Neo-Pentecostal and prosperity gospel teachings represent the clearest and most present danger to the evangelical faith in Africa today. We have chosen, therefore, for this volume to be focused on these two dangerous groups.

To Whom?

This book is targeted to several different groups. First, we hope that evangelical theological institutions such as Bible colleges and universities, divinity schools, departments of theology, and seminaries will take heed of the warnings in this book and will seek to prepare their students to confront and reject false teaching wherever they find it. We hope and pray that across the continent these schools will develop contextualized, locally relevant, and indigenous curriculum to address in a head-on manner the local manifestations of these issues. We pray that principals, presidents, academic deans, and other administrators will develop curriculum to address these issues. We also pray that individual lecturers will see the need to address these problems in their lesson planning and day-to-day teaching as they provide practical guidance and application in their various courses.

Second, given that all the authors of this book are Baptists, we pray that Baptist conventions, fellowships, and unions across Africa will all benefit from this book. We also hope that like-minded evangelical denominations will use this resource to defend the faith from these assaults on biblical Christianity. None of us can ignore the infestation and decaying rot of Neo-Pentecostalism and the prosperity gospel. This false teaching must be identified, cut out, and attacked wherever it is found—especially at the denominational level.

Third, we pray that pastors will benefit from this book as they seek to shepherd the men and women God has given them. A shepherd is both a guardian and a caregiver. In the imagery of the shepherd in Psalm 23, the staff is a tool for keeping sheep on the right path while the rod is a tool for warding off dangerous wolves. Both of these images—one of guidance and one of protection—should inform the work of pastors. Pastors should not be afraid to throw the rod at wolves that come in to devour their flock. Likewise, pastors should make use of their staffs to guide and direct their flock to the right path—the gospel. Doctrinal and theological discussions can sometimes lose sight of the fact that we are dealing with individuals who have backgrounds, stories, families, fears, and griefs that are unique to that individual. This book is for those men who will seek to pastor and care for their flocks in a way that shows sensitivity to those issues while remaining passionately resolute to proclaim the gospel that many churches and pastors have tragically often abandoned.

Finally, this book is for individual Christians who are tempted to abandon the gospel of Jesus Christ. The apostle Peter commanded all Christians to be able to give a defence of their faith.[4] We pray that this resource will help individuals to fulfill that command and also help them to encourage others to remain faithful to the gospel.

---

[4] 1 Pet 3:15.

Where?

Philip Jenkins has shown us that the worldwide center of Christianity is shifting southward.[5] This shift means that the next century's theologians will arise from places like South America, Asia, and Sub-Saharan Africa. The voices of the Sub-Saharan African church are speaking. The worldwide church needs to hear. As African churches and individuals "contend for the faith that was delivered to the saints once for all,"[6] we pray that this resource—which has been written and developed in African soil—will be a useful tool for these African shepherds and saints.

Who?

Every author in this book calls Africa his or her home. Many of the contributors are native-born Africans. Others are missionaries who have made their homes here. Some have been in Africa for many decades, and others have arrived more recently. All of the contributors are involved in African churches and are deeply concerned with both the current state of the church as well as its long-term health. We are also all individuals with our own experiences, opinions, and specific concerns. Given this diversity, it is safe to assume that the more than twenty authors will not all agree with one another on every point in this book. This diversity of opinion is to be expected and even celebrated as we sharpen one another.

---

[5] Philip Jenkins, *The Next Christendom: The Coming of Global Christianity* (New York: Oxford University Press, 2002); Philip Jenkins, "The Future of World Christianity Is African," TGC (The Gospel Coalition), August 7, 2020, https://www.thegospelcoalition.org/article/future-christianity-african/.

[6] Jude 3.

The debate concerning Neo-Pentecostalism and the prosperity "gospel" is not merely an academic one for us. Our families, friends, communities, and countries are suffering at the hands of charlatans, heretics, and wolves. We refuse to stand by while the Evil One seeks to steal, kill, and destroy the church of Jesus Christ.[7] History has shown us that once-vibrant, Bible-believing societies can become post-Christian wastelands much more quickly than one might imagine or even fear. We will not be bystanders in that slaughter.

WHAT?

This book represents the beginning of a comprehensive and cooperative strategy to seek to protect the gospel and safeguard the Scriptures from false teaching across Africa. While all forms of false teaching are concerning and problematic, we are particularly concerned with false teaching that masquerades as biblical preaching and teaching. This concern has driven us to address what we have identified as the biggest current threat to the evangelical faith in Africa—Neo-Pentecostalism and the prosperity gospel. These twin false teachings are not merely different flavours of the same fruit. These teachings are dangerous and damning lies. Instead of reconciling people to God in Christ, these false teachings pave the way to an eternal hell.

HOW?

This book represents our efforts to build on the work that Dr. and Mrs. Randy Arnett started before their untimely death in a road accident in

---

[7] John 10:10.

the Democratic Republic of the Congo in early 2018. Randy's book, *Pentecostalization: The Evolution of Baptists in Africa,* sparked thinking, conversations, and concerns across this great continent—especially among Baptists.[8] Randy and Kathy spent most of their adult lives in Africa. They loved Africa, and they loved Africans. Even greater than their love for Africa and Africans was their love for Jesus, Jesus's bride, and the Word of God. We pray that this book will build upon the Arnetts' legacy and passion for truth.

This book is divided into three sections. The first section deals with the history and development of Neo-Pentecostalism and the prosperity gospel. The second section seeks to give biblical responses to various Neo-Pentecostal and prosperity gospel practices. The third and final section is directly based on Randy's recommendations for the foundation of church planting and church development in his final chapter of *Pentecostalization.*

If the Lord wills, this book represents the first phase of a multiphased/multi-year educational series that will address the dangers of Neo-Pentecostalism and the prosperity gospel in Africa. By God's grace and for His glory, our organization, AB316, will seek to both develop and facilitate the development of all manner of resources that will provide individuals, churches, and institutions the tools they need to protect the gospel and safeguard the Scriptures from these dangerously false teachings.[9]

---

[8] Randy Arnett, *Pentecostalization: The Evolution of Baptists in Africa* (Eldon, MO: CreateSpace, 2017).

[9] Please see the AB316 website, at http://www.ab316.org.

CONCLUSION

Nearly one hundred years ago, American theologian J. Gresham Machen declared that "naturalistic liberalism is not Christianity at all."[10] By this declaration, Machen was saying that Liberalism is not an alternate form of Christianity that one can critique on certain points of doctrine and engage in a debate. Instead, Machen was saying that Liberalism is an altogether different religion. The difference between Christianity and Liberalism was not like the difference between Methodism and Presbyterianism. The difference was like the distinction between Islam and Hinduism—two completely different religions with completely different presuppositions and approaches to the search for Truth.

The authors of this book contend that the evangelical church in Africa (and indeed around the world) must rise up and say the same thing about any and all aberrant faiths and false churches. This particular volume will lay this charge against the various movements and groups that can be categorized under the heading of the prosperity gospel and Neo-Pentecostalism. These two (overlapping) groups represent a religion that has abandoned the gospel and is now preaching a gospel that is no gospel at all. This message has been stripped of its power to save, its power to transform, and its power to reconcile. Only by returning to the gospel can the church in Africa be a useful tool in her Master's hands. May God grant us the grace to "contend for the faith that was delivered to the saints once for all."[11]

---

[10] J. Gresham Machen, *Christianity and Liberalism*, rev. ed. (1923; repr., Grand Rapids, MI: Eerdmans, 2009), 52.

[11] Jude 3.

PART 1

HISTORY AND DEVELOPMENT

Chapter 1

An Overview of the History of Neo-Pentecostalism in Africa

Matthews A. Ojo, PhD, Nigeria

Christianity was first introduced to Egypt and Roman North Africa (presently Libya, Tunisia, and parts of Algeria) in the third century AD from Palestine and Asia Minor. However, the military conquests of the Muslim Arabs in the seventh century almost wiped out the Christian faith, with only the Coptic Church in Egypt remaining as a minority religion. Between the fifteenth and eighteenth centuries, Portuguese commercial voyages brought Roman Catholic missionaries to the West African coast, São Tomé, Príncipe, Congo, and Angola, but conversion was limited to a few in the palaces of the indigenous rulers. However, it was the sustained evangelical missionary activities initially promoted from the United Kingdom—and later from other European countries and North America beginning in the early nineteenth century—that resulted in the planting of Christianity in Africa.

Among the factors that assisted in the Christianization of Africa were the evangelical awakening in Europe, the abolition of the slave trade, the search for legitimate trade to replace slave trade, missionary advances, the settlement of freed slaves in Liberia and Freetown, the subsequent founding of European colonies in Africa, and European settlements in East and Southern Africa. By the end of the nineteenth century, Christianity was firmly established in most parts of Africa with the introduction of Western school systems, the establishment of medical missions with the building of hospitals and dispensaries, the introduction of industrial missions to give marketable skills to African converts, the emergence of trained African clergy, on whose shoulders the new phase of Christian advance rested, and the emergence of the educated elite who later became political leaders of independent Africa.

Christianity is a literary religion, and the power of literacy produced translations of the Bible into various African languages. The British and Foreign Bible Society, founded in London in 1804, helped greatly in the translation and publication of the Bible or portions of it in many African languages.[1] The cumulative effect of this literacy and the promotion of indigenous languages was a development that, according to Lamin Sanneh, stimulated indigenous assimilation and produced indigenization with its variety.[2]

The response of Africans to the introduction of Christianity varied. Initially, nationalist agitation caused secessions from the mission churches in the 1880s to produce Ethiopianism. In the first two

---

[1] T. A. Beetham, *Christianity and the New Africa* (London: Pall Mall Press, 1967), 54.

[2] Lamin Sanneh, *Translating the Message: The Missionary Impact on Culture* (Maryknoll, NY: Orbis Books, 1989).

decades of the twentieth century, visionary prophet-healers emerged to promote an indigenous version of Christianity, later referred to as African Independent Churches. Interdenominational faith missions entered Africa in the early twentieth century. From the late 1930s, North American Pentecostal missions planted classical Pentecostal churches, which remained small and insignificant until the early 1970s.

BEGINNINGS OF THE PENTECOSTAL AND CHARISMATIC MOVEMENTS

Beginning from the early 1970s, a new form of Christianity emerged with the rise of Pentecostal and Charismatic movements. A Charismatic renewal in the early 1970s among students in Evangelical Christian Union groups at Nigerian universities stimulated a new spirituality that emphasized a radical conversion experience similar to that of the apostle Paul. Baptism of the Holy Spirit and speaking in tongues as subsequent and definite experiences were added to this emphasis on radical conversion. With a strong emphasis on literal interpretation of the Bible, they also condemned the nominalism in the mainline Protestant and Catholic churches. Later, the new spirituality also emphasized the power to heal all kinds of diseases and perform miracles just as Jesus did in the Gospels. Parachurch organizations emerged from this Charismatic renewal, and they promoted evangelism, power over all demonic forces, and healing for all.[3]

---

[3] Matthews A. Ojo, "The Charismatic Movement in Nigeria Today," *International Bulletin of Missionary Research* 19, no. 3 (1995): 114–18. See also Matthews A. Ojo, "The Contextual Significance of the Charismatic Movements in Independent Nigeria," *Africa: Journal of the International African Institute* 58, no. 2 (1988): 175–92.

Generally, in East Africa, Neo-Pentecostalism partly benefited from the fading *Balokole*, or East African Revival, which had flourished as a lay pietistic movement in the mainline Protestant churches in the region from the 1930s. Others built upon such revivalist ethos. For example, one major religious episode in Tanzania was The Big November Crusade, a non-denominational revival programme first held in Dar es Salaam in November 1986 with the cooperation of the mainline Protestant churches. This event promoted crusade evangelism, but it later stimulated independent Charismatic ministries when some preachers emphasized the manifestations of the Holy Spirit.[4] In addition, the Charismatic renewal spread to secondary schools and higher institutions, where it caused divisions in the Christian Union groups. However, by 1982 the gap between the Charismatics and evangelicals had narrowed.

In Kenya, one can track a number of trajectories to understand the emergence of Charismatic Christianity among college and high school students and the founding of independent Charismatic churches from the 1970s. First, indigenous Pentecostals like Joe Kayo, who had been converted in a T. L. Osborn crusade around 1957, preached among young people and eventually established the Young Ambassadors Christian Fellowship, which soon metamorphosed into an independent Charismatic church, the Deliverance Church of Kenya, in November 1970. Similar groups also emerged by the late 1970s. Second, the Kenya Students Christian Fellowship, an indigenous evangelical student group, and the Fellowship of Christian Unions (FOCUS), which linked several

---

[4] Josiah R. Mlahagwa, "Contending for the Faith: Spiritual Revival and the Fellowship Church in Tanzania," in *East African Expressions of Christianity*, ed. Thomas Spear and Isaria N. Kimambo (Oxford: James Currey, 1999), 296–306.

national evangelical Christian Unions, facilitated the spread of the Charismatic renewal across borders starting in 1974. By the mid-1970s, the campuses of Kenyan higher institutions had witnessed the renewal. The emphasis on personal salvation experience, intense prayer life, and healing taught in various camp meetings encouraged the formation of several evangelistic outreaches.[5] In Uganda and Ethiopia, political instability and the harassment of students in higher institutions partly delayed the emergence of the renewal in these countries until the early 1980s. Lastly, the thrust of Nigerian Neo-Pentecostal missionaries into Kenya from the late 1970s further built upon the existing Charismatic revival activities and encouraged more Pentecostal innovations.

Southern African countries like Zimbabwe, Malawi, and Zambia experienced the renewal from the early 1980s through evangelistic visits and distribution of literature by Charismatics from other countries. In South Africa, apartheid gave white classical Pentecostals the lead until the late 1980s, when blacks established a number of Neo-Pentecostal churches in Johannesburg. Visits from Ghanaian and Nigerian evangelists in the 1990s stimulated further growth in Neo-Pentecostalism.[6] French-speaking Africa witnessed the Charismatic renewal only from the

---

[5] Philomena N. Mwaura, "The Role of Charismatic Christianity in Reshaping the Religious Scene in Africa: The Case of Kenya," in Afe Adogame, Roswith Gerloff, and Klaus Hock, *Christianity in Africa and the African Diaspora* (London: Continuum, 2008), 180–92. See also Damaris S. Parsitau, "Radical Christianity in Kenya: A Case Study of Deliverance Church in Nakuru District" (master's thesis, University of Nairobi, Kenya, 1997).

[6] Allan Anderson, "New African Initiated Pentecostalism and Charismatics in South Africa," *Journal of Religion in Africa* 35, no. 1 (2005): 66–92.

mid-1980s, largely as a result of the missionary activities of Nigerian Pentecostal and Charismatic groups.

Apart from its evangelical background, the revival manifested Pentecostal spirituality mixed with African participatory ethos. From the early 1980s in Lagos, Nigeria, these itinerant evangelists preached regularly in public conveyances as the buses moved from one place to the other. Richard van Dijk, a Dutch scholar who examined similar religious phenomena in Malawi in the 1980s and early 1990s, described these evangelists as "young puritan preachers."[7] This face of Christianity, and particularly its expression among Africans in the Diaspora in Europe and North America, has attracted the attention of the media and scholars of religion.

Although an indigenous initiative, foreign imports, mostly of American televangelists and faith preachers, came later in the forms of evangelistic visits, distribution of literature, sponsorship of church planting efforts, and networking. Moreover, open-air evangelistic services held by Westerners introduced new evangelistic methods and partly gave impetus to Africans in setting up their own Pentecostal organizations. A clarification is needed here. Pentecostals are those Christians who believe in the baptism of the Holy Spirit as a definite experience after conversion, either accompanied with speaking in tongues or not, and who belong to the classical Pentecostal churches where these beliefs have been institutionalized. On the other hand, Charismatics, or Neo-Pentecostals,[8] also accept the beliefs of baptism of the Holy Spirit with or without speaking in tongues as private experiences, but many have their membership

---

[7] Richard A. van Dijk, "Young Puritan Preachers in Post-Independence Malawi," *Africa: Journal of the International African Institute* 62, no. 2 (1992): 159–81.

[8] The two terms are used interchangeably.

in mainline Protestant churches, or from the 1990s in the independent Charismatic churches.

The explosion of Pentecostal and Charismatic movements since the 1970s constitutes major growth points for Christianity in contemporary Africa as the new churches proliferated under apostles, prophets, general overseers, and self-styled bishops. This new evangelism was also promoted by and through literature, crusades, camp meetings, "Fire or Holy Ghost or Power" conferences, "Holy Ghost Nights," healing and deliverance services, and so on, which were constantly and generously advertised in the media. By the mid-1980s, the young Puritan preachers were already establishing their own groups as bases for their new evangelism, and in the new millennium, some were broadcasting on digital satellite television.

Indeed, by the early 1990s, many of these groups had become independent Pentecostal and Charismatic churches, adding a new zeal to African Christianity. From about ten independent Charismatic organizations in the mid-1970s largely restricted to Nigeria, the number grew to more than 5,000 groups across Nigeria by 2000. By 2000, the membership had become substantial with about 8 million of the estimated 48.42 million Christians in Nigeria,[9] about 2 million of the Christian population in Ghana,[10] not less than 400,000 in Cameroon and Côte d'Ivoire, about 300,000 in each of Benin and Burkina Faso, about 150,000 in

---

[9] Figures worked out from Annual Percentage Growth statistics and other reports released by the National Population Commission of Nigeria between 2002 and 2007.

[10] Data culled from the *National Church Survey, 1993 Update* (Accra: Ghana Evangelism Committee, 1993), 1–15.

Togo, and about 2,000 in Niger Republic.[11] It is remarkable that within four decades the Pentecostal and Charismatic movements have moved from being a fringe religion into a position of social and religious prominence in many countries, as they presented themselves as alternative centres of power to solve human problems that the centralized state failed to address.

THE DYNAMICS OF TRANSNATIONAL RELIGIOUS NETWORKS AMONG NEO-PENTECOSTALS

Perhaps the greatest Pentecostal leader to foster the expansion of Neo-Pentecostalism to other African countries was Benson A. Idahosa (1938–98), founder of the Church of God Mission International Incorporated, which was established in Nigeria in 1970. Claiming a divine mandate to preach the gospel all over the world, he inaugurated the Idahosa World Outreach in the mid-1970s as an organ to advance his evangelistic campaigns. He was the first African evangelist to promote the prosperity gospel, and he demonstrated this with his flamboyant lifestyle and by his emphasis on faith, miracles, and prosperity. By the mid-1980s, Idahosa had traveled to about seventy-six countries, and during these evangelistic campaigns he initiated networking with other African Pentecostals.[12]

---

[11] Data condensed from information gathered during personal field works in West Africa between 1996 and 2000. See also Patrick Johnstone and Jason Mandryk, *Operation World: 21st Century Edition,* 6th ed. (Carlisle, UK: Paternoster Lifestyle, 2001), 140–41, 208–9, and 624–25.

[12] *Redemption Faith* magazine (official voice of Idahosa World Outreach), November 1985, 8–9.

In the early 1980s, when he began his television programme, *Redemption Hour*, he was already emphasizing prosperity, which he had imbibed from his American mentors: T. L. Osborn, Oral Roberts, Gloria and Kenneth Copeland, and Gordon Lindsay. Second, it was through Idahosa's Bible school, All Nations for Christ Bible Institute (ANCBI), in Benin City, Nigeria, which some Africans attended on scholarship, that a new class of prosperity preachers in many parts of Africa was created. For example, among the graduates in 1988 were fifteen students from Ghana, seven from Chad, two from Zimbabwe, three from Kenya, two from Cameroon, four from Côte d'Ivoire, and one each from Sierra Leone and Togo.[13]

Most of Idahosa's disciples returned to their countries with strong Pentecostal convictions and became pioneers and "giants" of Pentecostal awakenings. Among these was Nicholas Duncan-Williams, who in 1979, upon his graduation and return to Ghana, established the Christian Action Faith Ministries International as Ghana's first indigenous Charismatic church. The associate bishop of the Christian Action Faith Ministries (CAFM), Bishop James Saah, also trained at ANCBI and for about a decade served as the editor of the *Redemption Faith* magazine while working with Idahosa in Nigeria. Bishop Charles Agyin-Asare also trained in Nigeria in 1986 and later established the World Miracle Bible Church, one of the largest Charismatic churches in Ghana.[14] Likewise, Pastor Suleiman Umar also trained at ANCBI and upon his return to Niamey, Niger Republic, established *Eglise Vie Abondante* in 1990 as the first

---

[13] *Redemption Faith* magazine, March–April 1988, 8.
[14] Paul Gifford, "Ghana's Charismatic Churches," *Journal of Religion in Africa* 24, no. 3 (1994): 241–65.

independent Charismatic church in the country.[15] In Kenya, Margaret Wangari, the founder of Anointed Christian Fellowship, Banana Hill, who had been a healing evangelist from her high school days, also trained at Idahosa's Bible school in the early 1980s and was further mentored to become the first female Pentecostal champion in the country.[16]

Another key African leader is David Oyedepo, who became the leading pastor of the Living Faith Church in Nigeria in 1984. Oyedepo was ordained by Idahosa as a Pentecostal bishop in 1988. Among his bold thrusts in Africa was the African Gospel Invasion Programme (AGIP), which he initiated in late 1995 and through which he established thirty branches in the state capitals of other African countries and promoted the emphasis on prosperity and "productive faith." In 2002, he further initiated the Africa Maximum Impact Summit, which according to him is a campaign to bring change to Africa. The first two summits were held in Lusaka, Zambia, and Nairobi, Kenya, in June 2002, while the third one was held in August 2002 in Accra, Ghana, and another one in Yaoundé, Cameroon, in September 2002.[17] Oyedepo's emphasis on material prosperity indirectly tapped into the discourse of modernity and offered a motivation to many young Africans seeking upward social mobility.

---

[15] Interview with Pastor Suleiman Umar, Niamey, Niger Republic, March 1997.

[16] See Bishop Margaret Wangari, "Woman Without Limits—Bishop Margaret Wangari Ngugi (PART 1)," Rev. Kathy Kiuna, May 25, 2017, YouTube video, 51:12, https://www.youtube.com/watch?v=-kg6h17o6vU; and "Woman Without Limits—Bishop Margaret Wangari Ngugi (PART 2)," Rev. Kathy Kiuna, June 5, 2017, YouTube video, 51:13, https://www.youtube.com/watch?v=T0g3EF6rZ44..

[17] *The Winners' World*, July 2002, 1–2.

GROWTH AND STRUCTURAL CHANGES WITHIN NEO-PENTECOSTAL MOVEMENTS

The phenomenal growth of Pentecostal and Charismatic movements in Africa since the 1970s is partly linked to the movements' mode of transmission as a transnational phenomenon. There are substantial transnational networks, some of which are missionary in intention, fostered by Nigerian and Ghanaian Pentecostal and Charismatic churches in other African countries and beyond as they compete for geographical extension. Improvement in road and telecommunications networks and the subsequent promotion of economic integration across Africa have opened new possibilities for trans-border expansion for religious movements.

Neo-Pentecostal groups originally were inter-denominational or non-denominational and operated only during the weekdays, with their members still claiming to be members of the existing Protestant churches. By the early 1980s, several had become new independent Charismatic denominations. This change was marked by the beginning of Sunday services. Soon after, paid clergy, mostly associates of the founders and later some others who were trained in their own Bible schools, emerged. By the early 1990s, some had erected their own church buildings. More important, the messages shifted from personal evangelism to baptism of the Holy Spirit, healing, miracles, and prosperity. All were seen as paradigms for personal empowerment. To a large extent, these changes were conditioned by the socio-economic changes in the society. Also, the routinisation partly streamlined and created doctrinal and structural partitions among the Pentecostal organizations.

Recent attention has been drawn to the impact of Neo-Pentecostalism on the theology and ecclesiology of mainline Protestant churches in

Africa.[18] In fact, as noted by Randy Arnett in his study of this issue, many Baptist churches in West Africa since the 1990s have reflected Neo-Pentecostal teachings and practices even when some of these expressions are not biblically normative but are syncretistic variations of classical Pentecostal teachings and worldviews of African Traditional Religion.[19] Responses to this challenge of Neo-Pentecostal emphases have been varied, but generally concerns have been expressed on how to uphold the evangelical faith in this contemporary era.

ESSENTIAL FEATURES OF NEO-PENTECOSTALISM

Charismatic organizations show interesting variety. Some are large while others are small. Some continue to grow across the continent and are attracting media attention, while many have atrophied and died or merged with bigger groups. Consequently, each has its uniqueness and often appeals to different classes of people. Hence, Pentecostal and Charismatic movements exhibit many characteristics that make them different from any existing religious movements.

First, Neo-Pentecostal organizations have a large membership of mostly educated young adults who are mobile and fluent in the English language (or French in the Francophone countries). This class of educated elite generally is mostly facing the challenges of succeeding in the contemporary competitive world, and Pentecostal emphases such as the

---

[18] The first of such studies is Cephas N. Omenyo, *Pentecost Outside Pentecostalism: A Study of the Development of Charismatic Renewal in the Mainline Church in Ghana* (Zoetermeer, NL: Boekencentrum, 2002).

[19] Arnett, *Pentecostalization* (see intro., n. 8).

doctrine of prosperity and success provide the stimulation for personal upward social mobility.

Second, Charismatic Christianity is largely an urban phenomenon and a middle-class religion. Pentecostal and Charismatic organizations address their messages to the contemporary problems of the urban areas, such as joblessness, unemployment, loneliness, inadequate health care, poverty, and so on. Besides, urban areas provide much of the economic resources needed to run the massive organizational structures of some of these Neo-Pentecostal churches.

Third, the movements promote a religion that is market-oriented, success-directed, very optimistic, imbued with a can-do mentality, and Charismatic in style. These groups often are made up of ever growing multi-ethnic congregations largely using English as a medium of communication.

Fourth, despite their modern outlook, African Pentecostalism is steeped in primal worldviews that have been made elastic to accommodate existential questions about life, whether in its traditional moorings or in its modern perspectives. Hence, with their emphases on demonic oppression, spiritual warfare, and healing and deliverance activities, it is evident that Neo-Pentecostals continue to grapple with power in its various manifestations.

Fifth, the administrative structure found in most Neo-Pentecostal organizations is hierarchical and centralized. It is common to have power and authority concentrated in the hands of the Charismatic founder or leader. Written constitutions are hardly used as guidelines because the founder could often override the constitutional provisions anyhow. Organizational discipline is very limited; hence, those who disagree with the founders/leaders often leave to establish their own churches. Although women predominate the laity, men largely dominate the leadership of Neo-Pentecostal organizations. Furthermore, the Charisma of the founder or leader keeps the organization together, and these leaders are seen by members as preachers, healers, prophets, counselors, and so on. To the members, the pastors are not ordinary men. They are "men of God," "the anointed," "Papa," "Daddy G.O.," "the Anointed men of God," "the men with power-packed messages," and lately "the Rev. Dr." or "Evangelist Dr." They are also "the Holy Spirit-soaked demon destroyers," the bishops and archbishops, who are chauffeured with bodyguards. The founders have achieved a kind of celebrity profile through the command of numbers, effective use of the media, and flamboyant lifestyle. However, a few have fallen foul of the law and have been charged in court for various offenses, including inflicting bodily harm, rape and sexual exploitation, money laundering, human trafficking, and so forth.

Sixth, in the 1990s, some political leaders identified with and courted Neo-Pentecostals to garner sectional support and also tried to use the platform of Charismatic Christianity for political purposes. The most prominent example was Frederick Chiluba, president of Zambia from 1991 to 2001, who in December 1991 declared Zambia "a Christian nation" and received much support from Pentecostals and some evangelicals.[20] However, this Pentecostal identity did not prevent corruption and intolerant attitudes toward political opposition or change the predatory nature of governance in Africa.

Lastly, Neo-Pentecostals are modern in style and often appropriate the media, technologies (such as video, satellite broadcasting, the Internet, and modern musical instruments), and global marketing

---

[20] Isabel Apawo Phiri, "President Frederick J. T. Chiluba of Zambia: The Christian Nation and Democracy," *Journal of Religion in Africa* 33, no. 4 (2003): 401–28.

techniques to propagate their faith as they compete for membership. Generally, services in Pentecostal and Charismatic churches are lively, warm, and usually participatory, though often noisy, with clapping and dancing to choruses during praise worship sessions. Somehow, worship in Pentecostal churches has restored to the centre of the liturgy genuine praise and a deep spirituality.

Conclusion

The dynamism and innovation of the Pentecostal movements have been helpful. Hence, across Africa, there has been a substantial religious awakening as a result of Pentecostal spirituality. However, certain excesses and doctrinal inaccuracies have been associated with some of their teachings, and these have given concern to some evangelicals. Nevertheless, Neo-Pentecostalism is still spreading in many countries, partly because its doctrinal emphases have been made contextually relevant to the contemporary situation facing millions of Africans.

CHAPTER 2

THE PROSPERITY GOSPEL AMONG NEO-PENTECOSTALS IN AFRICA

MATTHEWS A. OJO, PHD, NIGERIA

Since the 1980s, the prosperity gospel has become one of the major doctrinal emphases of contemporary Christianity in Africa. Borrowed from the American Word of Faith movement and Pentecostal televangelists, it became a popular concept by the mid-1980s, and was termed "prosperity gospel" by the media and scholars of religion. The newness of this emphasis stems from the fact that biblical metaphors of success and material prosperity have taken on new meanings within the competitive modern market economy in Africa. This emphasis shows how Pentecostalism has responded to the popular demands of Christianity for economic relevance in the African society.

Simply put, the prosperity gospel is a re-reading and misinterpretation of certain verses in the Bible. According to prosperity gospel

Unless otherwise noted, Scripture quotations in this chapter are taken from the King James Version.

proponents, God and the atoning death of Jesus Christ are understood to have promised a state of well-being, of abundance, of victory over social stagnation, of abundance of money and materials to meet the needs of Christians. As a result, Christians can live a life of spiritual and material abundance in the world.

Lacking any exegetical or contextual interpretation, and using proof texting of the Scriptures as a method, Pentecostals and Neo-Pentecostals have taken certain passages as support for the doctrinal emphasis on prosperity. The most quoted biblical passage is 3 John 2, "Beloved, I wish above all things that thou mayest prosper and be in health, even as thy soul prospereth." Similarly, Ps 35:27 is often quoted: "Let them shout for joy, and be glad. . . . Let the LORD be magnified, which hath pleasure in the prosperity of his servant." Deuteronomy 8:18 is also a popular verse: "But thou shalt remember the LORD thy God: for it is he that giveth thee power to get wealth . . ." Other verses include Deut 7:14; 8:6–9; 28:1–14; Josh 1:8; 2 Cor 8:9; 9:6–8; Gen 12:2; Zech 1:17 and Hag 2:6–8.

Prosperity preachers also insist that Christians enter into the realm of prosperity based on individual understanding of God's promises because God has given humans access to the Abrahamic covenant. Hence, one's salvation launches one into the realm of God's abundance (i.e., material benefits are the result of exercising faith). Christians who are not prospering could be harbouring unbelief or are unaware of God's promises and the laws of success, or maybe they are not paying their tithes, have accepted the lies of the devil, or are bogged down by sin and curses.

As the emphasis gained attention in the mid-1980s, so also emerged many publications from Pentecostal pastors, who initially promoted this emphasis. Generally, most of these pastors started from the premise that salvation ushers in spiritual well-being for the believer. For example, by knowing and accepting Christ as one's personal Saviour, one could get material benefits that include good health, wealth (money, houses, vehicles, etc.), and the ability to meet one's needs as they come.

The doctrinal emphasis on prosperity has continued to elicit public interest because it has partly been associated with the growth of Pentecostalism in Africa since the mid-1980s. For instance, Paul Gifford has argued that the doctrine was an American export to Africa and represents a foreign religious commodity.[1] Birgit Meyer has revealed how the hidden obsession with wealth and power has provided powerful stimuli for Ghanaian Pentecostals in defining the devil amidst the capitalist world economy.[2] Recently, Gifford has noted that the emphasis on success and wealth as this-worldly concerns among Ghanaian Pentecostals partly built on traditional religious imagination and also tied into modern capitalist economy.[3] In another approach, Kwabena Asamoah-Gyadu and Kingsley Larbi have argued that Ghanaian Pentecostals and Charismatics coming from the Akan worldview try to interpret the prosperity gospel as flowing from a holistic view of salvation.[4] Other opinions abound on this debate.

---

[1] Paul Gifford, "Prosperity: A New and Foreign Element in African Christianity," *Religion* 20, no. 4 (1990): 373–88.

[2] Birgit Meyer, *Translating the Devil: Religion and Modernity among the Ewe in Ghana* (Trenton, NJ: Africa World Press, 1999), 237–38.

[3] Paul Gifford, *Ghana's New Christianity: Pentecostalism in a Globalizing African Economy* (London: C. Hurst, 2004).

[4] J. Kwabena Asamoah-Gyadu, *African Charismatics: Current Developments within Independent Indigenous Pentecostalism in Ghana* (Leiden, NL: Brill, 2005), 201–32. See also E. Kingsley Larbi, "The Nature of Continuity and Discontinuity of Ghanaian Pentecostal Concept of Salvation in African Cosmology," *Asian Journal of Pentecostal Studies* 5, no. 1 (2002): 99–119.

DOCTRINAL EMPHASIS OF
PROSPERITY EXPLAINED

Some prosperity preachers insist that the emphasis flows from the concept of salvation, while others argue that prosperity is part of the blessings available to believers as part of God's covenant with Abraham. According to the Pentecostal preachers who lay great emphasis on prosperity, failure, poverty, unhappiness, and all forms of difficulties are considered curses that should not be associated with Christians. Rather, Christians should be successful and prosperous.

"Prosperity," according to David Oyedepo, "is a state of well-being in your spirit and body. It is the ability to use God's power to meet every need of men. . . . In prosperity you enjoy a life of plenty and fulfilment. Prosperity is a state of being successful; it is life on a big scale."[5] Oyedepo further stated that Christians do not enter into the realm of wealth and plenty as a result of prayer or fasting, because that entrance is not a promise but a covenant. Instead, Christians enter into the realm of prosperity based on correct understanding of the power of God through the covenant. Accordingly, Christians can get rich if they tap into the power of God. "God has from the beginning created . . . you to prosper. God has capsules in the Bible, the unfailing laws of success. God is not partial. He wants everybody to prosper." Therefore, "you must understand that you have the sole responsibility for your prosperity and good success."[6]

---

[5] Sunday Jide Komolafe, *The Transformation of African Christianity: Development and Change in the Nigerian Church* (Carlisle, UK: Langham Monographs, 2013), 166.

[6] David Oyedepo, Living Faith Church, Weekly "Faith Digest," no. 89/20, 3. See also David Oyedepo, *Signs and Wonders Today: A Catalogue of the Amazing Acts of God among Men* (Ota, NG: Dominion, 2006), 165–69.

However, there is a limit to the capacity of humans to get wealth, because the unsaved (i.e., non-believer) could get prosperous materially, and some through unrighteous means.[7]

The second aspect that is more emphasized in the contemporary era is material prosperity or financial prosperity, defined as having enough resources, which can be money, houses, cars, children, a promotion, jobs, and so on. Financial prosperity, though it has its source in God, is the work of one's hands. Some leaders pointed out that the vehicle through which God prospered Old Testament men such as Abraham, Job, and Solomon was the work of their hands. Thus, responsibility is placed upon every Christian to engage his or her hands in worthwhile things.

Conditions for accessing prosperity include having knowledge of the Word of God, obeying and serving God, being righteous and living in holiness, and not allowing riches to have control over oneself. Some Pentecostal pastors teach that the good and godly motive of being prosperous is for the propagation of the gospel. It is a false Christianity that equates poverty with piety, but at the same time it is bad to be devoted to materialism. The worship of materialism is mammon, and a "rich fool" is a person who is possessed by material wealth.

Generally, success and prosperity are perceived among Pentecostals as forms of healing when the Christian overcomes failure, poverty, and backwardness and lives a life of sufficiency and abundance. To be prosperous, one is expected to give liberally and sacrificially toward the

---

See also David Oyedepo, *Making Maximum Impact* (Ota, NG: Dominion, 2000), 1–72.

[7] Harford Anayo Iloputaife, *Dynamics of Biblical Prosperity* (London: Victory Publications Inc. of Faith Revival Ministries World Outreach, 1995), 9–11, 15–17.

course of the gospel, or "plant seed-money" or sow "seed of faith," as some Neo-Pentecostals say. Some preachers emphasize that the more one gives to God, the more abundantly the person receives in return. In fact, this aspect of the teaching has attracted much criticism from evangelicals. The sexual scandal, mail fraud, and wire fraud associated with the US prosperity preacher Jim Bakker and the PTL Club between 1987 and 1992 caused much discomfort for the prosperity preachers, even in Africa.

There are different refinements about the teaching on prosperity among Neo-Pentecostal preachers, but generally the following list represents the consensus within the constituency:

1. God promises prosperity in the Scriptures, and it is available to every Christian who accepts the scriptural truth.
2. Because prosperity is integral to the covenant with Abraham— "to bless and make him great," Christians also stand as inheritors of that covenant. Hence, the popular chorus, "Abraham's blessing are mine, I am blessed in the morning, I am blessed in the evening, Abraham's blessings are mine."
3. Material wealth and financial prosperity are necessary benefits of true spirituality that Christians must enjoy. Therefore, God approves when Christians are blessed materially.
4. Understanding and acting by faith on the Word of God is the path to prosperity.
5. Those who contribute generously in tithes, offerings, donations, and so on to the church or God's works ultimately receive abundant blessings from God because the quantity and quality of harvest is a function of the quantity of "seed" sowed.

6. If a Christian consistently lacks or is poor or has no material wealth to his benefit, this could be considered an illness that needs healing.

7. Christians who are undergoing suffering or sickness are out of the will of God. Unbelief and not tapping into the abundance of God's resources are sin.

8. Speaking positively, that is, "name it and claim it," can lead Christians to higher grounds of prosperity.

9. Christians should be strategic and business-minded in the gospel ministry so that they can make profit while serving the people.[8]

Preachers of prosperity often provide the principles or keys to use in entering the covenant of prosperity. Among these keys are dreaming big and expanding one's horizon, believing, obedience to God's command, sowing seeds or giving bountifully and sacrificially, partaking in "miracle meal," giving positive confession, exercising faith unconditionally, using anointing oil, claiming the power in the blood of Jesus, and so on. In the Living Faith Church, members regularly partake of the Eucharist, which is interpreted as shutting the doors against afflictions and failures and guaranteeing victory and success. Overall, this emphasis among Neo-Pentecostals promotes the notion that one must not live below the optimum level, but instead one must strive to add value to the resources that God has made available to humans and continually endeavour to improve economically and socially.

---

[8] For details of how Oyedepo became wealthy, see Oladimeji Olutimehin, *Business Secrets of David Oyedepo: How from Poverty He Became the Richest Pastor on Earth—You Too Can* (Akure, NG: Kingdom Books & Media, 2015).

HISTORICAL DEVELOPMENT OF THE PROSPERITY GOSPEL

As the Charismatic renewal was undergoing denominationalisation in the 1980s into stable religious organizations with bureaucratic structures, the movement adopted a great emphasis on healing, which is composed of four major areas. First is physical healing, which is basic to all Pentecostal groups. Second, there is healing constructed specifically within the African worldview of evil, witchcraft, and the world of spirits. Within this realm, Pentecostals obtain healing when malevolent forces are cast out. This process is termed "deliverance." Third, the progressive nature of Pentecostalism is reflected in what is termed success and prosperity, which is healing the socio-economic difficulties of the individual, and hence the believer can appropriate the blessings of Christianity. Lastly, Pentecostals extended their healing activities over the political and socio-economic conditions of a nation. This process is termed "prayer for the nations." However, prosperity gained much ground in the mid-1980s and became a distinct doctrinal emphasis.

Winning and fruitfulness are constant themes in sermons of churches stressing prosperity to a particular class of Christians. In actuality, most Neo-Pentecostal churches are urban in nature and appeal to the educated middle class. The churches' entrepreneurial organization, sophisticated marketing techniques, and modernizing tendencies have facilitated the seeming success of this emphasis on prosperity.

Although subsequent development of the prosperity gospel was broader in scope, it was Archbishop Benson A. Idahosa (1938–1998), a Nigerian, who first propagated this doctrinal emphasis on a large scale among African Pentecostals in his continent-wide evangelistic programmes beginning from the late 1970s.[9] Writing in 1987, he noted:

> God created men and women for a better life than many are experiencing. . . . God never intended that anyone should go through life imprisoned by their own superstitions. He opens the door of success to every believer who will dare to step out and go after the good life. No one in God's family was ever destined to exist in sickness, fear, ignorance, poverty, loneliness or mediocrity. God's abundant goodness will be enjoyed and utilised by those who discipline themselves, become decisive, bold, adventurous, believing, daring, risking and determined.[10]

By the time he died in March 1998, many other burgeoning African Pentecostal evangelists had accepted the teaching and had broadcast it wide through their radio broadcasts, television programmes, open air evangelistic meetings, tracts, Bible study outlines, booklets, and audio tapes. More important, testimonies or personal stories of individual spectacular successes are publicly advertised to strengthen the validity of their doctrinal emphasis on prosperity.

---

[9] For more on Benson Idahosa see Matthews A. Ojo, "Nigerian Pentecostalism and Transnational Religious Networks in West African Coastal Region" in *Entreprises Religieuses Transnationales en Afrique de l'Ouest,* ed. Laurent Fourchard, André Mary, and Rene Otayek (Paris: Editions Karthala & Ibadan: IFRA, 2005), 395–415.

[10] Benson Idahosa, *I Choose to Change: The Scriptural Way to Success and Prosperity* (Crowborough, UK: Highland Books, 1987), 9, 14.

The greatest apostle of the prosperity gospel is David Oyedepo, the founder of Living Faith Church (popularly known as Winners' Chapel), who was ordained by Idahosa in 1988. In 1995, he embarked on an expansion strategy from Nigeria into other African countries, and by 1997, branches had been established in thirty other African countries. Oyedepo teaches that Christians are destined to experience abundance and material wealth in the world; therefore, they should aspire to be prosperous, and they should be known for their prosperity in society, such as by driving good cars and wearing costly dresses.

In practical terms, messages with this emphasis have been motivational, very assuring, and depict instances of triumphalism. Indeed, the founders often proved the efficacy of the messages with flamboyant and expensive lifestyles. Some travel to the West for medical checkups, and some have bought private jets. There are also structures and educational investments, like privately owned universities, to advertise this. Members often give testimonies of what they termed "supernatural financial breakthrough." Spiritual retreats have moved from the old evangelical camp meetings in the countryside to success seminars in downtown five-star hotels. Generally, there are corporate images of success to project this emphasis and to launch members on the quest for upward material and social mobility.

THE POLITICAL AND SOCIO-ECONOMIC CONTEXTS OF THE PROSPERITY GOSPEL

What sustains this new doctrinal emphasis and the apparent quest for material wealth is partly the socio-economic and political upheaval in Africa, as well as the deteriorating economic situation in Africa in the 1980s and 1990s. The predatory nature of governance in Africa, the widespread corruption of the elite, and the growing incidence of poverty throughout the continent despite several interventionist programmes, including the Millennium Development Goals, seem to have driven the masses to untold suffering. By the late 1970s, a section of Pentecostal churches in Nigeria had legitimatised their existence by attributing the poor economic development to the forces of Satan as they continue to wreak havoc in the lives of individuals and in the African nations in general.

In another way, the attraction of "corrupt" wealth has partly given currency to the emphasis on prosperity, which has afforded Neo-Pentecostals a means of responding to the economic conditions and the social values around them. While Pentecostals may argue that there is consonance in their emphasis with biblical prescriptions of wealth and well-being, the dissonance is manifested in the Neo-Pentecostals' pursuit of prosperity as though economics and social structures do not matter. The miraculous wealth without any commensurate productive activities also finds some congruence in the magic wealth that has become the dominant theme in the contemporary African home video films.

In Africa, wealth is a means to recognition in society and the means toward political power. People have used various means to acquire wealth. Hence, the emphasis on prosperity legitimizes the quest for materialism and the associated power and prestige that have characterized the values of African society since the 1980s. Neo-Pentecostals, through their doctrinal emphasis on prosperity as a new spirituality, have helped to lend new meanings to the quest for materialism, which traditionally has been a subject of condemnation in evangelical Christianity.

Lastly, the social capital that the Neo-Pentecostal emphasis on prosperity has generated in terms of the drive and motivation to invest and succeed, to eliminate poverty by hard work, to create economic networks that can facilitate entrepreneurship, and the promotion of frugality and economic risk-taking are reflective of the so-called Protestant ethic. However, no stimulation for large-scale economic development or enduring religious values has yet emerged to justify the economic implication of the prosperity gospel on the large society.[11]

CONCLUSION

The continuing popularity of the prosperity gospel among Neo-Pentecostals and African Christians, as already pointed out, arose from new interpretations of biblical metaphors in rapidly changing socio-economic situations. Hence, the emphasis on prosperity has become a powerful metaphor in negotiating wider concerns, which they consider important to themselves within their socio-cultural background and contemporary situation. While concentrating on biblical symbols of illness and poverty, Pentecostals and Charismatics have employed healing in its wider context to define and confront the contemporary situation of overwhelming the evil of poverty and backwardness within their society. The evils they are challenging are not only literal sicknesses, but also the failures of the economic and political systems and the social services, as well as the extensive dislocation created by successive governments in modern Africa. Hence, the emphases on prosperity and success have taken account of the traditional causative factors of poverty and also come to terms with the dislocation of contemporary life in a capitalist economy.

---

[11] For critique of the Protestant ethic and the prosperity gospel, see Paul Gifford and Trad Nogueira-Godsey, "The Protestant Ethic and African Pentecostalism: A Case Study," *Journal for the Study of Religion* 24, no. 1 (2011): 5–22.

CHAPTER 3

THE CHALLENGES OF NEO-PENTECOSTALISM IN AFRICA

REV. MAMITIANA NIRINTSOA, MADAGASCAR

The Neo-Pentecostal movement began growing outside the major denominations during the first half of the twentieth century. This movement, which has spread across the countries of Africa, concerns the integrity of the gospel of Jesus Christ. This study will analyze the importance that Neo-Pentecostals place on experiential evidence by contrasting it with the evangelical understanding that the Word of God is the ultimate authority in the believer's life. This study will give examples that Neo-Pentecostals have contravened the accepted limits of contextualized theology.

ANALYZING THE FORMS OF THE NEO-PENTECOSTAL MOVEMENT

The Neo-Pentecostal movement is powerfully changing the face of Christianity. The overemphasizing of individual spiritual gifts and the experience of being filled with the Spirit distinguish their practice. Emotion and experience play a huge role in their movement. This movement especially stresses a variety of miraculous gifts of the Spirit, such as visions and dreams, miracles, spiritual power, divine healing, and speaking in tongues, as well as the belief in the word of faith, sometimes called health and wealth gospel, which teaches that God promises people health and wealth in addition to these various gifts of the Spirit.

Neo-Pentecostalism views salvation both as an event and a process at the same time. The whole point is to grow closer to God and to grow fuller in the experience of God's Spirit in their lives, which they call the baptism of the Holy Spirit. While most evangelicals believe that salvation is both an event and a process, Neo-Pentecostals interpret it differently. What they trumpet in everyone's ear is that salvation is the first event, where they receive some of what God intended them to have. Most evangelicals believe baptism of the Holy Spirit happens at the moment of salvation. Neo-Pentecostals argue that it is the most important of the many subsequent events in the life of believers. These events may include sensing the physical presence of God coming into their lives. One distinctive experience in Neo-Pentecostalism is being slain in the Spirit. They believe the Spirit has fallen on a person who is speaking in tongues, shaking, or falling as though dead.

Neo-Pentecostalism also brings an emphasis on spiritual warfare or power evangelism. The focus is on the man of God speaking from the pulpit. The audience attends in order to receive these extraordinary blessings. One of the reasons this movement proliferates in numbers is that they claim it is the power of the Holy Spirit working in them. Through them, people seek extraordinary gifts and blessings rather than seeking God Himself.

Neo-Pentecostalism has no education requirements for leadership. Anyone who claims to be filled with the Holy Spirit may start a church, anytime, anywhere. They may also give themselves a title such as apostle or bishop or any other name that seems to have biblical authority. However, they are self-acclaimed and often bring scandals into the church. This movement also moves quickly across cultures, claiming the rapid spread is due to the Holy Spirit's movement being fluid, adjustable, and adaptable.

Neo-Pentecostals have gained power in Africa because they respond to the people's needs, especially those who have faced or are facing traumatic experiences. They preach the message that having the Spirit come into their lives will give spiritual power to people who are otherwise powerless. They also promise wealth and health, prosperity, and success. The emphasis of their meetings tends to be for people to come forward to be prayed for so that they might receive the Holy Spirit, receive miraculous healing, and receive one form of miracle or another. These manifestations have become the magnet that draws people to follow this movement because they are desperate for experience and some extraordinary and supernatural manifestation of gifts or blessings.

One major characteristic of Neo-Pentecostalism is the "man of God" concept. In a particular service, the men who are leading the church present themselves as having an extra power within them, and so the people come to them to be prayed for. This shift into the "man of God" concept is a significant one; it involves proclaiming that the man who stands in front of the church is not only a prophet who proclaims the Word but also a priest who brings God's blessings to them. They focus on people with desperate needs and desire for change. They promise wealth, prosperity, stability, and health if people follow them. Instead of inviting people to respond to the message of the gospel, they invite people for prosperity and the promise of wealth and health. The message of the gospel has changed from deliverance from sin and God's wrath to the hope of healing, prophecies, and deliverance from demons—and these draw the crowds.

CONCERN FOR THE NEO-PENTECOSTAL MOVEMENT

In his views on the African churches, the late African theologian Byang Kato acknowledged that the African church is facing theological and ideological threats from the inside and the outside. These threats may jeopardize the development of African churches and can lead to the danger of syncretism and liberal theology throughout Africa. Kato's legacy is "let the African Christians be Christian Africans." He longed for African Christianity to not only be genuinely biblical but also genuinely African.[1]

The churches now ought to be concerned about this Neo-Pentecostal movement. It is rapidly and powerfully changing the Christian faith. However, it seems that in Africa, this movement has gone even further. Nearly all Africans believe and respect God. However, their belief in His existence has been mixed with the traditional African religions.[2] They believe that the African traditional religions are even more powerful if they mix them with God. This seems to be natural in the African mind because of the power that a shaman or witchdoctor has in their lives.

The man of God concept is similar to allowing the shaman to bring life and blessings into their lives. By claiming to have received power

---

[1] In the June 4, 2009, edition of *Christianity Today,* "Let African Christians Be Christian Africans," Carolyn Nystrom tells about the legacy of Byang H. Kato (1936–1975), https://www.christianitytoday.com/history /2009/june/let-african-christians-be-christian-africans.htm.

[2] Yusufu Turaki, *Foundations of African Traditional Religion and Worldview* (Nairobi: WorldAlive, 2006), 53–54.

from God, the "man of God" can potentially create a situation where abuses can occur within the movement. Abuse is taking place as leaders control church members through fear. The leaders are elevated with great respect because they are the "Lord's anointed." No one is allowed to speak negative things to God's anointed because something horrible or a curse will happen in their life.

Why has this movement grown? This movement parallels African Traditional Religion. Through generations upon generations, a system has developed in which only particular people, such as the shaman or the witchdoctor, have the authority and power to bring curses or blessings. They are the problem solvers. Hence, when Neo-Pentecostalism came onto our doorstep, the way its followers do things related to the African traditional belief system.

THE ABUSE AND MISUSE OF SCRIPTURE IN THE NEO-PENTECOSTAL MOVEMENT

One of the major problems of Neo-Pentecostalism is failure to respect Scripture and study it for what it means. Scripture is the bedrock of the Christian faith. The moment anyone abuses or misuses Scripture, he is stepping off of that bedrock and is twisting Scripture. Taking a verse out of context or changing the meaning for a personal gain is not acceptable. Let the Word of God speak for itself, as it has the final authority on any practice and faith.

The Neo-Pentecostal movement uses the Word of God to convict people. They take people through Scripture and even point them to Christ for forgiveness. Above that, they tell people that for them to be blessed, they have to bring money, which they call "seed," to the church. The bigger the seed they bring, the bigger the blessings they will receive. The actual results make people more miserable, because while the "man of God" promised a miracle, nothing is happening in people's lives.

One of the passages that the Neo-Pentecostal leaders love to use is Mark 16:14–21. There is a word in this passage that the movement uses that we need to recognize, "signs." This word "signs" is a keyword. The Bible deliberately uses it to speak primarily concerning something that is bound to happen, and when it happens, it has spiritual significance. For example, in Isa 7:14 (NASB), the prophet says: "Therefore the Lord Himself will give you a sign: Behold, a virgin will be with child and bear a son, and she will call His name Immanuel." When a declaration like this happens, it is a message that God is about to do something extraordinary and supernatural—don't miss that event. A sign has to do with an event; it happens, and then after that, it's gone. This is the context in Mark 16:17 (NKJV). Jesus sent His disciples and said, "These signs will follow those who believe." This was only to the disciples who were with Jesus, not to all who would become Christians. In Acts 2 also signs and miracles were performed but ceased. The event did not continue.

Some denominations are still arguing about the continuation of these miraculous signs and wonders and gifts of the Holy Spirit. The question we need to ask is, What are the results? What is the proof that the blind can see, the lame can walk? If those things happened, those healed would not hesitate to testify. We need to allow Scripture to speak for itself in its technical sense. We are not expected to walk on water like Peter. That was a specific command for Peter. We cannot perform a miracle to feed 5,000 with a few loaves of bread and fish, to rebuke winds and waves that are disturbed, to heal the sick miraculously, and to raise the dead. The apostle Paul himself refers to these events as the signs of the apostles in 2 Cor 12:11–12.

The Neo-Pentecostal movement exhibits another misuse of Scripture. It is the overemphasis on the world of demons and the binding and loosing of these fallen creatures. Have you attempted to go into the passage of the Bible that teaches about binding and loosing? When you go to passages such as Matthew 16 and Matthew 18, there is nothing about binding and loosing demons. What is the context? These passages refer to church discipline, not demons. That is the context. It should concern the church when people start to abuse Scripture, using verses here and there to develop their own theological idea. It would upset you if you said something to someone who repeated it saying something quite different. How much more with the Word of God! It is the same when a person is twisting the Word of God and making it say what it does not say at all. That is manipulation, which the Scripture condemns.

THE PURE GOSPEL IS MISSING THE NEO-PENTECOSTAL MOVEMENT

What is lost in Neo-Pentecostalism is the gospel. The gospel is preaching to people about repentance and having faith in the Lord Jesus Christ. They have replaced the message of the gospel with a different message. If they want to use passages like Mark 16, the message is unambiguous. Go into all the world, proclaim the gospel, whoever believes and has been baptized shall be saved. That is the message, yet that is missing in the Neo-Pentecostal movement. When you look at their crusade posters and banners, the message of salvation has been replaced by the promise of deliverance from all kinds of hardship in life.

A message solely about deliverance from pain and suffering is unbiblical. Where is the conviction of sin? Where is the cross of Christ? Where is the mentioning of the payment made on Calvary? Does repentance take place? Do people put their faith and trust in Christ? Where are all these gospel elements? They are all missing in the Neo-Pentecostal movement—not only missing, but replaced with a different message such as wealth, health, and prosperity.

One problem of the overemphasis on demons and evil spirits is that everything is blamed on them. The Bible calls us to be responsible for our sins. However, for the Neo-Pentecostal movement, everything is connected to an evil spirit. For example, an unfaithful spouse has a spirit of lust, and therefore needs deliverance. Different evil spirits are blamed and consequently individuals are not learning to be responsible for their own sins. Responsibility is key. Christians need to be responsible for their actions rather than blaming evil spirits. The Bible is the filter of any practice in the church; every message and action should be filtered through the Scripture.

A CALL TO COME BACK TO THE SUPREMACY OF SCRIPTURE

The Bible is God's divine revelation. The Holy Spirit verbally inspired the original autographs. The Scriptures, in their original manuscripts, are infallible and inerrant. They are the sole, full, and final authority on all matters of faith and practice. Again, one of the major problems of Neo-Pentecostalism is the failure to simply respect Scripture and study it for what it means.

How the Bible is viewed in some parts of Africa is wrong. Promises are taken out of the context of the Bible in order to match the African context. They come with a form that sounds Christian, using Christian words from the Bible to draw crowds. This is a warning for all African churches. Instead of preaching the gospel and driving out the darkness, this Neo-Pentecostal movement has opened a significant door at the back of the church and has let in the African traditional religions.

This "man of God" concept relates to the traditional African beliefs, which is why it draws crowds in Africa. The Neo-Pentecostal movement is a form of African Traditional Religion. The witchdoctor's approach to the people is like the Neo-Pentecostals' approach to the church, which has abandoned the message of the gospel. In Africa, the shamans or the witchdoctors control and manipulate people's lives with authority and extraordinary power. This has now been translated in the Neo-Pentecostal movement with the man of God concept. They appeal to people's overt physical needs when they speak of liberation or breaking free or prosperity and draw people to them, but they often ignore Scripture. People only want and expect God's promises and what He will give.

Prophetic leadership, protection from witchcraft, and prophecies concerning health and wealth are all messages that will draw crowds. If you want your promises to be blessed and to be true, you go to the pastor and seek his approval of them. This is how cults are formed. They now identify pastors as prophets like in the Old Testament, contrasting the role of a pastor in the New Testament. The man of God concept automatically elevates the pastor to the one who performs a miracle. Being the anointed of God, people will listen, obey, and will not say anything bad or negative against the pastor because they do not want to bring bad luck on themselves. It is no wonder that there are all kinds of abuses in the church. Fear cripples the people following this movement.

The Bible as a revelation from God to people is needed as an authoritative and normative guide for every practice and faith. God has communicated Himself to people authoritatively and infallibly. The Scripture, however, must critique culture and never the reverse. The words of the man of God can be questioned, filtered, and examined through Scripture.

God's truth serves as the standard to be achieved. God's Word is the authoritative and normative guide for every practice and faith.[3]

CONCLUSION

The Neo-Pentecostal movement is still the number one problem that causes many to stumble in Africa, and it requires a biblical response, guidance, and perspective to bring transformation and true Christianity. Jesus has promised that in the world, we will face trouble and suffering.[4] The church has to expect and believe that challenges will come, in our lives, in our communities, and in our workplaces. We should be concerned when these truths have been taken away from the life of the church; we have to be concerned when people are paying more attention to wealth, health, and prosperity rather than focusing on God. Let us get back to the Bible, the *sola Scriptura*.

---

[3] See Keith E. Eitel, *Transforming Culture: Developing a Biblical Ethic in an African Context* (Nairobi: Evangel Publishing House, 1986), 171–73.

[4] John 16:33.

PART 2

BIBLICAL RESPONSES

CHAPTER 4

SPIRITUAL POWERS

SCOTT MACDONALD, THD, ZAMBIA

The concrete-floored, wood-walled, and tin-roofed church building resounded with around two hundred African voices. Prayer time had commenced, and while a few prayed quietly, the overall tenor of the event was a cacophony of worshipers shouting declarations and exorcising demons. The boisterous scene nearly accorded with the 1 Kings 18 encounter at Mount Carmel, though the ruckus echoed the intercessory tone of the prophets of Baal, not the measured request of Elijah.

As I stood behind the pulpit next to the pastor, I strained to focus on the prayers of the people, which were simultaneously gushing forth in English, Chinyanja, and ChiBemba. No one was praying for the lost. No one was praying for the salvation of the nations, the

Unless otherwise noted, Scripture quotations in this chapter are taken from the English Standard Version.

exposition of the Scriptures, or the perseverance to endure in trial. "I cast out the demon of poverty!" "I bind the spirit of sickness!" These rang out like spiritual bullets designed to cut down the powers that harassed their lives.

My eyes instinctively opened. I glanced at the members who were exorcising demons (though I saw no one exhibiting possession symptoms), but my gaze fell upon the worship leader. He stood at the intersection of the cross-shaped floorplan, and his arm was chopping back and forth with force, as if he was wielding an ax against unseen spiritual assailants.

After the prayers subsided, his choice of music was fitting. "*Satana, Satana,*" the name of Satan, was prominent in the majority of the songs. In music and in prayer, the theme was set: Christians are at constant war with spiritual forces, and our tumultuous services revolve around that conflict through declarations and exorcisms.

We would not be surprised if this commotion described a Pentecostal church in Africa, but this was a Baptist church in Lusaka, Zambia, where Baptists are proud to be known as "People of the Book." But was this worship by the Book? Was this demonology by the Book? Do Christians meet together to repel evil spirits with declarations and exorcisms each week?

The confusion is evident throughout Africa, and much of it arises from the similar vocabulary. African Neo-Pentecostalism (ANP) has adopted many of the same terms (e.g., demons, Satan, exorcism, Jesus, deliverance, salvation, healing) that are present in other Christian groups. Yet we marshal the same words while imbuing different meanings and rendering different practices. Thus, we are forced to inquire, "What does African Neo-Pentecostalism believe about spiritual powers?"

AFRICAN NEO-PENTECOSTALISM
BELIEFS ABOUT THE DEMONIC

ANP, encompassing and invading innumerable Christian sects throughout Africa, displays some consistent convictions about the demonic. Much could be said about its theological relationship to African Traditional Religion (ATR), but for the sake of brevity, let us outline a pair of ANP convictions concerning the fallen spiritual powers.

First, demons are hostile forces that bear the primary blame for human suffering, poverty, and problems. Although a Western form of the prosperity gospel might attribute difficulties to sin or to demons and also prescribe faith declarations (e.g., "I believe God for a new car!"), ANP incorporates and accommodates the spiritual realm in keeping with a traditional African worldview (e.g., "I cast off the tormenting spirit of economic suffering and claim a new car in Jesus's name!"). Difficulties are traced to malevolent spirits. As if God had allowed Satan to test the whole world and not merely Job, the loss of employment, family, and peace is an assumed affliction from the powers.

Second, victory over demons is secured primarily through regular spiritual declarations to bind and cast them out. Spiritual warfare is a reality for every serious reader of Scripture, but the question is, "How does one fight?" ANP responds with an exorcism-focused formula. Sometimes with the assistance of a spiritual expert or a "man of God," the demon of the particular affliction is named (e.g., "demon of joblessness"), and then its influence can be curtailed through binding. Finally, the demon is expelled, while the name of Jesus Christ is repeated liberally throughout the process. This continues weekly at church services and deliverance meetings, and other specialists and prophets (and perhaps even a *ng'anga*, an ATR practitioner) may be visited, until deliverance is achieved.

BIBLICAL BELIEFS ABOUT THE DEMONIC

But do the Scriptures prescribe such a perspective and response toward the demonic? Again, we must struggle for clarity, seeking objective guidance. In demonology, the temptation to let experience lead is formidable, yet clinging to biblical authority and sufficiency, we must examine some scriptural emphases concerning the demonic so that our experiences may be interpreted by revelation, not vice versa. Let us examine five truths.

First, demons deceive. From the beginning, Satan was a liar (John 8:44). He and his servants are experienced in the foul art of deception. The opening pages of humanity's rebellion are inscribed in the ink of his lies—"Did God actually say . . ." But the wickedness continues.

The demonic powers are still wielding words to deceive people. They spout lies of hopelessness and condemnation, accusing and harassing. They even fashion the corrupt, idolatrous, and blasphemous religions that ensnare billions of people. According to 1 Cor 10:20, demons stand behind the systems of false worship and power (including sorcery and witchcraft). Deuteronomy 32:16–17 states, "[Israel] stirred [God] to jealousy with strange gods . . . they sacrificed to demons that were no gods." The demons have doctrines (1 Tim 4:1), and all the nations, peoples, and individuals are entangled in part or whole.

Second, demons rule. In a number of places throughout Scripture, the fallen powers are mentioned as possessing dominion. Ephesians 6:12 states this blatantly: "For we do not wrestle against flesh and blood, but against the rulers, against the authorities, against the cosmic powers over this present darkness, against the spiritual forces of evil in the heavenly places." Evidently, a cosmic arrangement exists that permits the rulership of supernatural powers over the affairs of humanity. These are the spiritual slave masters to whom we were all enslaved prior to our adoption in Christ (see Gal 4:1–11), the demonic princes over the nations that oppose God's people (see Daniel 10). They instigate and enforce systems of fear, inhibiting the spread of freedom found in the cross.

Third, demons tempt. Satan tempted Jesus in Matthew 4, but do his comrades tempt us today? Of course they do! Just as Jesus was attacked with misquoted verses and the possibility of ill-gotten gain (e.g., dominion over the nations with a bend of the knee), so too we face temptation. We are tempted to take the fruit and gain knowledge. Remembering how David succumbed in 1 Chr 21:1 and ordered a Satanic census, we can be tempted to trust in human strength, not divine provision. We can be incited to sexual immorality by the insistence of Satan, as 1 Cor 7:5 articulates concerning the married: "Do not deprive one another [of sex], except perhaps by agreement for a limited time, that you may devote yourselves to prayer; but then come together again, so that Satan may not tempt you because of your lack of self-control." Since Jesus was tempted in every way like us (Heb 4:15), then it is possible that demons will tempt us as well.

Fourth, demons "demonize." In accordance with their strategy to dominate, enslave, and indoctrinate, evil spirits inhabit and harass individuals. Perhaps one could call this "possession" as long as we recognize that demons have no ultimate right to possess anything. The New Testament shows us that demonic beings can and do personally exert control in the lives of humans in the stories of the Gadarene demoniac in Mark 5 and the slave girl in Acts 16. Nearly every culture and religion on the planet affirms this reality. Any attempt to explain away these biblical stories is both difficult and fruitless.

But in the event of invasive demonization, what are the capabilities of the inhabiting spirits? The demonizing of a person can lead to self-destructiveness (Mark 5:5), additional voices (Mark 5:9), violence (Mark

9:18; Acts 19:16), and disability (Mark 9:25; Luke 13:11). Yet in the case of the slave girl, she appears to be a functioning individual with perhaps a more symbiotic relationship with the "python" demon. Inhabiting spirits are capable of substantial harm, but the variety of biblical examples should lead us away from hasty assumptions. They do not have to act the same way with every person.

Finally, demons lose. If we could imagine the events of Scripture passing before us like a play on a stage, one truth about the rebellious powers would stand above the rest—the demonic and their detestable director are doomed for defeat. In Genesis 3, the serpent heard his fate. And again and again, when faced with the King of kings, the demons lost; even a legion of them could not prevail.[1] Their end is set, for "the devil who had deceived them was thrown into the lake of fire and sulfur" (Rev 20:10). Satan and his horde have been cast as villains in the epic of salvation history, and while they cruelly lash out at humanity from under the foot of Christ, only defeat awaits them.

Yet, with ANP in mind, are demons primarily to blame for human suffering and poverty in the lives of African Christians? Standing upon the biblical witness in the story of Job, we can claim that they are able to cause suffering and poverty, under the watchful eye of our sovereign God. Various types of affliction *can* come from demonic sources, but an ANP perspective of the powers portrays demons as the normal source of problems in our world.

Should our problems be routinely blamed on the powers? The Scriptures respond with a resounding no. Obvious cases of demonization are certainly times when we can name the enemy without confusion. But in general, we do not know if and when demons are involved in

---

[1] Mark 5:9.

family deaths, joblessness, and poverty. We are not like Job; we lack direct revelation into our situation. However, we can replicate Job's evaluation, "The Lord has taken away."

James 4:1–10 also responds to the experiences of God's people. While we are called to resist the devil in verse 7, we cannot miss James's emphasis upon our human passions and our fleshly desires, along with the influence of the broken and sinful world. Could a spirit of division and dissention fall upon a church? Theoretically, yes! But where does James want us to look? We must examine our own proud and fleshly hearts. And as Rom 12:2 iterates, we must not be conformed to this world, but be transformed in our minds—the primary location of spiritual battle.

ENGAGEMENT AGAINST DEMONS

The Bible answers illness and health in a similar way. Could a demon come to disable a person? Yes. But this does not mean that we can assume every instance of sickness is a "demon of affliction." The man born blind in John 9 did not have a demon, nor had he or his parents committed a particular sin leading to his condition. Paul did not bind a spirit of stomach pain, but in 1 Tim 5:23 he prescribed a change in diet for young Timothy. While overt situations arise where the powers are undoubtedly involved, the Scriptures leave us the responsibility and freedom to address problems with multiple causes in mind, including our broken cultures and sinful hearts.

Exorcisms and declarations are a necessity in numerous times and places, for many a believer has experienced an unsettling nocturnal visit from a demon. The compassion of Christ should compel His people to pursue the release of the oppressed and demonized. But is binding and casting out demons our primary means for waging war with the powers?

While exorcisms were necessary in the lives of Jesus and the apostles, the central means by which they engaged the demonic forces of the age was through biblical preaching and outspoken evangelism. Matthew, Mark, Luke, and Acts divulge the details of some exorcisms. But the majority of God's revelation to His church—including their struggles with false teaching, immorality, and suffering—revolved around the proclamation of doctrine. The truth sets us free (John 8:32).

Be not surprised that Ephesians 6 and the rest of divine revelation instructs us to prepare for spiritual combat through the inculcation and proclamation of doctrine. In a world filled with conflict, we embark protected by the gospel, righteousness, faith, and truth while brandishing the Word of God, the Spirit-inspired Scriptures.

Demons rule, but we wear our armor. Demons deceive, and "the god of this world [blinds] the minds of the unbelievers." But we offer "the open statement of the truth" (2 Cor 4:1–6).

Demons tempt, enticing us with daily needs like food and worldly desires like power. But we retort, "Man shall not live by bread alone, but by every word that comes from the mouth of God" (Matt 4:4).

Demons "demonize," harassing the souls of many. Christians release the captive, remembering that we are seated "in the heavenly places in Christ Jesus" (Eph 2:6), which is "far above all rule and authority and power and dominion" (Eph 1:21).

Demons lose, and we rejoice knowing that the Lord accomplishes their defeat "by the blood of the Lamb and by the word of [our] testimony" (Rev 12:11). We may encounter poverty and trials in this life, but our battle is for the truth, not a problem-free life.

What about our churches? As "People of the Book," let us be persistent in our doctrine! Too many church services, revival meetings, and evangelistic outreaches have been lost due to a preoccupation with demonic powers and exorcisms. We must resist the temptation to become popular (and wealthy) deliverance experts at the expense of being faithful ministers of the gospel. Can we imitate the example of Paul, who focused on the preaching of the gospel in Philippi in Acts 16, even as he was pestered by a demon for days? Yes, the exorcism was eventually performed, but the priority was clear: deliver the gospel.

Let us hold to all of God's revelation—the entire Bible. While African Neo-Pentecostalism wears the clothes of doctrinal orthodoxy, the movement lacks the "whole counsel" of Scripture and its worldview (Acts 20:27). One can easily find a few popular verses regularly misused in ANP circles, but an emphasis on particular texts to the exclusion of other passages is just as dangerous (if not more so) as fabricating a completely false doctrine. The whole truth must resound in our churches, that our struggle against the powers might not be the empty shouting of declarations and exorcisms but the equipping of God's people in the gospel, righteousness, and the Scripture.

On the outskirts of Lusaka, Kabuta Baptist Church is multiplying. On Sundays, it is full. A number of new churches have already sprung from its evangelism and discipleship efforts. Years ago, the church was at a crossroads. A demonized man interrupted the service, and the zealous pastor publicly cast out the demon, freeing the captive in the name of Jesus Christ. But unbeknownst to the pastor, a few church members hurriedly departed, proclaiming these works of power performed by their pastor. Church attendance swelled.

Like false disciples of Christ scrounging for more bread, the crowds came. The dreams of many pastors were being fulfilled in that church. Yet the church had not expanded by the transformation of the gospel, but by the message of exorcism. In wisdom, the pastor recognized the crossroads, and he led the church away from those crowds, returning to a church service that focused on worship and the faithful preaching of the Scripture.

Demons no longer had the stage of the church—the gospel of Jesus Christ was lifted up. Necessary exorcisms still occurred elsewhere (since the Bible has no example of an exorcism occurring in a church service). And according to the gracious providence of God, the church has reaped a harvest of true converts.

Across Africa, we are at this same crossroads. Which way will we turn? What will we be known for—the message of exorcism or the transformative power of the gospel?

CHAPTER 5

DREAMS AND VISIONS

REV. MISCHECK ZULU, ZAMBIA

And afterward,
I will pour out my Spirit on all people.
Your sons and daughters will prophesy,
your old men will dream dreams,
your young men will see visions. (Joel 2:28)

DREAMS DEFINED

Nelson Hayashida gives *dream* its most common meaning as being the activity of the unconscious during sleep when scenes and/or voices are seen and/or heard.[1] According to the *Dictionary of Early Christian*

---

[1] Nelson Osamu Hayashida, "The Significance of Dreams and Visions among Members of the Baptist Churches of Zambia with Special Reference

Unless otherwise noted, Scripture quotations in this chapter are taken from the New International Version.

Beliefs, in the ancient world most persons believed that dreams were caused by the wandering of the soul while the body was sleeping. The early Christians generally held to the common view of their day.[2] Tertullian, an early church father, asks the question, "Where do dreams come from?" He then responds that the fact is the soul cannot rest or be altogether idle, nor does it confine its immortality to the still hours of sleep. Instead it shows that it possesses a constant motion; it travels over land and sea, it trades, it is excited, it labours, and it plays. Further, Tertullian introduces an interesting idea in that dreams are inflicted on us mainly by demons, although they sometimes turn out to be true and even favourable to us. However, all those visions and dreams that are honest, holy, prophetic, inspired, instructive, and inviting to virtue must be regarded as emanating from God, for He has promised indeed to pour out the grace of the Holy Spirit upon all flesh.[3] Another early church father, Origen, says it is a matter of belief that in dreams, impressions have been brought before the minds of many. Some relate to divine things, others to future events of this life. This may be with clearness or in symbolic manner.[4]

VISIONS DEFINED

Visions are the activity of the conscious state when the mind conjures up scenes and/or voices. This conjuring up is totally beyond the control of

---

to the Manyika Baptist Association and to Selected Urban Areas" (PhD diss., University of Edinburgh, 1993), 7.

[2] David W. Bercot, ed., *A Dictionary of Early Christian Beliefs* (Peabody, MA: Hendrickson, 1998), 220.

[3] Bercot, 220.

[4] Bercot, 221.

the person. While he or she is awake, some power or supernatural occurrence brings pictures and/or voices into the mind. Hayashida continues to say that visions sometimes arise from a trance or semi-conscious state, though not always. An experience is considered a "vision" if it fits the above definition.[5] The *Dictionary of Bible Themes* defines visions as mental pictures used by God to convey messages or reveal future events. They are normally received in private by individuals who are often prophets.[6]

DREAMS AND VISIONS IN THE BIBLE

There are several accounts of dreams and visions, supernatural appearances, and other such occurrences in the Scriptures. Dreams and visions in the Scriptures have been seen as means or ways by which God reveals Himself to man and communicates His purpose. Within the Old and New Testaments they offered insights into everyday realities or provided opportunities to those particular generations by connecting the earthly and the divine, as well as by connecting the present and the unknown future. Dreams and visions highlighted or predicted events either of a personal nature or universal in outlook. It should be stressed that many of these occurrences were understood by the recipients (Israelites) as divine revelations, yet the significance and meaning of others could not be immediately understood. Thus, it is necessary to consider some examples from both the Old and New Testaments.

---

[5] See Hayashida, *Significance of Dreams and Visions,* 8.

[6] Martin H. Manser et al., eds., *Zondervan Dictionary of Bible Themes* (Grand Rapids, MI: Zondervan,1996), 50.

DREAMS AND VISIONS IN THE OLD TESTAMENT

Dreams. References containing dreams are numerous in Genesis and Daniel, with other recorded dreams in Numbers, Deuteronomy, Judges, 1 Samuel, 1 Kings, Job, Psalms, Ecclesiastes, Jeremiah, and Joel.[7] We have an example of Joseph, whose story includes a number of dreams— both his and those of others (Gen 37:5–11; 40:6–22; 41:1–40). Having initially gotten into trouble by directing the benefits of his dreams to himself at the expense of his parents and brothers, Joseph seemed to have matured in the ability to interpret his dreams and those of others. So, when he was in Egypt and the subject of dreams came up, Joseph focused everyone's attention on God rather than using the situation to make himself look good. He turned it into a powerful witness for the Lord (Gen 40:8; 41:38).

Visions. Through visions God gave spiritual insight to prophets. These visions feature prominently in Ezekiel and Daniel, with other occurrences being in Genesis, Numbers, 1 Samuel, 1 and 2 Chronicles, Psalms, Job, Isaiah, Jeremiah, Lamentations, Hosea, Obadiah, Nahum, Habakkuk, Joel, and Zechariah.[8] Whatever the vision, it was clear that it was God who spoke even in the midst of false visions by the lying prophets. Visions in the Old Testament had prophets and seers as recipients.

---

[7] For example, see Num 12:6; Deut 13:1–3; Judg 7:13–15; 1 Sam 28:6, 15; 1 Kgs 3:4–15; Psalm 126; Ecclesiastes 5; and Joel 2:28.

[8] For example, in addition to the passages in the previous footnote, see also 1 Samuel 3; Isaiah 2; Jer 1:11–13; 24; Hos 12:10; Obadiah; Nahum 1; Hab 2:2–3; Zechariah 1–6.

DREAMS AND VISIONS IN THE NEW TESTAMENT

Dreams. Dreams recorded in the New Testament mostly occur around the birth of Christ (Matt 1:20; 2:13, 19). The conception and the birth of Jesus are supernatural events beyond human logic or understanding. God wanted certain individuals to grasp the significance of what was unfolding before them. The angel declared to Joseph that Mary's child was conceived by the Holy Spirit and would be the Son of God, revealing an important truth that God was fulfilling toward humanity. Note that these messages helped in the following ways:

- For Joseph to understand the pregnancy (Matt 1:20)
- That the wise men should not return to Herod (Matt 2:12)
- That Joseph should flee to Egypt with Mary and the baby Jesus (Matt 2:13)
- That Joseph should return home from Egypt because it was now safe (Matt 2:19–20)
- That Joseph should not establish a home in Judea (Matt 2:22)
- That Pilate should have nothing to do with Jesus during His trial (Matt 27:19)

Visions. Most visions in the New Testament are found in the book of Acts. Additionally, the book of Revelation has sustained details of vision occurrences. The apostles as well as other Christians and prospects for the gospel, Jews as well as Gentiles, were guided and led to specific encounters by the visions they experienced. Worth noting is Paul's conversion in Acts 9. Here God broke into a life in a spectacular manner, bringing him to conversion through that unique experience. God was about to step up the gospel transmission to both Jews and non-Jews. In addition, Luke highlights the following vision occurrences:

- The vision of Zacharias (Luke 1:22)
- The vision of Ananias (Acts 9:10)
- Cornelius's vision (Acts 10:3)
- Peter's vision (Acts 10:9–16)
- Paul's vision experience (Acts 18:9)

DREAMS AND VISIONS AND JESUS CHRIST

There is no scriptural record about Jesus having dreamt during His life. It is in Matthew we find the record that while in the midst of the trial of Jesus, Pilate got word from his wife: "Don't have anything to do with that innocent man, for I have suffered a great deal today in a dream because of him" (Matt 27:19). Pilate did not respond to the warning delivered to him by his wife with the understanding that God spoke to her in a dream.

With regard to visions the following is recorded about Jesus's baptism experience: Matt 3:16–17; Mark 1:9–11; Luke 3:21–22. These bear record of the same account, stating that as Jesus emerged from the water, He saw heaven open and the Spirit of God in the form of a dove descended on Him, followed by a voice from heaven that said, "This is my Son, whom I love; with him I am well pleased" (Matt 3:17). While the text in Luke indicates the dove came "in bodily form," or "in physical appearance," I still believe that this occurrence can be placed in the category of a vision.

FALSE DREAMS AND VISIONS

It should be noted that while there were legitimate dreams and visions through which God communicated to the people, there were also false dreams and visions that were misleading. These peculiar and spectacular dreams and visions occurred through the ministries of soothsayers and diviners, for example, in the time of the prophet Micah (3:5–8). These "seers" led people astray and warned of their sure disgrace and demise. In the same way, Jeremiah (23:25–26, 28) sent out a warning to the false dreamers who prophesied lies in the name of God when these were simply delusions of their own minds. The ultimate end for those who peddle prophecy through false dreams is spelled out in Deuteronomy (13:1–5): the death penalty shall be meted out for misleading people. Thus, God takes seriously the misleading of His people through counterfeit dreams and visions. Those who mislead men and women of God shall one day experience His wrath.

THE ROLE OF DREAMS AND VISIONS IN CHURCHES OF AFRICA

Men in many cultures of Africa look upon those who provide leadership in religion as great men of God. They are considered to have a special message from God, and they can tell others those mysterious things from God only known to them. In addition, they have the ability to tell others how to live and please God and what to expect from Him. Like the prophets of the Old Testament, there has emerged in these days people who claim to possess God's special word and revelation as part of their being entrusted with God's message. These men and women claim to possess an exalted position of supremacy sometimes close to that of Jesus Christ, all on the premise that ordinary men and women cannot fully grasp or understand God.

John S. Mbiti says that it is a widespread feeling among many African societies or peoples that man should not, or cannot, approach

God alone or directly, but that one must do so through mediation of special persons or other beings. In this case, societies have seers, prophets, and oracles. It seems their main duties are to act as ritual elders, to give advice on religious matters, to receive messages from divinities and spirits through possession or dreams, and to pass on the information to their communities.[9] This is understood to mean that God shows people what is going on in the spiritual world through a medium—in this case, a man who provides guidance to the true spiritual state of the church and of individuals.

Also worth noting is that religion has deep roots in people's lives. Therefore, in order to make it function properly in society, there are often men and women who have religious knowledge and serve as the link between their fellow human beings on the one hand, and God and spirits and invisible things on the other.[10] Hence, their calling is a special experience and leads to their valued high position. For example, among the Gikuyu of Kenya, the seers are ritual elders who are supposed to be in direct communication with God, who gives the instructions in dreams and guides people in performing the necessary rituals and invocations to God.[11]

Mediators are very important in Africa. Many functions and activities are built around the function of that mediator. Of course, a mediator's function is between two people or groups with a view to bring them together into an agreement. Thus, we need answers to crucial questions

---

[9] John S. Mbiti, *African Religions and Philosophy* (London: Heinemann Educational Books, 1983), 68.

[10] John S. Mbiti, *Introduction to African Religion* (London: Heinemann Educational Books, 1982), 152.

[11] John S. Mbiti, *Concepts of God in Africa* (London: SPCK, 1970), 222.

such as "who can represent mankind before God, and vice versa, who can represent God to mankind?" This is ultimately the role that religious men and women take while those who follow non-Christian religions often believe that ancestor spirits, divinities, prophets, or other specialists will act as mediators between human beings and God.[12]

The role that dreams and visions occupy in African churches, both traditional (mainline) and Charismatic (Neo-Pentecostal) including African Independent Churches (AICs), is so significant that they are ultimately considered the means to the connection and continuity between individuals and other aspects of spirituality. In fact, many dreams led and continue to lead to the founding of new religions and independent churches in Africa.

There are three distinct manifestations of revelations that function among Neo-Pentecostals in Africa. They are prophecy, discernment of spirits, and dreams and visions. Randy Arnett explores this manifestation of dreams and visions, which consist of personal revelations that provide direction or understanding.[13] These are commonly reported by the founders of churches and ministries. These dreams and visions also give direction to the organization and contribute to the founder's authority as the following examples will show.[14] They highlight the individual's calling through a dream.

John Ng'ang'a so called the impoverished Christian Kikuyu out of the worldly society of colonial Kenya that the manner of his calling to prophethood is surely worth noting: "'One night in a drunken stupor,

_____

[12] Wilbur O'Donovan, *Biblical Christianity in African Perspective* (Carlisle, UK: Paternoster Press, 1996), 258.

[13] Arnett, *Pentecostalization*, 40 (see intro., n. 8).

[14] Arnett, 40.

Ng'ang'a had a dream. In his dream God called him to leave his drunkenness, receive salvation, be baptized and then pray for his people that they might be liberated from their rulers.' Ng'ang'a obeyed the heavenly word and founded a movement that continued on the fringes of Kenya Christianity for years."[15]

Then there are those who claim to experience a vision in their calling, such as W. Wadé Harris (c. 1860–1929), a "young Grebo Anglican catechist and political activist" in Liberia. "The Angel Gabriel came to him in a vision calling 'him to be a prophet, to preach a gospel of repentance, to destroy "fetish worship" and to baptize those who obeyed.'" Harris saw himself "as a prophet of that heavenly kingdom soon to come to earth. . . . When he died in 1929, Harris had his final earthly vision of the coming kingdom."[16]

I was recently listening to testimonies of four men who were being interviewed in view of their impending ordination to the gospel ministry, and three of them attributed their calling to a dream or series of dreams that led them to conclude that the Lord was indeed laying a claim on their lives to serve Him. These are in mainline churches, and many others have had the same experience and share similar testimonies.

God used many ways to send His messages to people in Old Testament times. The writer of the book of Hebrews says, "In the past God spoke to our ancestors through the prophets at many times and in various ways" (Heb 1:1). God's word was found in the prophets, persons

---

[15] Mark Shaw and Wanjiru M. Gitau, *The Kingdom of God in Africa: A History of African Christianity,* rev. ed. (Carlisle, UK: Langham Global Library, 2020). See also O'Donovan, *Biblical Christianity in African Perspective,* 289.

[16] Shaw and Gitau, *The Kingdom of God in Africa*; O'Donovan, *Biblical Christianity in African Perspective,* 292–93.

He had chosen to proclaim His Word to the world. The revelation of the prophets came in a timely manner, fitting the age to which the message was designed.

There are many in Africa today, especially in Neo-Pentecostal practicing churches, Charismatic churches, AICs, and some mainline churches, who claim to be prophets of God who are able to receive communication from God through visions and dreams. Therefore, they seek to give special revelation to their people.

With the growth of Christianity and the founding of many churches, rightly hearing God's voice is critical. How does God guide and lead Christians today? Can dreams and visions be relied upon as God's revelation in these days? Do all dreams and visions come from God? How can one know?

When a Christian thinks God is guiding through these means, such guidance must always be compared with the truth of the Bible. God will never give guidance or a fresh revelation that stands in contrast to His eternal and authoritative Word. It stands forever and is forever applicable.

CHAPTER 6

ILLNESSES, CURSES, AND AFFLICTIONS

CONRAD MBEWE, PHD, ZAMBIA

In this chapter I deal with the perplexing realities of illnesses, curses, and afflictions, especially in our African context. I first address the question of where, according to our traditional beliefs, illnesses and afflictions come from. The understanding is that they are almost always a result of curses. We also see in this chapter how culturally we tend to work toward the removal of a curse, which is supposed to lead to the removal of illnesses and afflictions. However, I then look at the Scripture. How does it explain where illnesses and afflictions come from? Were they part of life from the dawn of creation? Finally, I suggest the best way for us to deal with illnesses and afflictions in view of what the Scriptures teach.

Unless otherwise noted, Scripture quotations in this chapter are taken from the English Standard Version.

CURSES AS MAIN CAUSES OF ILLNESSES AND AFFLICTIONS

As Africans, we are educated to believe that suffering comes into our lives because a fellow human being with mystical powers from the spiritual underworld has cast a spell—a curse—which is now being carried out against us. It is strongly believed that in the realm of the spirits of the ancestors there are malevolent forces arrayed against us. In order to get out of this state of suffering, we conclude, we must find someone with greater powers to undo the curse that we are under. We either go to the witchdoctor or the man of God. These are the power brokers who, in our understanding, can reverse the curse and end our suffering. Let us examine this belief, because we need to get back to the biblical understanding that was mentioned earlier in this chapter.

We are made to understand that illnesses are caused by ancestral spirits being upset with us, rightly or wrongly. They are a direct consequence of spiritual attacks either by demons (i.e., fallen angels) or by bad spirits in the realm of the dead. This belief becomes even stronger when a person has gone to the hospital for treatment and the illness is not being cured. This is seen as irrefutable evidence that the illness is from the spirit world.

This is also how conditions such as barrenness, infertility, and miscarriages are explained. Forces in the spirit world prevent a pregnancy or prevent the pregnancy from being carried to full term. Another category of misfortunes often attributed to the spirits of our ancestors is when a person has an accident or is harmed by a wild animal. If a person is bitten by a snake or attacked by a lion, that creature has been sent in his direction by a curse. No misfortune comes our way unless the spirits of our fathers permit it.

How do our traditional beliefs explain why ancestral spirits should be angry with one person and not another? Apart from an immediate curse that is put upon the person who is now suffering, there are other explanations. Sometimes it is due to what the parents of that individual did long ago. This is equated to the statements made in the Bible about God punishing people "to the third and fourth generations" (e.g., Exod 20:5; 34:7; Num 14:18). These are referred to as generational curses. You may be totally innocent yourself, but if your parents or grandparents did wrong and a curse was placed upon them that included "the third and fourth generation," you will still suffer the consequences.

Often, however, ancestral spirits are said to be unhappy with someone as a direct consequence of something they have done. They may have broken a taboo. This marks them out for punishment from the spirit world.

GOD'S CURSE AS THE CAUSE OF ILLNESS AND AFFLICTIONS

In contrast to all this, what does the Bible teach us about illnesses, curses, and afflictions? To begin with, as human beings we naturally do not want to suffer. That was how the Creator made us in the beginning. We were wired for a life of joy in the immediate presence of God as all our senses take in the beauty of the rest of creation around us. So, the statement that God made when He finished the work of creation brings joy to our hearts. We read in Gen 1:31 (ESV), "And God saw everything that he had made, and behold, it was very good." That was certainly a world that did not have suffering written all over it, as ours does.

When you look around, the situation has drastically changed. Life is filled with a lot of "very bad"—the exact opposite of what we read in Gen

1:31. The change took place in Genesis 3 when Adam and Eve listened to the lies of the serpent and ate the fruit that God had told them not to eat. God had warned that the day they would eat of it they would surely die. Satan, through the serpent, persuaded them that this was not going to happen. They ate the forbidden fruit and, sure enough, death came into the world.

The story is well-known. God cursed creation. He said:

> Because you have listened to the voice of your wife and have eaten of the tree of which I commanded you, 'You shall not eat of it," cursed is the ground because of you; in pain you shall eat of it all the days of your life; thorns and thistles it shall bring forth for you; and you shall eat the plants of the field. By the sweat of your face you shall eat bread, till you return to the ground, for out of it you were taken; for you are dust, and to dust you shall return. (Gen 3:17–19)

This curse changed the trajectory of human experience. Work was no longer full of unalloyed joy. It was now full of pain and toil. Many hurtful frustrations—represented by the phrase "thorns and thistles"—are now experienced in the context of work and of life generally. Life is about sweat and suffering until we breathe our last and die. The sad and stubborn reality is that we find ourselves in this period. We do not like it because we were wired for a life of joy, but whether we like it or not, this is our experience. We fall sick, and death is all around us. We, too, will soon die.

The explanation that the Bible gives for why we suffer illnesses and afflictions of all kinds is very different from that which is taught to us in our African culture. Both explanations speak of curses. However, whereas in the traditional context the curses are from human beings or spirits, in the biblical context the curse is from God the Creator. As a result of the fall of mankind in Genesis 3, the whole world is under a curse (Rom 8:20–25).

WHY IT IS SO IMPORTANT TO BELIEVE IN GOD'S CURSE

What bearing does this have on the way in which we deal with these misfortunes of life? How we understand the source of our illnesses and afflictions will inform the way in which we seek to remove the curses.

In the traditional understanding of what causes human suffering, you inevitably find that individuals and whole communities go to witch-doctors (sometimes called medicine men or traditional healers) or "men of God" for help. These two groups are understood to have access to the spirit world and to prevail upon those spirits. For many people who are Christians but who still hold on to the traditional way of understanding human afflictions, the main difference is that the witchdoctor uses evil power while the "man of God" uses clean power, God's power. Yet, all of them chant words over and over again until they apparently get insight into what has really taken place in the spirit world. In that way they are able to diagnose the problem and even suggest the cure. The witchdoctor moves a few divination bones around on the floor as he discerns what has really gone wrong, while the man of God prays in tongues, that is, in a language no one understands.

Having found out the cause of the misfortune in the life of the client, the witchdoctor recommends the solution. This often includes the client paying for the service. In traditional circles, it may include sacrificing an animal to appease the angry spirits and providing a charm or a talis-man or an amulet that the client can wear to keep away the curse of bad spirits. Even where herbs are given as medicine, usually the witchdoctor would have done some rituals to consecrate or empower those herbs so that they have potency. The rituals often include dancing and beating of drums and singing.

What takes place in traditional circles is more or less what takes place in many churches today. Whereas in traditional circles they offer animal sacrifices and amulets, in church circles it is the claiming of the blood of Jesus as an imagined protective garment. Very loud prayers are offered as a way of securing the breakthrough in order to break the curse. This is essentially the process of removing the curse that was upon the life of the client. Once the curse is removed, it is understood that the blessings will begin to flow from above.

Where the curse is understood to be primarily God's curse, then the most important question that ought to be uppermost in the minds of those who are afflicted is whether this curse of God has been removed through them having a right standing with God. This right standing with God can only be ours if we are repentant toward God and have put our faith in the Lord Jesus Christ as our Saviour (Acts 20:21).

The Bible says, "Christ redeemed us from the curse of the law by becoming a curse for us—for it is written, 'Cursed is everyone who is hanged on a tree'—so that in Christ Jesus the blessing of Abraham might come to the Gentiles, so that we might receive t he promised Spirit through faith" (Gal 3:13–14). Although Jesus was absolutely sinless, He suffered the consequences of our sins so that in Him we might be accepted by God as righteous.

Since the curse has been removed from us through the death of Christ, we should have another explanation as to why God's children still suffer illnesses and afflictions together with the rest of humankind. It is to make us godlier and to bring us closer to God. The Bible says:

Count it all joy, my brothers, when you meet trials of various kinds, for you know that the testing of your faith produces steadfastness. And let steadfastness have its full effect, that you may be perfect and complete, lacking in nothing. . . . Blessed is the man who remains steadfast under trial, for when he has stood the test he will receive the crown of life, which God has promised to those who love him. (Jas 1:2–4, 12)

A biblical understanding of illnesses and afflictions also gives us eternal hope that one day when Jesus Christ returns "death shall be no more, neither shall there be mourning, nor crying, nor pain anymore, for the former things have passed away" (Rev 21:4). As we fight illnesses and afflictions, we know that for a child of God these are temporal. They will soon be a thing of the past when we are resurrected with new bodies at the return of our Saviour to earth.

SEEKING ANSWERS TO IMMEDIATE CAUSES

Does that mean we should not try to get out of our illnesses and afflictions because we see that God allows them to come our way in order to sanctify us? Of course not. We said earlier that we were wired for a life of joy. That is why illness and afflictions are described as trials. We should do everything that is legitimate to avoid illness and afflictions, and when we find ourselves in them, we should do whatever is legitimate to get out of them.

Many of our illnesses, for instance, are caused more immediately by bacteria, viruses, and fungi. In the cultural mandate that we find in Gen 1:28, we are told to "fill the earth and subdue it." This subduing of the earth includes our harnessing of the potential that is in the earth for our good and for God's glory. It is as a result of the creative ability that God has given us as human beings because we are made in His image. Through knowledge rather than superstition, we should find remedies for these bacteria, viruses, and fungi.

Science and Christianity are not in opposition to each other. Scholarship and faith are not enemies. The problem with the cultural view that our illnesses and afflictions are caused more immediately by angered spirits is that it undermines our capacity to seek solutions that are based on knowledge. There is no effort to subdue the earth. We only want to subdue spirits. Even where herbs are used—which probably heal due to their medicinal content—we still attribute the healing to the divination, the drums, and the dancing that the medicine man did before administering the herbs.

When we make science an enemy of faith, we do not subject the herbs to laboratory testing so that we can develop the knowledge of the herbs and make them more powerful. We do not come to a better diagnosis of the stage of an illness or understanding of the right dosage that can kill the bacteria without harming the body. We fail to ensure hygiene in the preparation of the medicine and in its administering. Also, as long as only the traditional healers know the herbs, we lack the capacity to make them more accessible to people further afield. This partly explains why Africa remains so underdeveloped.

Does it mean that there are never situations where illnesses can be caused by evil spirits or as a direct consequence of our sins? I think there are and, in those situations, medicines may prove ineffectual and only the prayers of faith of the righteous can prevail (Jas 5:13–15). However, even there, the Bible does not say that human curses or the curses of ancestral spirits are the cause. This is what we must reject. Those of us who are church leaders and mature believers should engage in biblical counseling and teaching rather than rushing to prayers of deliverance. We must encourage people to confess their sins and pray to God in all circumstances of illnesses and afflictions. We must also encourage them to seek solutions based on the creation mandate to subdue the earth.

CHAPTER 7

SPEAKING IN TONGUES

REV. BASIL BHASERA, ZIMBABWE

According to what we learn from the Bible, speaking in tongues can be understood as the ability to speak in an unknown language through the supernatural enabling of the Holy Spirit. The Greek word for *tongues* in the New Testament literally means "languages." This gift was first described as having manifested in Acts 2:4. It is written that "they were all filled with the Holy Spirit and began to speak with other tongues, as the Spirit gave them utterance" In this instance, Luke records that many people from far and wide were present, and some were able to understand and identify the new tongues (Acts 2:6–12). Prior to this passage, in Mark 16:17, Jesus told His followers that these "signs" shall follow those that believe, that they will cast out devils and "speak with new tongues."

Unless otherwise noted, Scripture quotations in this chapter are taken from the New King James Version.

We can extrapolate that this occurrence of believers speaking in tongues unknown to some that happened on the day of Pentecost, and in other places after that, was probably what Jesus was referring to. The same type of supernatural occurrence is recorded in other parts of the book of Acts as well, including Acts 10:45–46 and Acts 19:5–6. In all these instances we can deduce that they spoke in a language previously unknown to them and unlearned. It is crucial to note that in other instances following the day of Pentecost, it does not tell us that the witnesses could understand the new language.

In 1 Corinthians 14, Paul writes about this special gift, and notably he mentions that whenever this gift was in use another gift to interpret was needed. This further tells us that in this instance this gift was not understood by the hearers. This is probably how the gift of tongues has been understood until the present day, as a supernatural and unknown spiritual language that can only be understood once an interpretation has been given by someone who has the gift to interpret tongues.

HOW NEO-PENTECOSTALS HANDLE THE GIFT OF TONGUES

The most notable teaching about tongues in prosperity and Neo-Pentecostal churches is that it is a sign of the indwelling of the Holy Spirit in an individual. It is most commonly taught that after one has made a profession of faith in Jesus, he or she must then receive the Holy Ghost. Evidence that this has occurred is the speaking of an unknown tongue. This teaching among Pentecostal circles is mainly derived from Acts 2:1–4 and hinges on the notion that if a believer does not yet speak in tongues, the person has not received the gift of the Holy Spirit. This secondary experience is within Pentecostalism believed to be the baptism of the Spirit mentioned in the New Testament: Matt 3:11; Mark 1:8; Luke 3:16; Acts 1:5; Acts 11:16; and 1 Cor 12:13.

It is also mainly believed that in form, tongues are an unknown, unintelligible language spoken by the inspiration of the Holy Spirit. In the second chapter of the book of Acts, it is recorded that those upon whom the Holy Spirit descended like tongues of fire spoke in a language that was heard by all who were present but was unknown to some. Pentecostals also derive their belief about the form of tongues from passages such as Acts 2. According to their interpretation, unknown languages were spoken as a result of the Holy Spirit coming upon believers; hence that is the way it ought to happen in their congregations today.

Another feature pertaining to how the gift of tongues is handled in Neo-Pentecostal churches is that it is believed to be for everybody. Everyone can and should possess the gift. Among Pentecostals and Neo-Pentecostals there is also the belief that tongues are to be spoken corporately and it is a congregational practice even when there is no interpretation of the tongues.

The late Kenneth E. Hagin, a prominent prosperity preacher in the United States, stated in his article "Seven Reasons Why Every Believer Should Speak in Tongues" that "speaking in tongues is an initial evidence, or sign, of the baptism of the Holy Spirit."[1] This was Hagin's first point in his article. Secondly, he suggested that speaking in tongues puts every believer in "direct contact with God, who is a spirit." So because

---

[1] Kenneth E. Hagin, "Seven Reasons Why Every Believer Should Speak in Tongues," Kenneth Hagin Ministries, accessed 10 June 2020, https://www.rhema.org/index.php?option=com_content&view=article&id=1053:seven-reasons-why-every-believer-should-speak-in-tongues&catid=53:holy-spirit&Itemid=145.

of this "when you speak in tongues, you are talking to Him by divine, supernatural means." Another prosperity preacher who also gives five reasons why a believer should speak in tongues is Kenneth Copeland. In a short introductory paragraph in his article entitled "5 Benefits of Praying in Tongues," he states that "when you are baptized by the Holy Spirit, you receive a gift from God—the gift of speaking (or praying in tongues)."[2]

An African prosperity teacher, Chris Oyakhilome, popularly known as Pastor Chris, also teaches in his article entitled "The Importance of Speaking in Tongues" that it is more important for a believer to pray in the Spirit than to pray in the believer's own language. He states emphatically in this article, "every Christian should want to pray in tongues; it is very, very important because of what it does for you. If you don't do it, you lose all that, you miss all the benefits."[3]

HOW THE GIFT OF TONGUES WAS UNDERSTOOD IN THE NEW TESTAMENT CHURCH

If we look at the Bible, we can get some wisdom by analyzing how New Testament Christians understood and handled this gift. It is prudent for us to note that before the New Testament era, the prophet Isaiah mentioned this phenomenon in Isa 28:11, "For with stammering lips and

---

[2] Kenneth Copeland, "5 Benefits of Praying in Tongues," Kenneth Copeland Ministries, accessed 10 June 2020, https://www.kcm.org/real-help/prayer/apply/5-benefits-praying-tongues.

[3] Chris Oyakhilome, "The Importance of Speaking in Tongues," Affirmation Train, January 20, 2018, available from https://www.affirmation-train.org.

another tongue will he speak to this people" (KJV). Isaiah uttered this prophecy in his appeal to God's people that they return to their God to escape the coming judgment of captivity that the prophet Jeremiah foretells one hundred years later. This "sign" would be significant to God's people, the Jews. Paul makes it clear to us, as we read his words, that this is how the issue of tongues was understood and ought to be handled: as that which Isaiah referred to concerning God's judgment on His people Israel. First Corinthians 14:21–22 says:

> In the law it is written, with men of other tongues and other lips will I speak unto this people [the Jews]: and yet for all that will they not hear me, saith the Lord. Wherefore tongues are for a sign, not to them that believe, but to them that believe not: but prophesying serveth not for them that believe not, but for them which believe. (KJV)

I believe that we have here the foundational information with which we ought to understand what tongues meant to the early Jewish Christians and writers of the New Testament.

Tongues, it seems, were meant to be a specific sign for unbelieving people who were also Jews. As the New Testament begins to play out after the death of Christ, we have our first encounter with the phenomenon in Acts 2. Jews from all over the world, where they had been scattered, gathered to celebrate Pentecost, a purely Jewish feast. In Peter's sermon he speaks to the crowd who had just witnessed the first incident of tongues, and he addresses his audience with these words: "Ye men of Judea, and all ye that dwell at Jerusalem" (Acts 2:14 KJV). Peter seems to be addressing his kinsmen here, and as the sermon commences, he makes it clear that what had just happened is what the prophet Joel had prophesied. As Peter begins to expound what the prophet Joel was warning Israel about, we understand him to be saying that this is a sign of things to happen in the last days. In verses 19–21 Peter describes a very apocalyptic scene in which the sun will be turned into darkness and the moon into blood as the day of the Lord comes. It seems that Peter is suggesting that one aspect of this sign was for them to remember the judgement that was prophesied to come on those who do not believe.

Further on in the nineteenth chapter of Acts, we catch up with Paul, and he has encountered some Jews who have been living abroad in foreign lands. It is most probable that they were disciples of John the Baptist, directly or indirectly influenced by his teaching, because they had been told to believe in Christ who was to come. Paul needed not to convince them of Christ, but upon learning that they knew nothing of the Holy Spirit, he prayed that they may receive the gift. When the Spirit came upon them, they spoke in tongues and prophesied. Again, it is in the presence of Jews that the gift manifests itself.

We can be sure that the apostles understood the gift to be a sign that would be relevant to the Jewish people because their prophets had predicted its coming. As much as they encountered this miraculous display of tongues, there is nothing in their teaching that suggests that they thought it was for everyone, or that it ought to be done communally outside of the context of God speaking directly to His people or as a sign to unbelievers who would be gripped by the manifestation of that which had been foretold to be a reminder of God's coming judgement.

Paul clearly spells out how the New Testament church understood the gift of tongues in 1 Corinthians chapter 14. Paul begins in the early parts of this chapter to offer an enlightening comparison between the gift of tongues and the gift of prophecy. He suggests that it is surely better to speak that which one can understand rather than something which cannot be deciphered. Paul's admonition here is to prophesy rather than to speak in tongues. The end goal is that all who hear what you say may be edified, but speaking in an unknown language will not achieve this unless you interpret the tongue and speak that which is intelligible.

It is within this passage that Paul presents a powerful case against the corporate speaking of tongues. He reminds the church why the gift was given; it is a sign to unbelievers. From verse 22 onward Paul makes the case for the futility of speaking in tongues when the whole church comes together. In verse 23 (KJV) he asks a question to prod the reasoning of his hearers, "Will they not say that ye are mad?" Who are the "they" that Paul is referring to? He has just stated that tongues are a sign to unbelievers, and in the next bit he mentions the unlearned and unbelievers. It is this latter group that he clearly feels will suffer the futility of tongues, for they will not benefit anything from it. Does Paul contradict himself here regarding unbelievers? I say not. As I suggested earlier, I believe he is talking about two different groups of unbelievers. The first group is those of the house of Israel to whom this gift holds meaning as a sign that was foretold by their prophets. The second group is Gentiles who would have no connection with this sign because they have no historical context to connect with it.[4]

---

[4] For support of this interpretation see David Cloud, "Tongues Were a Sign to Unbelieving Israel," Way of Life Literature, February 6, 2013, available from https://www.wayoflife.org/reports/tongues_were_a_sign.html and George E. Gardiner, *The Corinthian Catastrophe* (Grand Rapids, MI: Kregel, 1974), 35–36.

Baptism of the Spirit: What the Bible Really Teaches

We are also baptized by the Spirit. Texts in the New Testament about this "baptism" are often what the Pentecostal churches have mishandled. It seems the baptism of the Holy Spirit in the Pentecostal movements is synonymous with receiving the gift of tongues. Does the Bible really teach this? Let us take a look at a few Scriptures. Ephesians 4:4–6 says, "There is one body and one Spirit, just as you were called in one hope of your calling; one Lord, one faith, one baptism; one God and Father of all, who is above all, and through all, and in you all." The literary context of this trio of verses is easy to follow, because in the beginning of this letter to the Ephesians, Paul lays out some basic but crucial aspects of salvation. In chapter 1 he clarifies the position of the believer: that he is chosen and sealed. In chapter 2 he emphasizes the mode by which his salvation is transacted—by grace through the work of Christ. In chapter 3 he proposes that we are united in one body and equal in the body.

When we find this mention of "baptism," Paul is talking about our unity in relation to other believers, in other words, to the church. Why does Paul use this expression? I think it is the most appropriate to describe how we become part of the body of Christ: through a death of the old man with Christ and then being resurrected into the new birth by Christ's own resurrection. This is in fact the main purpose of this ordinance, and why we adhere to it. He carries on swiftly to explain that even though this is the case, we are baptized by the Spirit into one body. Each one of us was given grace according to the measure of Christ's gift. It is clear that Paul never suggests or hints at the idea of baptism of the Spirit being anything other than the Spirit's mysterious work in knitting together every believer into the body of Christ in unity with the rest.

In 1 Cor 12:13, we likely have the most explicit explanation about Spirit baptism in relation to the gift of tongues, because in this context Paul is writing specifically about the gifts of the Spirit. But again, Paul is consistent and states the exact meaning of the baptism of the Holy Spirit as he does in his letter to the Ephesians: "For by one Spirit we were all baptized into one body—whether Jews or Greeks, whether slaves or free—and have all been made to drink into one Spirit." There can be no mistaking that Paul is yet again describing this inexplicable work of the Holy Spirit as a baptism, one that is spiritual and requires no priest or rabbi to perform. Paul never associates this spiritual baptism with the immediate manifestation of any spiritual gift, nor does he ever suggest that it happens post-conversion as a secondary event. Instead he teaches that while we may be all in the body together, different gifts shall be bestowed on whomever the Spirit chooses for the purpose of supplying the body what it needs to do the work of Christ.

If this is the case, then why would the gift of tongues be given to every single member of the body? Paul argues the same just a couple of verses later in verse 17: "If the whole body were an eye, where would be the hearing? If the whole body were hearing, where would be the smelling?" Paul's rhetorical questions seem to be addressing the very same mishandling of spiritual gifts that we find ourselves trying to deal with today, and in verse 30 of the same chapter he spells it out for them: "All do not have gifts of healings, do they? All do not speak with tongues, do they? All do not interpret, do they?" (NASB). Paul is begging for logic with these questions. It was clear to Paul that this matter had to be clarified, as it indeed needs to be today. When we look into the Scriptures, we must do so with an earnest desire to find the Bible's truest teaching on any subject. One thing is clear: when it comes to the issue of tongues, the Pentecostals and Neo-Pentecostals have not done so. We cannot decide to bypass the strenuous but intricate and surgical hermeneutical approach to all Scriptures that mention the gift of tongues, which I have no doubt if done diligently, will arrive at no conclusion that favors the current handling of tongues by Pentecostals.

CONCLUSION

Tongues are a sign for unbelievers; they were never for believers. Peter says so in Acts 2 and Paul reiterates the same in 1 Cor 14:21–22.

Tongues were only to be used if accompanied by interpretation; otherwise, they must not be used at all (1 Cor 14:28).

Those speaking in a tongue must only speak in turn, and not all at the same time (1 Cor 14:27).

Those speaking in tongues should be limited to at most two or three people, and not more than that (1 Cor 14:27).

There is definitely an admonition to handle the use of this gift within certain parameters that were obviously meant to safeguard its misuse. It is these safeguards that are cast aside carelessly. It is Paul's conviction that it is more harmful to the body if the gift was used wrongly than if it was not used at all. He would rather have had the Corinthians shut down the gift than handle it with ignorance or even maliciously for their own recognition-seeking motives. For all intents and purposes, going mute on the gift of tongues would make them a healthier congregation under the circumstances. It is also clear that concerning this biblical teaching and caution about tongues, Neo-Pentecostals have largely abandoned it.

CHAPTER 8

PROPHECY

JULIUS D. TWONGYEIRWE, PHD, UGANDA

Throughout history, God's people in each generation have had to clarify His unchanging message in changing times, so as to remain faithful to God and relevant in their day. Today, the authority of some personalities, some denominations, and their traditions are still exalted above the Scriptures. Also, our generation is faced with a contest of discernment for God's voice amidst the vast spiritual noise and clamor of prophetic claims. Many people are not sure whether they are being attracted to myths and tales or to God-exalting, human-humbling messages in the name of prophecy. There is a greater need than ever before to rearticulate biblical truths so that God's Word refines and defines our generation so they can comprehend prophets and prophecy and be faithful to God in our own generation.

Unless otherwise noted, Scripture quotations in this chapter are taken from the New International Version.

PROPHECY IN THE BIBLE

What does the Bible say about prophecy? The first person to be called a prophet was Abraham, and it was God who gave him this title. This story is found in Gen 20:1–7. A heathen prince had taken Abraham's wife, and God commanded him to restore her, saying of Abraham, "He is a prophet" (v. 7). There must have been other people before Abraham who were prophets, including Enoch (Gen 5:24) as affirmed in Jude 14, but all through history, God appointed prophets from diverse backgrounds and many walks of life. Ezekiel and Jeremiah were priests; David was first a shepherd, then a warrior, king, a poet, and a prophet as well. Amos was a herdsman, Elisha was a plowman (1 Kgs 19:15–21), and Daniel was a government administrator (Dan 2:48). More than one hundred named prophets are mentioned in the Bible. In addition, numerous others prophesied, such as the seventy elders of Israel (Num 11:25) and the one hundred prophets rescued by Obadiah (1 Kgs 18:4).

The time of Elijah and Elisha was marked by a high level of prophetic activity, and a school for prophets thrived during their lifetimes (1 Kgs 20:35). The influence and authority of God's prophets did not come from their rank, education, wisdom, or wealth, but entirely from the fact that God chose them to be His messengers.

So, we may define a prophet as one appointed by God to bring God's truth to God's people in a specific situation. Prophets were also called "seers," because of their spiritual insight or ability to "see" the future. In the Bible, prophets often had both a teaching and a revelatory role, declaring God's truth on contemporary issues as "forth tellers" and revealing details about the future as "fore-tellers." They were "ministers of God's Word" by role. They were to reveal the nature and attributes of God to people (Deut 5:4–10), to make known the commands and laws of God (Exod 20:1–17), to call God's straying people back to obedience to God's laws (2 Chr 24:19), and to exhort God's people to sincerity in worship (Jer 7:1–11). Prophets were called to warn God's people of His judgment upon sin, both personal and national (Jer 36:30–31), and to foretell future events that God had willed or decreed (Jer 30:1–3), including the coming of the Messiah, our Saviour (Isa 9:6). Prophets recorded the history of God's dealings with men for future generations (Deut 31:9–13; 1 Cor 10:6, 11), and penned the Word of God (Exod 17:14; 34:27; Jer 36:27–28), among many other roles.

Prophets were not permitted to inherit that title or regard it as an official post to be filled by anyone specially trained for it. But because prophets were so influential, it is not surprising that false prophets also appeared, pretending to be God's messengers in order to support their own ambitions for authority and personal advancement.

Because of this, God gave clear instructions to the people to examine the credentials of all who claimed to be prophets (Deut 18:9–22). Given his role as a messenger of God, a prophet was under God's authority to deliver God's message to God's people for divine purposes.

SELF-PROCLAIMED PROPHETS

Today, falsehood that is embraced as "prophecy" thrives unabated in an inadequate understanding of both the biblical role of prophecy and its practice. Much of what is different in today's prophecy begins as a matter of where authority and sufficiency lie. Under the guise of prophetic and apostolic ministry, today's "man of God" has generally assumed greater honour and authority than the Word of God. Prophecy is thus audience-driven, looking upon the world rather than God, to find out what the public's itching ears would like to hear. The trend of unqualified men gathering members for feeble messages, myths, and spiritual entertainment with ministries named after them continues to yield victims. The search for God's truth from the Bible is replaced by the declarations from "the anointed man of God" who unleashes his own dreams and visions upon hearers. The undermining of biblical authority, reliability, and sufficiency serves to exalt whomever it is that claims to be God's messenger, but only before people.

Many of today's prophets are thus self-seeking, having replaced the God-ordained process of discipleship with their power-packed events and "spiritual instants," which promise recovery from sin and its effects on humans, but of course in vain. They claim instantaneous healings and solutions for different situations, without capacity to accommodate broken relationships, stubborn habits, immoral character, and other shortcomings on sin-laden lives. They emphasize miracles that fit the temporal nature of their events instead of helping people to cultivate character for a life that will spend eternity with God, undermining God's call for a lifelong sanctification.

Much of today's false prophecy takes advantage of Bible illiteracy in a fleshly search for spiritual experience. Thus, this false teaching inclines itself to excluding guilt, shame, sin, repentance, and consequences of sin from its declarations in order to maintain "excitement in Christ." This kind of subjectivism places spiritual demands on adherents, to dream dreams and to see visions, often at the neglect of the Scriptures. This subjectivism tends to instill a fear of the unknown past, an uncertain present, and an unpredictable future in its assumed generational curses that call for endless "deliverances." In turn, the deliverance and interpretation of life then elevates a spiritual guru for mediation in the name of a prophet.

In this way, false prophets exchange the gospel hope as centered on Christ and His accomplished work for a wishy-washy, self-centered, self-exalting psychotherapy. The so-called prophets are not proclaiming the gospel for sound faith in God but are turning people away from the glory of the eternal God to material prosperity in false assurance. This disregards the future—whether immediate or eternal—by focusing on the present for the God of only the here and now.

How have we come to this? We know through history that the church on the move is always prone to wander from faithful Word ministry, especially when people have lost a hunger for truth. We are now in an era when people are inclined to be "feelers" more than they are "thinkers." So, the search for greater spiritual experience is often at the cost of neglect of scriptural instruction. A combination of ungodly cravings that characterize itching ears and redefining the gospel in material prosperity have led to theological starvation in the church today.

As Jeremiah decried in history (Jer 23:9–32), today's prophets are once again the stumbling block between God and His people, making false spiritual diagnoses and utterances as they did before. This is how the sway of these self-seeking spiritual gurus has surpassed the influence of the Word of God, making the Bible a closed book and thus muting God's voice among many. Today's prophecy is disparaging and misrepresenting the work of Christ, causing people's faith to rest on wrong principles, only to produce deficient and ungodly lifestyles.

Since falsehood in today's prophecy takes advantage of Bible illiteracy, there is a lack of spiritual discernment. Discernment is related to wisdom, and the Word of God itself is said to discern the thoughts and intentions of one's heart (Heb 4:12). Even some of the sincerest God-seekers seem to lack the ability to properly distinguish between the biblical and the unbiblical. They lack the ability to "weigh up" the spiritual status, moral standing, or consequences. True discernment means not only distinguishing right from wrong in terms of ethics; it means distinguishing the primary from the secondary, the essential from the indifferent, and the permanent from the transient. Those who discern learn to think God's thoughts after Him with a sense of outlook through God's own eyes.

But discernment is for the growing and mature. The stunted and lazy cannot share in it but remain in danger of resting their faith in the pronouncements of false prophets. Also, zealous but undiscerning Christians become enslaved to others, caged to their own uneducated conscience, and thus incarcerated to an unbiblical pattern of life. We have many warnings against false prophets (Matt 7:15; 24:24; Rev 16:13; 19:20; 20:10), to avoid being led astray by "test[ing] the spirits to see whether they are from God" (1 John 4:1). The church's capacity for spiritual examination of false teachers is a needed protection against deviations from spiritual health, as believers test before they trust.

Since falsehood in today's prophecy confuses relevance and faithfulness in preaching, we need to come to terms with kingdom priorities in regard to God's message, God's methods, and our motivation in service. The hunger for tangible ministry results seems to allow no time to cultivate understanding of the culture around us, or the way to bring God's Word to it. The desire to see quicker results in evangelism and church planting often compromises the gospel by appealing more to cultural preferences as a way of persuading the statistically driven human agendas. This has bred broad Christian presence with minimal Christian influence in society.

Once result-oriented activism outshines God-given methods for the church on mission, preachers aim at being culturally relevant rather than scripturally faithful—thus propagating falsehood in our congregations. The excesses of cultural sensitivity must be checked by biblical faithfulness in seeking the Giver, and not only His gifts. Kingdom priorities remain key. Today's expedient prophecy is superficial, under priorities of a human agenda that fail to exclude error. A sustained abiding in Christ is the only stance that can lead to bearing fruit that will last (John 15:16).

Since falsehood in prophecy often thrives unchallenged, there is now a greater need for "Word ministry" that is not only geared to exhortation but an incessant rebuttal in refuting doctrinal error. Preachers who want to have a life-giving ministry that ensures a healthy church on mission have no viable option other than preaching and teaching Scripture with at least two voices: the voice for the sheep and the voice for the wolves. It is within this reality that today's biblical preacher must advance gospel ministry with boldness and fearlessness.

Similarly, faithful prophets of old had a dangerous calling. People frequently mocked, rejected, persecuted, and even killed them. Stephen, the first martyr of the new covenant, pointedly asked, "Was there ever a prophet your ancestors did not persecute?" (Acts 7:52 NIV). Even Jesus lamented that Jerusalem had killed the prophets God sent to them (Luke 13:34). As Isaiah described the stance of his nation (Isa 30:9–10), the prophets of God were often despised and their message unheeded. In order to deal with false prophecy, preachers must be prepared to refute error with greater confidence.

So, are there prophets today? The role of a prophet was to reveal truth from God. We have the completed revelation from God in the Bible. The prophets and apostles were the "foundation" of the church through their Word ministry (Eph 2:20), and we are no longer building this foundation today. The very words of the biblical writers are the words of God (1 Cor 2:13; 2 Tim 3:16). But this is not true of the words that come from every revelation claiming the gift of prophecy. Whatever prophecies are given today do not add to Scripture. Instead, they ought to be tested by Scripture, which is closed and final in authority.

GOING BACK TO SCRIPTURE

The teaching of the apostles was the final authority, and no other prophecies have such authority (1 Cor 14:37–38; 2 Thess 2:1–3). Faithful biblical preaching is prophetic and apostolic in a certain sense. Although no one today occupies the office of a prophet, God still speaks today, and the role of a prophet is played by preachers who are in complete agreement with what God has already revealed in the Bible. Passionate exposition is being thinned in many churches, with ritualism, motivational speaking, dramas, movie clips, and conversational interactions replacing biblical preaching.

So, how can the church remain hungry and open to God's voice—His warnings, His promises, and His commands—amidst the many loud and enticing voices? Can the church recover faithfulness to the Word and regain eagerness for God's voice? How can the church reclaim this ground enough to sustain the urge for us to contend for the faith that was once for all entrusted to God's holy people? For indeed, as Jude puts it, certain individuals have secretly slipped in among us (Jude 4).

We must reaffirm that the church is the "creature" of the Word of God.[1] The Word of God comes to people primarily through sound teaching and the authentic preaching of the Bible message. Therefore, the church must revisit prophecy according to the Bible to gain understanding and reassert the authority and sufficiency of Scripture. False prophets and apostles are trying to usurp the voice of God in regard to the human predicament. Additionally, the church must teach the Bible in order to reform and regain her capacity for spiritual discernment.

---

[1] Matt Chandler, Josh Patterson, and Eric Geiger, *Creature of the Word: The Jesus-Centered Church* (Nashville, TN: B&H, 2012).

Then, the church must be strategic in shaping the minds and hearts of upcoming preachers through expository preaching.

There is also a need to sustain inquiry into how and why Pentecostal Christianity has been well received among traditional religionists. This can guide the effort to true biblical discipleship, which cuts through worldview elements that include demonization, sickness, and spiritual assaults in the spirit world, building up authentic communities of faith. Recovery from prophetic falsehood calls for contextual hermeneutics that account for worldview elements that are peculiar to ethno-cultural arrangements, in order to cope with their spiritual inquiry. Once the cultural context is thoroughly examined, then particular inclinations can receive a biblical response, leading to gospel transformation.

In this way, the contextualized gospel will yield indigenized ministries, with people at home in Christ, like a plant in its soil. Indeed, by God's power and will, today's church can nurture a heritage of faithfulness that is passed on through godly lives over generations to come. The church must turn away from false prophecy by embracing expository preaching, which expresses the exact will of the glorious Sovereign and allows God to speak, not man. Expository preaching retains the thoughts of the Spirit and brings the preacher into direct and continual contact with the mind of the Holy Spirit, who authored Scripture. This ought to be the precedent for true prophecy. May Christ build and uphold His church!

CHAPTER 9

MIRACLES OF HEALING AND DELIVERANCE

REV. KEN MBUGUA, KENYA

Neo-Pentecostalism is rife in our age. It is unlikely that a believer on the continent could live out his faith without having to contend with the teachings and beliefs of this movement. In pursuit of a theologically mature and strong church that is not tossed to and fro by every wind of doctrine, we write these essays in the hope that the church in Africa will be equipped with God's truth as it resists the winds of false doctrine.

As with many of the distortions of biblical teachings, the teachings of healing and deliverance in the Neo-Pentecostal movement have shadows of truth that have been corrupted by unbiblical views. For most errors of this ilk, a biblical theology approach in addressing the matter can go a long way in mending or at least exposing the error without rejecting the

Unless otherwise noted, Scripture quotations in this chapter are taken from the English Standard Version.

biblical hope offered to saints today. Before we look at the distortion in Neo-Pentecostalism, let us take a look at the role that miracles of healing and deliverance play in the narrative of Scripture.

THE GOODNESS OF GOD'S PHYSICAL CREATION

It has often been said that the first eleven chapters of the book of Genesis lay down an all-important foundation for the truths that come thereafter. The first critical truth taught there is that God created a physical universe, a physical man and woman, and called it all good.

There is goodness in things physical, goodness in the blessing of order in and through creation. There is goodness in the beauty of the heavens and in the diversity of animals in the sea, land, and air. There is goodness in the changing rhythms of day and night. There is goodness in the food in the garden, in physical work of tending to the garden and exercising dominion over the earth. There is goodness in the pleasure of marital physical union. There is goodness in the mineral riches found in the garden. The earth and the fullness of it were God's and they were all good.

It is important to note at the beginning of the story of the Bible that God not only made things invisible, He also made things visible. He is not only God of the spiritual, He is also God over the physical. The physical is not of less importance than the spiritual. All belong to God, and all are good.

It is not uncommon to hear those defending against the excesses of Neo-Pentecostalism demean the goodness of physical things. It is easy to speak as though the more one believes in God, the less one is expected to care about the physical world.

The God who cares about our love, joy, peace, patience, and kindness also cares about our bodies, our daily bread, our clothing, our relationships, our illnesses, and our work. The world that God made was not only spiritual, it was also physical.

In this perfect physical world of blessing, there was no place for miracles of healing or deliverance. There was neither sickness nor brokenness of any kind. Everything worked just as it should. The story of the Bible presents an ideal that is superior to that of experiencing a miracle. A world that is both spiritual and physical but knows no brokenness, not even in the slightest degree, is put forward as the ideal that all believers long for. Not a world where the sick get healed but a world where there is no sickness at all.

THE FALL AND MIRACLES OF HEALING AND DELIVERANCE

God's good creation was corrupted by the entrance of sin into the world. The deceiver managed to convince mankind that it was possible to separate goodness from God; in other words, that it was possible to obtain good by going against God or better yet, that God was not to be trusted to determine for mankind the difference between good and evil.

The result was the fall of man. We fell from God and all that is good in Him. Good was replaced with evil and blessing by the curse. Nothing was spared, not our bodies or our relationships or our work. The curse corrupted everything and everyone. Health was often replaced by sickness, peace replaced by war, love replaced by hate, blessing replaced by the curse, and life replaced by death.

THE ENTRANCE OF DEATH

This is the book of the generations of Adam. When God created man, he made him in the likeness of God. Male and female he created them, and he blessed them and named them Man when they were created. When Adam had lived 130 years, he fathered a son in his own likeness, after his image, and named him Seth. The days of Adam after he fathered Seth were 800 years; and he had other sons and daughters. Thus all the days that Adam lived were 930 years, *and he died.* (Gen 5:1–5, italics added)

The phrase "and he died" rings loud in Genesis 5. From the first verse to the thirty-second verse, the phrase appears eight times:

Gen 5:5: "and he died"
Gen 5:8: "and he died"
Gen 5:11: "and he died"
Gen 5:14: "and he died"
Gen 5:17: "and he died"
Gen 5:20: "and he died"
Gen 5:27: "and he died"
Gen 5:31: "and he died"

The curse of death is the inescapable reminder that all things are broken in this world. All other experiences of brokenness in this life, evidenced in struggling marriages, sick bodies, or dysfunctional society, simply point to the effect of the curse that mankind is under. The power of that curse is most clearly seen in death.

The darkness that descends into creation is bleak without any trace of hope in it. The corruption is total, leaving no aspects of creation untouched. If there is to be hope, it has to come from outside the decay and rot that the world now experiences. Physical brokenness is real and cannot be refuted with vague statements that refuse to acknowledge the tragedy of loss, the bitterness of pain, and the evil of death, the ultimate sickness that mankind needs to be healed from.

Technology cannot fix this brokenness; economic revolutions, political changes, and advances in medicine are all impotent in the face of death. They might offer some momentary relief, but all capitulate and crumble under the tyranny of death. We need to be rescued. A little relief will not do. We need full and complete deliverance; we need final and eternal healing.

AND THEN THERE IS ENOCH . . .

The passage has one anomaly in it, Gen 5:21–24, "When Enoch had lived 65 years, he fathered Methuselah. Enoch walked with God after he fathered Methuselah 300 years and had other sons and daughters. Thus all the days of Enoch were 365 years. Enoch walked with God, and he was not, for God took him."

Enoch disrupts the death and despair in the passage. All men seem to be under the curse, but here is one who somehow escapes it. The Bible gives us a glimmer of hope that perhaps there is a way out for mankind. We do not have to forever live under the curse of death. Hebrews 11:5 will point us to faith as the answer that the whole narrative of Scripture aims to. What Enoch experienced is what in many ways mankind longs for and often seeks in science or deliverance services. Enoch's story gives us cause to hope.

MIRACLES AND OUR HOPE FOR DELIVERANCE

Miracles in the Scriptures do that which technology and all other earthly solutions to brokenness cannot do. They offer God-given hope that a full reversal of the fall is possible, not merely some ease and relief. Miracles give us hope that a world that works as it was designed to work, a world where sickness and death do not reign, is possible. Miracles in the Scripture are designed to give hope.

MIRACLES IN THE DELIVERANCE OF ISRAEL

The book of Exodus shows us the plight of God's people. In this cursed world, mankind does not show love to those made in God's image. Evil abounds and God's people are not spared from it. Israel lives under the oppression of Egypt, and they cry and groan to the Lord for deliverance.

> During those many days the king of Egypt died, and the people of Israel groaned because of their slavery and cried out for help. Their cry for rescue from slavery came up to God. And God heard their groaning, and God remembered his covenant with Abraham, with Isaac, and with Jacob. God saw the people of Israel—and God knew. (Exod 2:23–25)

THE FINGER OF GOD

God grants His people deliverance through ten miraculous plagues. The power of God is put on such clear display that Pharaoh's magicians concede that the power manifested in Moses's miracles is something more than the magic they were practicing: "Then the magicians said to

Pharaoh, 'This is the finger of God.' But Pharoh's heart was hardened, and he would not listen to them, as the Lord had said" (Exod 8:19).

This display of God's power shows us that the One who created the heavens and the earth also has the ability to bring destruction. There is hope in the display of power through the miracles of the plagues. Mankind does not have to live under the yoke of the curse. God can display His power (the finger of God) in such a way that the effects of the fall are thwarted.

MIRACLES NOT NORMATIVE

Even though God delivered the children of Israel by parting the Red Sea and causing His people to walk on dry ground, miracles are not normative. The children of Israel still needed bridges and boats in the Promised Land. The type of display of God's power manifested in miracles of healing and deliverance is not normative in the Bible or in the Christian life.

THE REST OF THE STORY

These miracles also did not spare God's people from the brokenness of this world, as displayed in their own rebellion against God and the tyranny of kings and nations against them. Even though in the next book (Deuteronomy), God basically offers them pre-fall blessings on the condition of perfect obedience (Deut 28:1–14), the rest of Israel's story is that of a people who relentlessly sin against God. As a result, they are unable to remain under the covenant blessings that He has offered them. The narrative of Israel shows us that the only way we can ever know the blessing that we lost is by escaping the sin that has brought a curse upon mankind. But how shall mankind be delivered from the sin that so closely clings to him and the curse that destroys all that is good around him?

The hope offered in the story of Israel in the Old Testament is the arrival of the kingdom of God, which will be ushered in by a descendant of King David who will sit on the throne that shall have no end. Under the reign of this King, God's people can once again receive all the blessings of the kingdom of God that were lost at the fall.

MIRACLES AND THE MESSIAH

When Jesus walked the earth, He repeatedly showed us through His miracles that He was able to reverse the effects of the curse. He healed the sick, fed the hungry, raised the dead, and cast out demons. Here was one who was demonstrating power and authority like no other; even winds and waves obeyed His voice. John 20:31 articulates clearly that the purpose of the miracles that John recorded was to show to us that Jesus is indeed the long-awaited Messiah, Saviour, and King in whom we must believe if we are to be saved from this fallen state that has enslaved us.

The people of God had at no time been awaiting a season of miracles as an end in itself. Miracles were always a sign of the arrival of the King and His kingdom. That is what they were anticipating and eagerly awaiting.

What the Scriptures offer us is not the promise of miracles but the promise of a Deliverer. Miracles only offer temporary relief in a broken world; the Messiah comes to usher in the new creation, which is fashioned after the goodness of our Creator.

MIRACLES STOP SHORT OF SALVATION

In Luke 11:14–32, Jesus exorcises someone who was demon possessed. But those around Him misunderstand what they have just witnessed.

Quite importantly, they misunderstand what power God has used, accusing Him of using the devil's power, to which Christ responds, "And if I cast out demons by Beelzebul, by whom do your sons cast them out? Therefore they will be your judges. But if it is by the *finger of God* that I cast out demons, then *the kingdom of God* has come upon you" (Luke 11:19–20, italics added).

MIRACLES—THE APEX OF THEM ALL— THE RESURRECTION

All the miracles in the Bible pale in comparison to the resurrection. The resurrection is the pronouncement that deliverance from all the effects of the fall has been accomplished (1 Pet 1:3–5).

MIRACLES IN NEO-PENTECOSTALISM

It is important to recognize first and foremost that the cries for miracles of healing and deliverance in Neo-Pentecostalism are legitimate and biblically warranted cries. The Bible does not expect us to be at home in a broken world.

> For the creation waits with eager longing for the revealing of the sons of God. (Rom 8:19)

The cry for deliverance from illnesses, financial struggles, and marital difficulties is a legitimate cry. God hears it, cares, and more importantly, has acted to make it possible for mankind to be restored to a place to never again know the effects of the curse. In some cases, these teachings are mingled with the teachings of the prosperity gospel, where miracles are peddled in exchange for money. In other cases, the miracles of healing and deliverance are offered by individuals who claim special anointing not available to normal saints, thus leading people to look to man for their deliverance from the pain of this life.

However, the solution that Neo-Pentecostalism offers to those who are hurting is an unbiblical one. The miracles we see in Scripture were only meant to point us to the Messiah who will usher in the new creation, where we shall be fully and finally relieved from all the brokenness of this world. Never in Scripture are saints promised that deliverance in this world.

Neo-Pentecostalism's teaching on miracles of healing and deliverance in many cases exposes a belief that the spiritual world controls the physical world. As with many other religions in the world, they attempt to manipulate the unseen world with hopes of accomplishing their desired end in the seen world. Christianity does not offer miracles; it offers salvation.

COUNSELING, DISCIPLING, SHEPHERDING, AND HOPE

Any teaching that belittles physical pain and suffering misunderstands the severity of the curse; on the other hand, any teaching that offers deliverance from all sickness and brokenness in this world is a distortion of what the Bible teaches. As believers, we are pilgrims, exiles in a fallen world. We have received our visas to the promised land where we shall never again know illness or death, but that day is yet to come. The saint sets his eyes on that Canaan, the Promised Land, the Eden that we lost, the Zion that is to come, the new heavens and new earth where sin and death will be no more. By faith we walk in this world as we patiently await the return of the King and the ushering in of His kingdom.

The church is called to mercy.

Churches are not called to peddle deliverance services; they are called to proclaim the Deliverer's sacrifice. The task of our ministries today then becomes not that of promising temporal fixes to current problems but that of prayerfully applying Christ to the hearts and lives of those we are called to. All the benefits available to the saint today are available only in Christ by faith.

Wait on the Lord.

The new creation is coming.

PART 3

CHURCH PLANTING AND CHURCH DEVELOPMENT

CHAPTER 10

HOLISTIC GOSPEL MINISTRY

THE MESSAGE OF COSMIC REDEMPTION AS A RESPONSE TO THE PROSPERITY GOSPEL

S. TREVOR YOAKUM, PHD, TOGO

One of the most insidious ways that Neo-Pentecostalism flourishes amongst Sub-Saharan Africans is through empty promises of well-being, wealth, and health. Sadly, perhaps one of the reasons that evangelicals have not been as successful in fighting these falsehoods over the years is that missionaries and pastors have, at times, presented a truncated gospel message. Having faithfully preached that Jesus Christ accomplished the salvation of our souls, we have neglected to mention the redemption of all of creation through His death, burial, and resurrection—a holistic gospel message. It is my contention that the proclamation of this holistic gospel message is the spiritual antidote to the Neo-Pentecostal

Unless otherwise noted, Scripture quotations in this chapter are taken from the New American Standard Bible.

contagion. In this chapter, I shall hope to prove my assertion by giving a fuller description of the holistic gospel and how it can positively impact Africans through their cognitive orientation and traditional belief structure. I shall also give concrete examples of a holistic gospel witness for a vibrant Christian response to Neo-Pentecostalism.

HOLISTIC MINISTRY

Holistic gospel ministry, as I am describing it, is gospel proclamation. It presents the saving message of Jesus Christ and invites hearers to willingly respond to the invitation of repentance of sin and belief in Jesus Christ as the One who saves them from the just penalty as transgressors of God's law. Holistic gospel ministry is also gospel demonstration in that it provides social ministry that addresses the physical, social, economic, and/or psychological needs of its listeners. Gospel demonstration is an expression of the conviction that Jesus Christ not only redeems souls but will also redeem the entire created order. A biblically informed understanding of gospel demonstration should not seek to redeem the created order in some sort of post-millennialist eschatological fulfillment of the kingdom of God. Rather, examples of gospel demonstration should be signs of how Christ shall "make all things new" in the age to come.[1] They should illustrate how we as believers anticipate the *Parousia* when Jesus Christ will "bring everything together in Christ, both things in heaven and things on earth in him."[2] As Enoch Wan writes in his own definition of holistic ministry:

---

[1] See Rev 21:5.
[2] Eph 1:10.

"Holistic ministry/missions" is understood to be "Christians motivated by their love for God and neighbors (within or without one's socio-cultural context), mobilized to be engaged in multi-dimensional services to HIM by serving others inclusively caring for the spiritual, psychological, social, physical, etc. well beings of others, with multifaceted (religious & charity, public & private, etc.) services and at multi-levels (personal and institutional, local and global), in the framework of reconciliation vertically with God, horizontally with humanity and hierarchically with the created order."[3]

Holistic ministry has been a controversial subject among mission agencies and ministry practitioners for decades.[4] I will attempt to show

---

[3] Enoch Wan, "Holistic Ministry/Missions: Reflections & Resource Material," *Global Missiology* 1, no. 3 (October 2005), http://www.enochwan .com/english/articles/pdf/Holistic% 20Ministry%20Missions.pdf.

[4] C. P. Wagner, *Church Growth and the Whole Gospel* (New York: Harper & Row, 1981), 101–4. Wagner identifies five different viewpoints concerning the relationship between gospel presentation and human needs ministry: (1) Ministry of mercy and social justice are the only legitimate ministries of the church; (2) Social concern is the higher priority, but evangelism is important; (3) Social concern and evangelism, deed and word, are absolutely equal in importance; (4) Evangelism is the primary function of the church; mercy ministry is important but is secondary; and (5) Ministry of the Word is all that the church does; ministries of mercy should not be the concern of the church.

See also Timothy J. Keller, *Ministries of Mercy: The Call of the Jericho Road*, 2nd ed. (Phillipsburg, NJ: P & R, 1997), 112. Keller disagrees with Wagner's five viewpoints in that all of them view mercy and evangelism as independent goals. Keller asserts, "The proper model is not (1) to see mercy as the means to evangelism, or (2) to see mercy and evangelism as independent ends, but (3) to see both word and deed, evangelism and mercy, as how holistic ministry, informed by orality studies in communication, can effectively engage the traditional African worldview. This worldview still bears the stamp of African Traditional Religion upon which Neo-Pentecostalism thrives. Holistic gospel ministry, proclaimed faithfully in the power of the Holy Spirit, engages the existential concerns of those who exhibit the traditional African worldview among both professing Christians and non-believers.

Holistic gospel ministry resonates with the African worldview according to the dominant cognitive orientation found in Sub-Saharan Africa. Missiologist David Hesselgrave notes that there is more than one way of thinking in any culture. In fact, there are three: conceptual (cognition by postulation, e.g., deductive and inductive logic); psychical (cognition by intuition), and concrete-relational, in which "life and reality are seen pictorially in terms of the active emotional relationships present in a concrete situation."[5] Furthermore, anthropologist E. M. Smith insists that people of all cultures think in each of these three ways.[6] The differences in culture are due to the priority given to one or another type of thought.

Most occupants of Sub-Saharan Africa exhibit the concrete-relational cognitive orientation. They view reality primarily in a visual, emotion-laden relationship with everything around them. This relationship with

---

means to the single end of the spread of the kingdom of God. To say that social concern could be done independently of evangelism is to cut mercy loose from kingdom endeavor. It must then wither. To say that evangelism can be done without also doing social concern is to forget that our goal is not individual 'decisions,' but the bringing of all life and creation under the lordship of Christ, the kingdom of God."

[5] David J. Hesselgrave and Edward Rommen, *Contextualization: Meanings, Methods, and Models* (Pasadena, CA: William Carey Library, 2000), 205.

[6] Hesselgrave and Rommen, 205.

all of life is expressed concretely rather than in the abstract. The implications of the concrete-relational cognitive orientation are manifest in their religious expression.

African Traditional Religion

In African Traditional Religion (ATR), beliefs are not doctrines or abstractions to which the believer must avow to be a member of the faith. Instead, these beliefs are lived out in the day-to-day life experiences of the believer. This concrete expression is not mechanical or rote but exists relationally. For the traditional African, one must live in a harmonious relationship among both the citizens of the seen world and the unseen world of spirits, deceased ancestors, and divinities. To do so is to experience wellness and wholeness within the community. Thus, many ATR practitioners will seek the blessings of the spirit world upon their crops, finding a mate, fertility, and finding deliverance from life crises.[7] This mentality persists even among many Africans who profess to be Christians. Following Paul Hiebert's levels of culture model, while they may express orthodox Christian beliefs at the explicit level, at the implicit level they will remain bound to the ATR system and, consequently, vulnerable to the seductive appeal of Neo-Pentecostalism and prosperity preaching.[8]

---

[7] "Christian Witness to People of African Traditional Religions," Lausanne Occasional Paper 18, Lausanne Committee for World Evangelization, sec. 5, thesis IV, part i, available from https://www.lausanne.org/content/lop-lop-18#5.

[8] Paul Hiebert, *Transforming Worldviews: An Anthropological Understanding of How People Change* (Grand Rapids, MI: Baker Academic, 2008), 33.

Based on the information presented, it is my conviction that a holistic gospel ministry can affect Africans (Christians and non-believers) at the deepest level of their being. Following Hiebert's levels of culture once again, holistic gospel ministry has a greater potential to affect Africans at the "implicit level" of culture, including worldview categories, logics, and epistemology.[9] Apart from gospel transformation at this "implicit level," evangelistic engagement of Neo-Pentecostalism risks a greater likelihood of abject refusal or, even worse, a syncretistic fusion of Christian and ATR beliefs and practices encouraged and even celebrated by prosperity preachers and their followers.

As we mentioned earlier, traditional Africans seek to live a harmonious life in balance with the seen world of daily life and the unseen world of divinities, deceased ancestors, and nature spirits. This emphasis on wholeness considers the concerns of the present day, as in crop yields, fertility, and the health of family members. Holistic gospel ministry proclaims the truth of end-time salvation even as it demonstrates how the kingdom of God has broken through to present-day realities through ministries of mercy. This dual emphasis resonates with people groups who share an ATR orientation. Effective evangelism that is faithful to Scripture and sensitive to the existential concerns of listeners should not speak only about the age to come; the gospel also has relevance for today. To augment this both-horizons effort to address the ATR worldview, such an endeavor should adopt a multi-dimensional approach. That means, of course that humanitarian ministries should be a part of the mission strategy. Christian workers should explain why they perform mercy ministries. The answer should not be simply to spark interest in

---

[9] Hiebert, 33.

their message. Instead, it should be to demonstrate the power of the life-giving message that they proclaim.

Alongside mercy ministries, Christian workers should proclaim the gospel in a way that impacts the worldview of ATR. With the assistance of orality studies, holistic gospel ministry can impact the cognitive, affective, and evaluative dimensions of the ATR worldview.[10] Following Hiebert's model of worldview, orality-based means of proclaiming the gospel message, including the creation, fall, and redemption of all creation, would impact the cognitive dimension. Indigenous art, informed by our understanding of orality and transformed by the gospel, focuses primarily on the affective dimension. And a creative use of African proverbs, parables, and sayings could be the orality-based method by which to address the evaluative dimension.[11]

BIBLICAL THEMES OF COSMIC REDEMPTION

Proclamation of the gospel, including the redemption of creation, is the way we may engage the cognitive dimension of the traditional African worldview. This method of gospel proclamation has clear objectives: (1) proclaim the gospel message; (2) use Scripture narratives as the source material; (3) follow the linear progression of redemptive history of creation-fall-redemption-consummation mediated through covenants; and (4) trace how God is intent on redeeming not only human souls, but indeed their souls, bodies, and the whole of creation itself. This redemption of all creation is seen as we trace the biblical theological themes of

---

[10] Paul Hiebert, *Anthropological Insights for Missionaries* (Grand Rapids, MI: Baker, 1985), 46.

[11] Hiebert, 46.

the image of God, the kingdom of God, and the temple, themes that teach this idea of cosmic redemption.

This oral method of proclaiming the gospel, at one level is nothing new, and yet it does present some new considerations for how we should recount the grand narrative of Scripture. Intercultural workers have used oral storytelling of biblical narratives for more than thirty years. Telling the overarching biblical narrative by following the covenants is less common but nothing novel. Tracing the biblical theological themes of the image of God, the kingdom of God, and the temple to portray God's unfolding plan of cosmic redemption, however, is a different approach to oral storytelling methods. We witness these three themes interwoven throughout the overarching story of God's plan to save lost humanity and restore a creation "subjected to futility" by "summing up of all things in Christ" (Rom 8:20; Eph 1:10). The effort behind highlighting this cosmic redemption in each of the story sets (creation, fall, redemption, consummation) is to engage a key component of the ATR worldview upon which Neo-Pentecostalism thrives.

Space does not permit me to demonstrate how these themes interconnect and underscore the idea of cosmic redemption. The following chart lists the Scripture references for the three themes of image of God, kingdom of God, and temple along the narrative arc of creation-fall-redemption-consummation. Practitioners can incorporate these story sets into their already existing stories to include this important element of God's saving plan:

Story Sets:

	Image of God	Kingdom of God	Temple
Creation	Gen 1:26–28	Gen 1:28–29	Gen 1–2, 2:15; 3:8; Ezek 28:13–14
			Ezek 47:1–12; Rev 21:1–2
			Gen 2:10; 3:24; Ezek 28:14–16
			Ezek 40:2–43:12; Rev 21:10
			Ezek 40:6
Fall	Gen 3:16–19	Gen 3:16–19	Gen 2:24
Redemption	1 Cor 15:45–49	Exod 19:3b, 6	1 Kings 6–7
	Col 1:15	Ps 8:4, 6–8/	Exod 40:34–35
	Eph 1:20–21	Gen 1:28/	2 Chr 7:1–2
	Rom 8:29	1 Cor 15:24–25	Ezek 10:18–19
	2 Cor 3:18	1 Chr 17:11–14	John 1:14, 32–33
		Dan 7:13–14	John 2:18–21
		Matt 4:17; 5–7; 28:18	Matt 4:23–25; 11:4–6/Isa 32:3–4
		John 3:5	Isa 35:5–6; 42:7, 16
		1 Cor 15:20–24	Acts 2:1–4
		Col 1:13–14	Eph 2:19–22
			1 Cor 6:19–20
Consummation	Phil 3:21	Matt 15:31–40	Rev 21:1–4; 9b–14
	1 Cor 15:25		
	1 Cor 6:2–3		
	Rev 21:1–4; 22:3		

TELLING THE BIBLE'S STORY

Using storytelling of biblical narratives can display the grand theme of cosmic redemption and thereby address the cognitive worldview dimension. In a similar way, the use of indigenous arts can address the affective dimension. The discipline that can assist us in this field of specialization is that of ethnodoxology. Ethnodoxology is "the theological and anthropological study, and practical application, of how every cultural group might use its unique and diverse artistic expressions appropriately to worship the God of the Bible."[12] Use of ethnodoxology will differ among all ministry contexts. For some places, dance will be the primary indigenous art. For others, it may be songs. Use the same story sets listed but in the art forms of one's local ministry setting, for example songs, poetry, parables, proverbs. Regardless of the indigenous artistic form, Christian ministry practitioners can implement the local indigenous arts to engage the affective dimension of the ATR worldview.

Use of the indigenous arts should be intentional and focused in its implementation. The content of some artistic media, for example, could use the story sets that we mentioned in the previous section concerning the biblical themes of the image of God, kingdom of God, and the temple. Blended together, songs, poetry, or parables could promote the message of cosmic redemption. The performers and the audience would then share an emotive experience in community that also promulgates

---

[12] "What Is Ethnodoxology?," Global Ethnodoxology Network, accessed October 5, 2018, https://www.worldofworship.org/what-is-ethnodoxology/. Those interested in learning more about ethnodoxology can visit the website at https://www.worldofworship.org/; also see Brian Schrag and Robin Harris, "Ethnodoxology's Time Is Here: How Engaging Local Artists Can Expand God's Kingdom," *Lausanne Global Analysis* 3, no. 1 (January 2014).

the worldview-transforming content of the gospel message.[13] This form would have cognitive content, to be sure, but would primarily engage the listeners at the emotional or affective dimension in their world.

Finally, orality-based strategies can engage the ATR worldview at the evaluative dimension. According to Hiebert, the evaluative dimension is at the center of worldview.[14] It encompasses the executive or volitional function of an individual. An orality-based strategy to engage the traditional African perspective is the use of African proverbs. Jay Moon, missions professor at Asbury Theological Seminary and former missionary in northern Ghana, has used African proverbs to engage his hearers in their decision-making processes.[15] Through the use of creative engagement, Moon demonstrates, Christian ministry practitioners can articulate African proverbs in such a way that they can winsomely engage their hearers with the wisdom of the gospel.

Imagine that a Christian worker wishes to engage a Neo-Pentecostal audience about their blind allegiance to a Neo-Pentecostal preacher. These charlatans do not want to bless the members of the local community; rather, they wish to exploit them. The Christian worker could refer to an Ewé proverb from Togo: "The rooster says, 'Your master is also your assassin!'" After an explanation of the proverb (the farmer who owns the

---

[13] In Togo, there is a community of Kotokoli believers who worship regularly in their own language and in their traditional music style. The work of an International Mission Board couple, almost thirty years ago, promoted this type of engagement.

[14] Hiebert, *Anthropological Insights for Missionaries*, 46.

[15] W. Jay Moon, *African Proverbs Reveal Christianity in Culture: A Narrative Portrayal of Builsa Proverbs Contextualizing Christianity in Ghana*, American Society of Missiology Monograph Series 5 (Eugene, OR: Wipf and Stock, 2009).

rooster intends to kill him for a future meal), the Christian worker could make an application to the people. The Neo-Pentecostal preacher that the congregation follows, like the farmer, seeks his own gain at their expense.

Moon illustrates how evangelists and other Christian workers can use proverbs for more advanced reasoning than the illustration above.[16] By using a traditional element of African culture, Christian ministry practitioners can engage their hearers at the evaluative dimension of worldview. To put this strategy into practice, however, requires that the Christian worker develop a repertoire of traditional proverbs. It is also preferable that practitioners use proverbs that are local and known by the members of the community.

Of course, Christian ministry is more than a grab bag of methods, techniques, and strategies. Our theology, consciously or unconsciously, drives our strategy. And hopefully, by the grace of God, our theology is faithful to Scripture. In this chapter, I have proposed some recommendations for engaging the scourge of Neo-Pentecostalism in Africa. A theology of holistic gospel ministry informed by multiple corresponding biblical themes underlies the strategies that I have proposed. I have not presented only what I have read from others. Rather, much of what I have recommended is based on my own experiences of ministering in three countries in West Africa over the last decade. And some of what I have proposed are things that I have done in part but wish to expand in the future. I pray that this material transcends a mere academic discussion and proves to be transformative in our engagement with Neo-Pentecostalism with the gospel of Jesus Christ.

---

[16] Moon, 49.

CHAPTER 11

SPIRIT-POWER PEOPLE

REV. EZRON MUSONDA, ZAMBIA

This chapter deals with spirit-power people, their call, emergence, and prominence on the Christian religious scene. It also explains their leadership style and how it is perceived by the people among whom they serve. In addition, it describes their perceived authentication, the foundation of their beliefs, how they have risen to prominence, the emphasis of their practices, and finally their Christology. The term "spirit-power people" refers to popular priests and prophetic individuals who form the leadership of African prophetic movements, Neo-Pentecostals, African independent churches, and Charismatic and other Christian revivalist groups whose prophetic pronouncements must be adhered to in order for one to prosper. Such leaders are perceived to have access to the spirit world, from which they derive their power to carry out and authenticate their ministries. Their access to the mysteries of the spirit world is said to provide them with the ability to understand the unseen realities that confront people today.

THE CALL

Spirit-power people are usually characterized by dramatic conversion. An example of such a person is William Wadé Harris (c. 1860–1929) of Liberia, who is noted to have experienced a trance visitation in which the angel Gabriel called him into the preaching ministry, and he continued to have these trance visitations later in his ministry.[1] In many cases, such leaders tend to express cultic authority by portraying themselves as having been instructed by God in a dream to carry out their ministry and as such to be the only channel of communication with God. They also tend to refer to Old Testament characters as their points of reference. In association with their call is the tendency to regard the basis of their supernatural call as a legitimate way of linking their leadership with the unseen personal powers.

LEADERSHIP STYLE

The leadership style of most spirit-power people is that of creating a cult around their leadership and personality by assuming the position of representative of unseen spiritual powers. Based on this perception, they regard their leadership in very high esteem and feel offended when equated with other church leaders, especially those who lead mission-planted churches. They repudiate the title of Pastor in preference for the title of Prophet or Apostle. They proudly present their well-being and prosperity as evidence of their salvation and favor with God and as a model to emulate by those to whom they minister. They tend to display

---

[1] Kwame Bediako, *Jesus and the Gospel in Africa: History and Experience* (Maryknoll, NY: Orbis Books, 2004), 85.

themselves and their powers instead of putting God ahead of them. They do so by drawing attention to the products that they use as channels of their blessings, such as anointing oil and water. These products are sometimes labeled with their own personal images and offered for purchasing in order to be used later to deal with people's problems.

In addition, they invite people to seek their counsel, prophecies, and intervention in matters that challenge their health, prosperity, and general well-being. Such counsel, when given, must be heeded. Failure to do so will lead the beneficiary to encounter disaster in his or her life. Since, traditionally, the African people regard God as far removed from them, spirit-power people become the focus of the people's attention in the same way that the traditional African worldview was filled by inferior spirits such as divinities, ancestors, and other nature spirits. Such a position lends them and their messages to be more concrete reality than the biblical text, especially with the cultural tendency to be more oral than literal.

ACCESS TO THE SPIRIT WORLD

The spirit-power person is regarded as one with free access to the spirit world. The privilege to have this access is believed to give such a one a connection with the unseen mysteries that affect the events of the seen world. Such a connection also makes the spirit-power person a genuine conveyor of the truth and one who is able to explain reality. Consequently, he must show forth spiritual manifestations that indicate his connection with the unseen mysteries in order to be accepted as credible and worthy of trust. Due to their perceived authority in spiritual things, many people have a misplaced trust in these specialists. Such a position brings about a sense of esteem from the people so that when confronted with challenging circumstances of life, they seek their help and insight regarding the cause of a particular situation.

The practices of spirit-power persons have similarities to African Traditional Religion in which people trust diviners, mediums, and priests who are believed to provide special understanding of things not seen. Since many people in Africa today—whether or not they are educated, live in cities, or work in business entities—continue to hold beliefs that are related to the African worldview, they tend to apply what they see in spirit-power people who serve as priests and prophets in Pentecostal and Neo-Pentecostal ministries to their own lives and circumstances. There are many causes that have led to the spirit-power people's rise to prominence.

THE RISE TO PROMINENCE OF SPIRIT-POWER PEOPLE

Among the major reasons for the rise of the spirit-power person in Africa is the obsession with power and its manifestations in people's personal lives, which has a deep-rooted connection with the traditional African worldview and particularly the oral background of the African people. Since African Traditional Religion is essentially utilitarian, people come before spiritual beings for purposes of deriving some practical benefit. The prosperity gospel that the Pentecostal spirit-power people preach is aimed at fulfilling the longing that the African has for the wholeness of life, especially with regard to health, well-being, and material prosperity. This longing for wholeness of life is the major explanation for seeking the spirit-power person, especially in relation to healing, deliverance from demonic oppression, evil curses, childlessness, and breaking away from every yoke of oppression.

The coming of Christianity into Africa, particularly Sub-Saharan countries, and the singling out of Satan as the adversary and major cause of suffering has made the spirit-power person turn his attention to the devil who battles against the destiny of believers. In many cases, terms such as "attacking the attackers" and "destroying the wicked foundation" are intended directly for the devil and his agents.

With the coming of Christianity in Africa, the traditional methods of dealing with the spirits that existed before the preaching of the gospel were overtaken by church-initiated methods, because the targeted spirits became associated with evil connotations and not ambivalent as before. Former Catholic archbishop of Lusaka, Zambia, Emmanuel Milingo testifies to the circumstance when he mentions that "the world in-between," as he refers to it, "came to assume an increasingly evil character—in the eyes of Zambians as of their missionary teachers."[2] Hinfellar also shows how, in the course of time, "the traditional ritual means of countering and overcoming evil became impoverished and inadequate, whereas the need for combating evil had not declined."[3] Such a scenario created a vacuum that the spirit-power persons had to cover up. Similarly, when the African convert related the new faith as propagated by mainline churches with their primal religious experiences, there was a sense of dissatisfaction that such churches disregarded the evident Charismatic experiences found in the Bible. When the spirit-power people came on the scene, during their teaching and preaching they emphasized the concrete trust they had in Jesus as the all-sufficient Lord and God who is able to meet

---

[2] Gerrie Ter Haar, *Spirit of Africa: The Healing Ministry of Archbishop Milingo of Zambia* (London: Hurst, 1992), 142.

[3] Ter Haar, 142.

the spiritual and physical longings and needs of the people who listened to them, including healing of their ailments.

Although the mission-planted churches spread horizontally and over wide areas in Africa, they disregarded the evident biblical experience pertaining to healing and other spiritual manifestations that formed the background of the African. Spirit-power people exploited this vacuum to create followers. Consequently, in order to legitimize their message, spirit-power people used the biblical experiences of Jesus's healing ministry and miracle performance as evidence to enhance their ministries.

The similarity of African Traditional Religion with the practices of Neo-Pentecostalism and similar movements lies in the fact that people trust spirit-power people in the same way they trusted the diviner, traditional priest, medium, and other specialists. As previously discussed, these traditional specialists were perceived to understand things unseen. Hence, with the additional credibility of preaching the Bible, Pentecostal and Neo-Pentecostal people were perceived as not only having access to the spirit world but as also having the power of the Supreme Being behind them.

EMPHASES OF THE SPIRIT-POWER PERSON

Spirit-power people display marks of authenticity in order to show their connection with the unseen powers. Their similarity with traditional specialists renders it necessary that they too show Charismatic manifestations, including the performance of miracles and fervent combat prayers that must exhibit efficacy and sufficiency to meet every need. Prayers are made in relation to repelling destabilizing demonic networks, deliverance from ancestral pollutions and idols and related associations, and protection from bad dreams (usually referred to as "dream pollution"), spiritual poisons, territorial spirits, and the like. They also emphasize their engagement in spiritual warfare other than that referred to above. In addition to offering fervent prayers, spirit-power people tend to emphasize holiness and purity of body and soul as a pre-condition for the effectiveness of their prayers and as proof to onlookers that such disposition will enhance answers to prayers that they offer on behalf of the people.

Other areas of emphasis in their ministries include the display of the evidence of speaking in tongues; prayers for explosive breakthroughs, moving one's destiny forward, living prosperous lives, and carrying out power evangelism; fulfillment of prophetic pronouncements; and display of the skill of connecting with the unseen through the use of terms such as the word of knowledge and discernment. Concerning prophetic pronouncements, the person of whom the pronouncement is made must accept that prophecy or else he or she would be befallen by misfortune. This attitude is similar to traditional specialists whose pronouncements must be accepted without question whether they sound reasonable or not. According to the spirit-power person, education, wealth, or fame does not count in spiritual matters. It is not surprising that some people have found themselves agreeing to eat grass or drink poisonous substances as prescribed by such prophets or apostles.

On the basis that Jesus came into the world to do three things, namely to save, to heal, and to deliver, deliverance activities are based on the framework of the manifestation of healing, not only diseases but every form of misfortune that harms the well-being of individuals. During such sessions, adherents are required to make every effort to pray for themselves because such prayers become permanent. Consequently, since everyone must pray for himself or herself, the practice of mass prayers is promoted such that those not used to the disturbing noise find it hard to concentrate during the time called "worship time." Since the target of their prayers is the devil, such prayers must be violent. Such deliverance sessions are considered to be very important on the basis that one can remove the ladder with which the enemies find their way into someone's life. Deliverance sessions must be authenticated by the testimonies of those who experience the deliverance with a view to enhance the efficacy of one's ministry and not for the glory of God.

Healing is emphasized because illness is attributed to unseen beings such as divinities, ancestral spirits, and possessing spirits. Healing also implies deliverance from the unseen spiritual forces that bring about such suffering. Healing sessions are legitimized by the use of Jesus's name, wielded like a magic wand in the hands of the spirit-power person. Similarly, the designation of Jesus as healer goes beyond mere healing. His name has a capacity to enrich those who embrace Him by bringing equilibrium to life so that it is appropriated in its fullness. In addition to the use of the name of Jesus and the Bible, they also revert to African religious idioms in order to create a familiar phraseology for easy communication of their intent. The tendency leads to all and sundry coming to receive the blessing whether they be believers in the Lord Jesus Christ or not.

Spirit-power people, especially those who belong to the Charismatic Revivalist movements, believe in the active presence of the Holy Spirit, not only in carrying out deliverance sessions but also as a means of exercising power and influence over congregants and the persons to whom their ministry is directed, as well as to legitimize their connection with God. The focus on the power of God promotes the strength and rapid growth of Neo-Pentecostal and Charismatic movements.

Another practice that is common among leaders of Neo-Pentecostal, Pentecostal, and Charismatic Revivalist movements pertains to the use of concrete symbols as a way of imparting blessings on the people. One such symbol is anointing. Though the Bible is used to teach the anointing of the Holy Spirit, in practice the emphasis is in its application through the use of concrete symbols, such as anointing oil.

The Message of Spirit-Power People

Most messages that are presented to the hearers relate to the issues of mystery, dreams, and spiritual warfare. Much of this is especially in relation to Satan and principalities, deliverance from illnesses, and witchcraft, the most dreaded spiritual evil in Africa. Meanwhile the chanting of the blood of Jesus is used to ensure that one's prayers are answered. Other messages pertain to assurance of material and spiritual prosperity and good health if only the hearer does what the prophet pronounces concerning one's destiny.

Conclusion

The chapter has briefly described the nature, call, leadership style, and source of authenticity and legitimacy of Charismatic revivalist ministries that are obtained through linkage with and access to the unseen personal powers, their rise to prominence among the people, their ministry emphases, and the character of their messages. Though they use the name of Jesus and quote passages of Scripture to justify their practices, their ministries are intended for self-glorification and are therefore devoid of the saving power of the gospel. Their messages do not contain the gospel that shows their hearers their lostness, their need for repentance, and their need to seek Jesus Christ in order that they might be saved.

CHAPTER 12

BIBLICAL RESPONSES TO NEO-PENTECOSTAL PRAYER PRACTICES

REV. PROF. EMIOLA NIHINLOLA, PHD, NIGERIA

Pentecostalism (as well as Neo-Pentecostalism or Charismatic renewal) is both a doctrine as well as an experience based on some practices. Neo-Pentecostal practices have affected virtually every aspect of Baptist church worship in Africa and include ecstatic prayer, speaking in tongues, shouting of "Praise the Lord," sharing of testimonies, singing of choruses, laying on of hands, and deliverance. Prayer, music, preaching, and teaching are the most important elements of corporate Christian worship, and these have all been significantly influenced by Neo-Pentecostalism. In this chapter, the following Neo-Pentecostal prayer practices and some biblical responses to them will be provided. Some of the prayer practices include starting prayer with "In Jesus's name," praying in tongues, all-night prayer, prayer mode or "tapage," prayer for deliverance, praying with elements and symbols, prophetic declaration, and imprecatory prayer.

NEO-PENTECOSTAL PRAYER PRACTICES AND BIBLICAL RESPONSES

One of the earliest forms of Neo-Pentecostal practice introduced in West Africa in the late 1970s was to start prayer with "In Jesus's name" or "In the name of Jesus," once or twice followed by a vigorous response of "Amen." This was a contrast to the traditional Baptist prayer, which usually started with a phrase like "Our Father in Heaven." The new prayer practice was critiqued and rejected by many Baptist leaders in many churches and organizations, but the practice has survived. The prevailing opinion is that to pray in the name of Jesus is to offer prayer that is consistent with the will, purpose, and character of Jesus (John 16:22–24). It does not matter if "In Jesus's name" is pronounced at the beginning or end of prayer.

The second form of prayer practice to be highlighted is *prayer in tongues.* The classical Pentecostal article of faith emphasizes the post-conversion experience of baptism in the Holy Spirit and the promotion of speaking in tongues as the initial and authentic evidence. Pentecostals do not only speak and pray in tongues; some also sing in tongues. Indeed, it can be said that a Pentecostal prayer session is not complete without speaking in tongues. While Neo-Pentecostals do not necessarily subscribe to the doctrine, they nonetheless give particular attention to spectacular and sensational spiritual gifts like speaking in tongues, prophecy, dreams and visions, faith, healing, and miracles (1 Cor 12:8–10, 28–30).[1]

---

[1] All of these various practices are taken up in other chapters in this same volume.

The elevation of speaking in tongues as the only authentic mark of one who has received the Holy Spirit is biblically defective. It is absurd to think that to pray in the Spirit is to pray in tongues (Rom 8:26–27; Eph 6:18; 1 Cor 14:15). Is to "walk in the Spirit" then to walk in tongues? Power for Christian living and witnessing is the evidence of a Spirit-filled life (Acts 1:8). Baptists and other evangelicals must avoid extremes of denial and excessive preoccupation with the gift of speaking in tongues. Congregational prayer with tongues, if any, should conform to scriptural regulation (1 Cor 14:27–28).

The next Neo-Pentecostal prayer practice to be highlighted is *night vigil,* or *all-night prayer.* Neo-Pentecostalism has introduced corporate all-night prayer sessions. The practice was resisted by Baptist leaders in the early 1980s in Nigeria on the basis of the argument that all-night church services are neither a consistent New Testament practice nor part of Baptist heritage. However, this all-night worship session is already being practised in many Baptist churches in Africa. Many contemporary Baptists have affirmed that night vigil has biblical support, as seen in the practice of the Lord Jesus Christ and the apostolic church (Luke 6:12; Acts 12:1–17). While night vigils have some logistic challenges (like disturbance of neighbours), the possible abuses do not invalidate the spiritual benefits.

Issues have been raised about the *prayer mode* in Baptist churches. In traditional biblical understanding, prayer is communion with God for the purpose of adoration, thanksgiving, confession, and supplication. In most Baptist congregational settings, the emphasis of prayer worship has been orderliness and solemnity (Hab 2:20). A very important feature of Neo-Pentecostal practice is to pray vigorously and loudly, depicting worship practices that suggest dynamism and liveliness.

The corporate prayer sessions introduced by many Neo-Pentecostal churches include various ecstatic practices like walking around with opened eyes, jerking, foot stamping, and finger snapping. Randy Arnett, a Baptist missionary in Africa until his death in 2018, reported that, in contrast with "normal" prayer, this "combat" spiritual warfare prayer is called *tapage* in some parts of West Africa and includes noisemaking with peculiar dramatic gesticulations of physical confrontation with the enemy, "clapping, beating the air with clenched fists, chopping the air with open hands, and hitting nearby objects such as wall, benches, or tables."[2]

From a biblical perspective, what matters ultimately for answered prayer is the condition of the heart. When the heart is right with God, prayers will be answered that are offered in any position (kneeling, standing, lying, walking), quietly or loudly, day or night, with closed or opened eyes. We must affirm first that some Neo-Pentecostal practices make the worshiper awake and alert. Second, the African emotional disposition is toward active, vibrant worship practices, as seen in traditional African religious worship. Nevertheless, biblical Christian worship does not typically promote loud and violent practices like the prophets of Baal (1 Kgs 18:26–29).

Prayer for deliverance is a specific form of Neo-Pentecostal worship practice that merits individual examination. Many Neo-Pentecostals pray to cast out demons from worshipers who may be oppressed, obsessed, or possessed by evil spirits. The person from whom the demon is cast out may be a professed Christian or a non-Christian. Deliverance prayer comes in different forms: some churches organize regular deliverance prayer for church members to keep their deliverance and healing;

---

[2] Arnett, *Pentecostalization*, 88–91 (see intro., n. 8).

sometimes prayer of deliverance is organized for a landed property, institution, house, or business premise that is perceived to be under a curse or in bondage. Some Christians attend special deliverance conferences, services, or crusades organized by Pentecostal churches in search for what is perceived as deliverance. In fact, some Pentecostal churches have labelled their churches as designated for deliverance, and they have had patronage over the years. In power evangelism, and also in frontier missions, deliverance practice may also take the form of prayer walking and spiritual mapping.

In the life and ministry of the Lord Jesus Christ, some assertions can be made with regard to prayer for deliverance. First, as Jesus preached and taught about the gospel of the kingdom of God, He delivered people from sin, evil spirits, sicknesses, and diseases (Mark 1:29–34). Thus, deliverance is a component of gospel preaching. Second, Jesus used the Word of God as the principal instrument for the deliverance and healing of people. However, in some cases He also used physical elements, like mud and saliva to open the eyes of a blind man (John 9:1–7).

This leads us then to consider the *nature and role of elements and symbols* in the prayer practices of Neo-Pentecostals. Neo-Pentecostals employ the use of a variety of elements and symbols to aid prayer, including laying on of hands, water, anointing oil, handkerchiefs, and calling or affirming the blood of Jesus. Neo-Pentecostal pastors and leaders lay hands on church members and worshipers for various purposes: to receive the Holy Spirit, to receive power, consecration for anointing and healing, and so on. Some pray over water and also use other elements to pray for people to receive blessings, prosperity, success, and breakthrough. This is one prayer practice that is sometimes subject to the abuse of commercialisation.

Before the rise of the Charismatic renewal in the 1970s, laying on of hands featured in Baptist church worship was limited to special occasions, like child dedications and the ordination of pastors and deacons. Many practices that are associated with the use of elements and symbols are scripturally justifiable, including laying on of hands (Mark 16:18) and anointing with oil for prayer (Jas 5:14–15). The practice of pointing hands toward the person or object being prayed for is another popular prayer symbol, but one that is difficult to justify biblically. God's people must be taught the reality of the power of God is complete without the symbols. The faith of people must be in God and not in the prayer elements and symbols (Luke 7:6–10).

Another prayer practice to be highlighted is *prophetic declaration*, especially for signs and wonders. One aspect of the religious life and emphasis of Neo-Pentecostals is the operation of Charismatic gifts like faith, healing, and miracles. While many Neo-Pentecostal ministers preach and teach pragmatically, most are weak in biblical exegesis. Instead, there is great enthusiasm and tendency to apply Scriptures to meet life needs. Along with this eagerness is the practice of blessing the congregation with prophetic utterances. This practice may take the form of word of knowledge, through which the preacher prophesies often about sudden miraculous provision, protection, and success for people. It should be asserted that it is an abuse of the gospel ministry for a worship leader to speak presumptuously and present his/her wish as a prophetic declaration. Some examples of prophetic declarations are:

- "The Lord says no worshiper or member of this congregation will die in this new year."

- "I decree that the first ten members of this church who can present a seed offering of $1,000 each will reap ten multiple fold and so become a millionaire within the next six months."

God cannot be coerced to honour an utterance He has not inspired. Many prophetic declarations have been made in vain, and these false prophets ought to be held accountable (Deut 18:20–22).

Biblical prophets usually call people to a right kind of living—obedience, purity, and service. They *forthtell* and *foretell*. Many of the predictive prophecies in the Bible include warning and judgement that will follow disobedience as well as blessings due to obedience. One major deficiency of many contemporary prophetic declarations in Africa is that they are often statements of promises and hope lacking in warning and judgement.

The final Neo-Pentecostal prayer practice to be examined is *imprecatory (sometime called violent or dangerous) prayer*. The Psalms in the Old Testament are poems and songs of worship in Israel. They are songs and prayers of life. One common type of psalm is an imprecatory prayer, which expresses anguish and suffering of people when threatened. An example is Psalm 35, a prayer for deliverance from violence (vv. 1–3) and injustice (vv. 11–18). Some Neo-Pentecostals build their prayer practice from the examples in Psalms.

Imprecatory prayers sometimes employ the imagery of war, with people asking God to fight for them to overcome their enemies and those planning evil against them (see Ps 3:7; 10:2). In contemporary Africa, some church leaders are designing and publishing devotionals specifically directed at enemies at home, at places of work, and in the larger society. The church is thus raising a generation of Balaams who wake up daily to curse others (Numbers 22). Who will deliver the people of God from this disorientation? Some examples of misused imprecatory prayers (from *Daily Encounter with God*, a Nigerian Baptist daily devotional) are:

- Every strange hand obstructing my advancement, wither now in Jesus' name (Ps 23:5).
- O Lord, disgrace every power contending with my lifting in Jesus' name (Ps 3:3).
- O God, let your hands be heavy on whoever is in possession of what belongs to my children; let them be forced to release them, cause the occupants of their seats of honour to be unseated in Jesus' mighty name (Gen 12:17–19).
- O God, my father, let the ground open up and swallow every demonic agent manipulating the lives of my children; put an end to the works of the devil in their lives (Num 26:10).

Many African Christians are overwhelmed with the presence and power of enemies, and then resort to the traditional African worldview to deal with the problem. All their difficulties and problems are attributed to some other persons. Many still live in the worldview of witches and wizards, where almost every form of community disaster is ascribed to witchcraft. Satan, demons, and human agents are responsible for every form of affliction, suffering, and adversity of people. One serious problem with this prayer practice is that it ignores hindrances to effective prayer like unconfessed sin (Isa 59:1–3), asking with wrong motives (Jas 4:3), ignorance of the will of God (1 John 5:14), etc.

One critical question to ask is whether it is right to make David's curses on his enemies the basis of Christian prayer (as found in Pss 35:1–8; 58:6–9; 59; 69:22–28; 137:7–9)? How do we reconcile this practice with the broad biblical revelation that vengeance belongs to God

(1 Sam 25:21–39; cf. Rom 12:14–21) and the teaching of Jesus to love our enemies and in fact do good to them so as to overcome their evil (Matt 5:38–48)? Contemporary African Christians need the grace and power to obey God as we engage principalities and powers in spiritual warfare to achieve kingdom purposes (Eph 6:12; Acts 13:4–12).

CONCLUSION

I would like to draw three conclusions from the highlight of Neo-Pentecostal prayer practices and brief biblical responses attempted in this chapter. First, evangelical Christian leaders and church pastors must not fail to guide and lead our people to study and respond biblically and practically to Neo-Pentecostal worship practices. Second, Baptist pastors and members have a duty to reject prayer practices and excesses that contradict biblical injunctions no matter how popular, attractive, pragmatic, or seemingly beneficial to physical church growth. Third, African Baptists need discernment, openness, sincerity, and courage to moderate, accept, adapt, and even adopt some Neo-Pentecostal prayer practices that may not be in our heritage but are nonetheless biblically justifiable.

CHAPTER 13

CRITICAL CONTEXTUALIZATION AND THE ABANDONED GOSPEL[1]

KEVIN RODGERS, PHD, KENYA

*L*ove your neighbour and hate your enemy . . . love your neighbour and hate your enemy . . .*" These were the words I heard coming from the children's Sunday school class, just outside the window of the local African Baptist church. As is often the case, they were repeating a Bible verse multiple times in order to memorize it and share it during the service. As we listened, my wife and I got more and more disturbed until she finally went outside and politely joined the class.

She opened the Bible and showed the teacher the next verse, Matt 5:44: "But I [Jesus] tell you, love your enemies and pray for those who persecute you." They went on to look at the entire paragraph together

---

[1] Some of this work is an adaptation of a chapter from my dissertation: Kevin W. Rodgers, *A Study of Theology of Place in Zambia and the Implications for Missions* (PhD diss., Southeastern Baptist Theological Seminary, 2011).

and discuss the context of the statement the children were learning. The teacher finally understood that she had pulled the statement from its context and was teaching it as normative truth for African children. She agreed that she understood what the passage was really saying. Yet we were incredulous when the teacher continued to make them memorize verse 43 out of context. As they proceeded into the church service, the children shouted, "You have heard it said, love your neighbour and hate your enemy!" and then they sat down.

I left the church that day a bit confused and uncertain as to what had just happened. It occurred to me that this was more than just poor hermeneutics; this was also about contextualization. Even though verse 43 was a quote from others that Jesus refuted in verse 44, verse 43 resonated more with her African worldview. Loving your neighbour and hating your enemy made perfect sense to this sweet Sunday school teacher; loving her enemies and praying for them was beyond her plausibility structures.[2] The inability to successfully contextualize the Word of God in an African context has led to much of the error that we see in the African evangelical world. The parts of the Bible that connect with the worldview are assimilated and spread (irrespective of sound hermeneutics), but the parts that challenge the worldview are often reframed or ignored.

---

[2] "Plausibility structures" is a term coined by sociologist Peter L. Berger in his book, *The Sacred Canopy* (Garden City, NY: Doubleday, 1967). Plausibility structures are the cultural contexts that determine what makes sense to an individual or is "plausible." These beliefs are embedded in cultural institutions and processes.

LACK OF CRITICAL CONTEXTUALIZATION

Randy Arnett, in his book *Pentecostalization: The Evolution of Baptists in Africa*, claims that the lack of critical contextualization is the primary factor that has led to African Baptist churches embracing Neo-Pentecostalism and the prosperity gospel, and correct contextualization can be the primary way to correct this theological drift:

> The lack of critical contextualization stands as one of the most obvious lessons of the process of pentecostalization. We find many cases of under-contextualization and over-contextualization throughout Africa. Consequently, we cannot emphasize enough the necessity of missiologically sound, biblically driven contextualization. The indisputable baseline for planting and developing Baptist churches lies in a strong understanding of the local worldview—not just the surface clutter—but the deep structures. The process of discipleship must engage the deep levels in order to have lasting transformation. As part of contextualization, the common issues of Traditional Religion deserve recognition and treatment: 1. Spiritual forces and powers 2. Dreams and visions 3. Illness, curses, and affliction 4. Healing and deliverance 5. Well-being and blessing 6. Spirit-Power people. Even though easily overlooked or dismissed, these issues persist and, if left unaddressed, turn people to Neo-Pentecostalism for answers.[3]

In short, Arnett blames much of the theological error in Africa today on the very ones who brought the gospel, but who failed to contextualize well.

---

[3] Arnett, *Pentecostalization,* 165 (see intro., n. 8).

While missionaries have been doing contextualization for years (be it good or bad), the word is a recent one. In the early twentieth century, missionaries spoke in terms of "indigenization." This was an attempt to self-correct the excesses of the Victorian era of missions when missionaries imported culture as well as the gospel. It was a worthy first step and yielded tremendous fruit in terms of national churches finding their own identities. Yet, in many ways, indigenization was an attempt to take what was Western, like worship styles, music, architecture, etc. and dress it in the traditional garb of the receptor culture.

Nicholls notes that in 1972 the term "contextualization" was coined by Shoki Coe and Aharon Sapsezian.[4] Indigenization has often been the work of outsiders trying to couch things in terms of *their* understanding of the receptor culture, whereas genuine contextualization considers the cultural perspectives of the receptors in the host culture. "Over the years, as missionaries studied languages more deeply, they came to realize that people in different cultures do not live in the same world using different labels, they live in different worlds."[5] Where indigenization involves framing the gospel in traditional cultural terms to facilitate communication, contextualization allows the entire culture and context to influence the way the gospel is expressed so that genuine meaning is transmitted.[6] Valid contextualization allows the receptor culture to contribute to the

---

[4] Bruce J. Nicholls, *Contextualization: A Theology of Gospel and Culture* (Vancouver: Regent, 1979), 21.

[5] Paul G. Hiebert, "Syncretism and Social Paradigms," in *Contextualization and Syncretism: Navigating Cultural Currents,* ed. Gailyn Van Rheenen (Pasadena, CA: William Carey Library, 2006), 32.

[6] John Corrie, "Mission and Contextualization," Trinity College, Bristol, February 22, 2010, available at http://library.mibckerala.org/lms_frame /eBook/corrie_mission_and_contextualisation.pdf.

conversation about how best to communicate supra-cultural truths in terms they can understand and apply.

THREE CULTURES NEEDED FOR CONTEXTUALIZATION

Eugene Nida is credited with the creation of the traditional "three cultures" model of contextualization.[7] These cultures refer to the biblical culture, the speaker's home culture, and the host culture. Nida believed one must understand the message of the Bible in terms of the biblical culture in which it was written to determine the supra-cultural truths of the text. Then he must understand his own culture so that he does not allow his cultural bias to affect his interpretation. Finally, he must understand the receptor culture, so he will know how to communicate those truths in ways that preserve biblical meaning and effectively communicate a "dynamic equivalent" meaning to the recipient in the receptor culture.

All aspects of the contextualization process are important, but the role of the receptor culture is of paramount importance for many reasons. First, the receptor culture is the locus of understanding. Even if the preacher effectively exegetes the supra-cultural truths of a text, careful to avoid inputting his own cultural biases, failure to correctly communicate that meaning in the receptor culture means he has failed to contextualize.[8] Second, the aspect of the receptor culture is the hardest

---

[7] David J. Hesselgrave, *Communicating Christ Cross-Culturally*, 2nd ed. (Grand Rapids, MI: Zondervan, 1991), 107.

[8] Donald K. Smith, *Creating Understanding: A Handbook for Christian Communication across Cultural Landscapes* (Grand Rapids, MI: Zondervan, 1992), 265.

piece of the contextualization process to unlock. Effective communication in another culture involves learning another language, learning the worldview of another people group, and weighing them against one's own cultural moorings and preconceptions. Third, the receptor culture is the determinant of action. The goal of most missionary, cross-cultural communication is to present lost people with the truths of the gospel and to effect personal and cultural change. If the receptor culture is not effectively engaged, then this cannot be accomplished. One can simply *transmit information* to the receptor culture, but to effect change, truth must be *understood* at the level of the receptor culture, because it is worldview that determines how people act.

There is a natural tension between these three cultures and varying perspectives on the role that receptor culture plays in determining meaning. These range from Roman Catholic anthropological models where human culture is the measure of truth and a medium for the revelation of God, to the classic decode/encode approach of missiologists like Hesselgrave who emphasize the pre-eminence of Scripture over all else. In addition, within the evangelical world you will find another sub-spectrum who disagree as to how much weight to put on the original meaning and how much weight to put on receptor culture understanding.[9]

---

[9] On the far-left side of this sub-spectrum would be someone like Charles Kraft. His magnum opus, *Christianity in Culture*, continues to be one of the most controversial books ever written on the subject. Ultimately, for Kraft, culture becomes the measure of the meaning of Scripture. Charles H. Kraft, *Christianity in Culture* (Maryknoll, NY: Orbis, 1979), 352. At the opposite end of the spectrum are missiologists like Hesselgrave who employ a classic decode/encode model of contextualization. For them the historical/critical understanding is preeminent over culture.

The simplest way to understand this spectrum is in terms of the locus of authority. D. A. Carson notes, "Broadly speaking there are two brands of contextualization. The first assigns control to the context [culture]; the operative term is praxis, which serves as a controlling grid to determine the meaning of Scripture. The second assigns the control to Scripture, but cherishes the 'contextualization' rubric because it reminds us the Bible must be thought about, translated into and preached in categories relevant to the particular cultural context."[10] In the past, some missionaries saw themselves as against the host culture and imported their own, more "biblical," culture, while others from a liberal or liberation perspective sought to totally embrace the host culture and refused to oppose any aspect of it as displeasing to God.

This is where the difficult art of contextualization has become so important. Contextualization is the tool that allows cross-cultural workers to distinguish between biblical truth and their own cultural biases, and then communicate those supra-cultural truths in a way that will be meaningful to the recipient from his own cultural vantage point. What is needed is a position that is as sensitive to the importance of the receptor culture as Kraft, and yet still values the authority and preeminence of Scripture as much as Hesselgrave. This position must emphasize the importance of dialogue between the speaker, the culture, and the text but with a mutual understanding that the text of Scripture is inspired and the source of truth. This position could best be described as an evangelical dialogical approach.[11]

---

[10] D. A. Carson, "Church and Mission: Reflections on Contextualization and the Third Horizon," in *The Church in the Bible and the World,* ed. D. A. Carson (Eugene, OR: Wipf and Stock, 2002), 220.

[11] Although Paul Hiebert is credited with the concept of developing the dialogical model of contextualization, others like David Clarke have recently built upon that. For the sake of clarity, "evangelical dialogical method" is

As the word suggests, the key component of a dialogical method is dialogue. The assumption is that theology and contextualization are best done in community and are not the sole preserve of a single individual. The identity of the participants in the dialogue is the key difference between an evangelical dialogical process and other approaches. In reality, the dialogue is not just between cultures, but between believers and God through His witness, the Bible. The Bible has primacy in the life of the church, and the goal of contextualization is for the community of faith to discover how the supra-cultural truths of God's Word relate to their personal lives and cultural milieu. Another key dialogical relationship is members of the community of faith dialoguing with each other, as they learn to self-theologize. Another important participant in this dialogue (which is often overlooked) is the historical witness of the church. Believers have been doing theology for thousands of years and their voice should be considered as believers wrestle with what God is saying to them in their context.

THE AUTHORITY OF THE TEXT

Before one can rightly contextualize the gospel in a receptor culture, the members of that dialogue need to agree on several fundamental premises. These preconceptions revolve around two core issues: the nature of the text and the nature of the dialogue. In relation to the text, the first pre-understanding must be that they recognize the authority and priority of Scripture. In addition, there should be established ground rules of biblical interpretation and hermeneutics. This ensures that believers in

----

a term this writer uses to describe an evangelical hybrid of the traditional dialogical model.

the receptor culture will be able to distinguish issues of context, prescription versus description, and the subtleties of application, significance, and meaning. Finally, when examining a text, the teacher must help the believing community interact with the contributions of other Christians in antiquity by considering historical theology.

A dialogical approach means that the community of believers is doing the work of theology just as much as the preacher. They are partners in this process and have a role to play. Carson suggests, "A truly contextualized theology is, in my view, one in which believers from a particular culture seek to formulate a comprehensive theology in the language and categories of their own culture, *but based on the whole Bible.*"[12] The communicator should also critically examine his role in the dialogue. It takes intentionality for a missionary to objectively examine his own cultural moorings and objectively examine the text in the light of a new culture. Finally, it takes humility as the teacher is willing to become the student, submitting himself to the dialogical process, recognizing that his students might have an insight that his own culture prevents him from seeing.

A final benefit to this model is that it helps the local church be more biblical. Even though individuals do theology, the priesthood of believers works in practice in hermeneutical community.[13] This dialogical method helps the church be the church God intended. It recognizes the individual's responsibility to do theology in a manner that is biblically sound and culturally appropriate, yet it teaches the individual the importance of doing this in community.

When dealing with issues like Neo-Pentecostalism and the prosperity gospel in Africa, this dialogical approach is vital. Arnett says that the problem

---

[12] Carson, "Church and Mission," 254.
[13] Hiebert, "Syncretism and Social Paradigms," 43.

is an epistemological one. Is epistemology of Neo-Pentecostalism and the prosperity gospel informed by Scripture or culture, or both, and how does one navigate that for sound contextualization? Historically there have been a variety of approaches in Africa related to Neo-Pentecostal tendencies:

> One approach simply ignores the Neo-Pentecostal divergences. A second approach takes the path of rational argument. In this case, people refute the aberrant faith and practice with reasoning, often based on systematic theology. This approach fails because *Neo-Pentecostalism values experience over syllogism.* A third, and similar, approach appeals to an incontrovertible authority, namely the Bible. These people engage Neo-Pentecostals with something akin to "The Bible says . . ." While Neo-Pentecostals recognize the Bible, their hermeneutic leads to alternative inter-pretations that reflect the Neo-Pentecostal's own understanding. Their worldview differs from yours. Neo-Pentecostals do not see the world the way you do. They do not think as you think. They do not reason as you reason. They do not value what you value. They do not trust what you trust.[14]

Arnett believes that African evangelicals value the Bible and even follow an author-centered hermeneutic. Yet they value "experience over syllogism," and the disconnect is an epistemological one. African cul-ture tends to connect more readily with Neo-Pentecostal doctrine and expression. In short, they value the text, but interpret the meaning of the text based on culture, experience, and worldview. From a cultural and epistemological standpoint, Africans tend to trust the "power person" and place great authority in him whether he be a witchdoctor, a chief,

---

[14] Arnett, *Pentecostalization,* 155–57.

or "the man of God." "The pivot point lies in authority and trust. Our task, then, is to change the foundation of belief from a person to the Bible. The process will involve critical contextualization with a focus on this epistemological problem."[15] For this reason, Arnett insists it is better to privilege biblical theology over systematic theology. Biblical theology focuses more on the story and narrative of Scripture, whereas systematic theology can be more logic/system oriented and, in some cases, more Western. Second, he endorses leveraging the idea of this spirit-power person by highlighting the concrete examples in the biblical narrative that appeal to the oral preferences of many Africans.[16]

Arnett advocates identifying a problem or practice and then creating dialogue with the church members to develop a biblical theology to address it:

> To begin, we seek the people passages that speak to the practice. At this stage, we answer the question: who, in the Bible, is related to this practice? Once we identify the key personages . . . we identify the key traits of the practice. We answer the question: how did these Spirit-Power people carry out the practice? What did the Spirit-Power people do? What did they not do? What is not mentioned? The latter question subtly addresses the extra-biblical practices that have evolved. Finally, we group these Spirit-Power persons into the different areas of the Bible to build a biblical theology. . . . The key is to avoid projecting an isolated practice in one era as normative for the whole Bible . . . we help the insiders

---

[15] Arnett, 157–58. By "our" Arnett is referring to anyone, regardless of nationality, who is doing the work of contextualizing and communicating the truth of Scripture.

[16] Arnett, 159.

evaluate the current practice in light of the Bible study . . . the insiders identify needed changes . . . the insiders make the transition by teaching, modeling and practicing the new way.[17]

This dialogical approach combines the concepts of concrete over abstract, narrative over didactic passages, dialogue over outsider opinion, and leverages the cultural perspective to create natural connections and organic applications in their minds. This approach is a recognition that the disconnect is as pedagogical as it is theological. Sound contextualization does not only address *what* people think, but *how* they think and *how* one communicates in ways that connect with them. For too long the West has communicated truth in ways that make sense to them but do not make sense to their African hearers. As a result, Africans have unanswered questions and unmet needs that have readily been answered by Neo-Pentecostalism and the prosperity gospel. They are not rejecting the truth; the truth is simply not getting past the veil of their worldview, and a false gospel is connecting more effectively. A robust, dialogical model of contextualization, employed by someone who knows the culture well and communicates effectively, is the key to removing the veil and letting in the "Light of the knowledge of the glory of God in the face of Christ."[18]

---

[17] Arnett, 160–61.
[18] 2 Cor 4:6 NASB.

CHAPTER 14

ESTABLISH SCRIPTURE AS THE FINAL AUTHORITY

REV. PATRICK DUBE, ZIMBABWE

The Word of God is of uppermost importance for the true believer in Christ Jesus. If we cultivate a high view of the Scriptures, we discover that the Word of God is solid and needs no external support systems to be put in place for it. As David declares in Ps 119:160, "Thy word is true from the beginning: and every one of thy righteous judgments endureth for ever." Notice how this verse covers the whole spectrum from "the beginning" (eternity past) to "forever" (eternity future). Psalm 119 is divided into twenty-two sections (according to the twenty-two letters of the Hebrew alphabet) of eight verses each. Its primary emphasis is the Word of God. It is also the longest chapter in the Bible. Is it any wonder that the longest chapter deals emphatically with the Word of God?

Unless otherwise noted, Scripture quotations in this chapter are taken from the King James Version.

Where we place the Word of God in our thinking will be reflected in our agenda for daily life. The prosperity gospel (which is not the true gospel) undermines the authority of Scripture by endeavouring to make the true gospel of Jesus Christ appealing to audiences. It first of all has a hidden agenda; then it looks for specific verses in Scripture to support its argument; it then takes Scriptures out of context based on a word or phrase that appears to enhance its agenda and ultimately misapplies the meaning of those Scriptures to suit its main thrust. To expose that hidden and often hideous agenda, this is what the holy Scriptures declare: "For the word of God is living and powerful, and sharper than any two-edged sword, piercing even to the division of soul and spirit, and of joints and marrow, and is a discerner of the thoughts and intents of the heart" (Heb 4:12 NKJV).

David exclaimed in Ps 119:9 (NKJV), "How can a young man cleanse his way? By taking heed according to Your word!" This clearly reveals the heart of David, a man after God's own heart. This also reveals David's motive for living, and that was to please God by living according to His Word. David wanted his heart (life) to beat according to God's heartbeat. The cry of his heart was to be found in line with the precepts of God. He did not allow his material benefits as king of Israel to deviate him from cultivating a godly relationship with God.

Did David have enormous resources of the material world? He definitely did but he possessed his possessions instead of being possessed by them. The innate philosophy of the prosperity cult is "Get all you can and can all you get!" Because this teaching is birthed in sinful desire, the teachers of these false and pervasive doctrines are bent on building privatized empires where they sit on the throne and Christ has no part in their agenda except when they use His name to rubber stamp their teachings and practices in an attempt to give them authenticity and veracity.

TRUE RICHES: THE WORD OF GOD

Those who are true disciples of Jesus need to know and understand that prosperity does not validate a person's salvation. Money, awards, promotions from an employer, or inheritance from relatives cannot be deemed as surety that God's blessing is upon a person's life. The blessing of salvation can be the experience of any person regardless of class, gender, race, or economic status. God is not a respecter of persons. Next, a biblical view of prosperity will teach people that the preacher's message is not validated by his own wealth. For example, many prosperity preachers will use their own net worth as proof that God is blessing them and, therefore, their message is trustworthy. This is unacceptable. Finally, prosperity does not validate a church's doctrine.

"Thy word have I hid in mine heart, that I might not sin against thee" (Ps 119:11).

"I will delight myself in thy statutes: I will not forget thy word" (Ps 119:16).

"Deal bountifully with thy servant, that I may live, and keep thy word" (Ps 119:17).

The fear of the Lord develops in us a deep respect for His Word; hence the Psalmist proclaims in Ps 119:38, "Stablish thy word unto thy servant, who is devoted to thy fear." If the believer has cultivated a deep-seated respect for the Word of God and the God of the Word, he/she will allow the Holy Spirit, who is the divine author of Scripture, to reveal the true meaning of His Word before attempting to interpret it. In our haste to push forward our personal agenda, we undermine the work of the Holy Spirit in aiding us to fully and accurately comprehend His Word. "For ever, O LORD, thy word is settled in heaven" (Ps 119:89).

Again David says in Ps 119:105, "Thy word is a lamp unto my feet, and a light unto my path." When the Word is a lamp to our feet, it gives light to our immediate proximity, where we stand, and when it is a light to our path, it gives light so that we can see what is ahead. When the proper hermeneutic is applied, it enables us to grow closer to God through His Word as David said in Ps 119:140, "Thy word is very pure: therefore thy servant loveth it," and in verse 133, "Order my steps in thy word: and let not any iniquity have dominion over me." It is clear that the Word of God is without error, and that is why David says he wants to order his life according to it. He knows that his life cannot go wrong when he follows the precepts of God.

Solomon, in his exercise of the gift of wisdom that God had endowed upon him, made this observation in Eccl 5:2: "Be not rash with thy mouth, and let not thine heart be hasty to utter any thing before God: for God is in heaven, and thou upon earth: therefore let thy words be few." The proponents of the prosperity gospel are hasty to make uninformed conclusions without much scholarly consideration. In the content of the prosperity gospel, God's covenant with Abraham is misconstrued, misinterpreted, and misunderstood with statements like, "If you'll sow a seed of faith like Abraham, God will surely bless you," or "If you speak it and live it by faith like Abraham, God will prosper you." These statements misrepresent the Scriptures and cause God's people to embrace this as a blanket guarantee.

If these aberrated versions of the Abrahamic covenant had any authenticity, then the multitudes who have embraced the prosperity gospel would become millionaires and property owners instantly. But the truth is that it is mainly the prosperity preachers who are benefitting from the offerings of those they deceive with their twisted doctrines that they propagate for personal gain.

TRUE RICHES: FAITH IN GOD

The Bible teaches that Christians are justified by faith (Rom 5:1), that Christians overcome the world through faith (1 John 5:5), and that Christians live by faith because of what Christ has done (Gal 2:20). Faith pleases God because it is the gift of God, is directly related to salvation, and is the evidence of trust in God for the believer. We do not trust in material things. We trust in the eternal God. Therein rests our faith!

Demonstrating trust in God's Word and finding it to be the most reliable and dependable source of faith, the weeping prophet declares in Jer 15:16, "Thy words were found, and I did eat them; and thy word was unto me the joy and rejoicing of mine heart: for I am called by thy name, O LORD God of hosts." What greater joy can one find in a corrupt world such as the one in which we live? The sinful nature of man has succumbed to the evil doctrines of materialism that draw man's attention and affection away from God to dead things that have no capacity to have a meaningful relationship with man.

When we cross over to the New Testament, we hear the prayer of the Master ring loudly through the corridors of time when He says in John 17:17, "Sanctify them through thy truth: thy word is truth." His deepest, innermost desire was and still is that the Word may have its way in our lives so that it may accomplish His perfect will in us and He will ultimately receive all the glory. It is the Word that will steer us on the path of righteousness so that we can live righteously and be pleasing to Him. The prosperity gospel emphasizes material blessings to the extent that its followers become consumed with the pursuit of the tangible things of this world instead of encouraging a pursuit of God for who He is rather than for what they can get from Him.

In the last book in the Bible, John writes down letters to the seven churches, dictated by Jesus. In Rev 3:8 Jesus says, "I know thy works: behold, I have set before thee an open door, and no man can shut it: for thou hast a little strength, and hast kept my word, and hast not denied my name." This seems to describe the modern church where the real church, the bride of Christ, is weak in some areas but in the aspect of adhering to the Word of Christ, the true church is not found wanting. The modern prosperity gospel is found wanting in that it does not adhere to the Word but rather uses the Word for conveniently pushing its agenda forward regardless of what the Scriptures actually say.

CONCLUSION

If we are to establish Scripture as the final authority, we must believe in the total inspiration of the Word of God (2 Tim 3:14–17). The authority of Scripture is horrendously eroded if the total divine inerrancy is in any way limited or discarded, or made relative to a view of truth contrary to the Bible's own. It is therefore imperative that every teacher of the Bible has embedded in his statement of faith an uncompromised declaration on the authority of God in Scripture and the authority of Scripture in God (2 Tim 2:15–19). We must affirm that the holy Scriptures are to be received as the authoritative Word of God (Rom 10:17; 2 Tim 2:9). We must consequently deny that the Scriptures receive their authority from the church, tradition, or any other human source. Our students are coming to our institutions with preconceived presuppositions about what we believe and how we behave.

We must therefore affirm that the authority of Scripture cannot be separated from the authority of God. Whatever the Bible affirms, God affirms. And what the Bible affirms (or denies), it affirms (or denies) with the very authority of God. Such authority is normative for all believers; it is the canon or rule of God. This divine authority of Old Testament Scripture was confirmed by Christ Himself on numerous occasions (cf. Matt 5:17–18; Luke 24:44; John 10:34–35). And what our Lord confirmed as to the divine authority of the Old Testament, He promised also for the New Testament, which was soon to be penned as inspired by God the Holy Spirit, who was promised to guide God's people into all the truth (John 14:16; 16:13).

We also must therefore categorically declare that one cannot reject the divine authority of Scripture without thereby impugning the authority of Christ, who attested Scripture's divine authority (John 5:39). It is wrong to claim that one can accept the full authority of Christ without acknowledging the complete authority of Scripture.

Like the disciples Peter (1 Pet 1:22–25), Paul (2 Cor 2:17; 4:2; 1 Thess 2:13; Heb 4:12; 13:7), and Stephen (Acts 7) centuries ago, our minds also need to be captive to the divine authority of the Word of God in our preaching and practices. Like the Berean wise men (Acts 17:10–13), we need to scrutinize, analyze, criticize, and finalize the modern pulpit ministry by asserting the authority of Scripture before we accept the teachings that are disseminated.

CHAPTER 15

INSIST ON VIABLE HERMENEUTICS

A RETURN TO CHRISTOCENTRIC INTERPRETATION IN AFRICA

REV. NICHOLAS A. MOORE, ZIMBABWE

The discussion of the proper methodology for biblical interpretation is not new to the African continent. During the period of history known as Late Antiquity (late 200s to 700 AD), the two major centers for biblical theology and exegesis were located at Antioch (Syria) and Alexandria (Egypt). The leaders of the Alexandrian school advocated for an allegorical interpretation of the Scriptures while those at Antioch held to a more "literal," if occasionally typological, exegesis.[1] Although there

---

[1] See Gerald Bray, *Biblical Interpretation: Past and Present* (Downers Grove, IL: IVP Academic, 1996), 79.

Unless otherwise noted, Scripture quotations in this chapter are taken from the English Standard Version.

is much gain in exploring the methodologies of these historical schools, for our present purposes the most poignant observation is that at the core of their divergence was the question of *how* Jesus Christ should be seen as central in all biblical exegesis. Whether by allegory, typology, or some combination of the two, the ancient exegetes understood something the Bible seemed to testify about itself—namely that "all the promises of God find their Yes in him" (2 Cor 1:20). The question over which they wrestled was *how?*

As we approach the issue of how to distinguish true, historical, orthodox Christianity from its many counterfeits in the African context, we may find ourselves asking an even more basic question than that of our ancient African and Near Eastern forebears. That question is not *how* Christ may be seen as central to biblical interpretation, but *whether* He is even to be seen as central in the first place. To be fair, virtually no expression of faith purporting to be "Christian" would likely deny the platitude that "Christ is central" to their readings of Scripture. But what lies at the heart of this effort to rightly identify and "contend for the faith that was once for all delivered to the saints" (Jude 3) is the question not of platitudes but of practice.

THE PROBLEM

Christianity is a text-driven faith. Throughout the history of the church, no matter where false teaching has arisen, rarely (if ever) has there been an outright rejection of the Scriptures. Certain portions, passages, and precepts of Scripture have been challenged at various times, but the nature of the Christian faith is such that to outright and categorically reject the document known as the Bible is to depart from the faith. One may well foray into cultism or other religions, but to reasonably identify as "Christian" has always meant affording some measure of credence to the biblical witness. The problem, though, is that just as Christians are aware of this basic fact, so is their enemy.

From the earliest pages of the Bible, we are introduced to a creature referred to as "the adversary" or "the devil" who is an opponent both to God's truth and its adherents. But the first word Scripture uses as a descriptor for him is the Hebrew term *'ārûm* (Gen 3:1). We tend to translate this as "crafty" (carrying a negative connotation), but the word is used more often elsewhere to describe those who are "prudent" (Prov 12:16, 23; 13:16; 14:8; etc.). For all we can say about Satan, the Bible admits he is "prudent." And his "prudence" is displayed in the manner by which he approaches Eve with a temptation to sin against God. In this earliest temptation, the enemy does not recklessly propose an outright rejection of God's word. Instead he merely proposes an alternate interpretation. As Russell Moore writes, "The old Serpent of Eden comes to the primeval woman not with a Black Mass and occult symbols, but with the Word she'd received from her God—with the snake's peculiar spin on it."[2] Satan does not deny that God had instructed the man and woman not to eat—he merely questions God's motive in doing so.

Similarly, in the rest of the Old Testament we find many "prophets" and "preachers" who indeed bear the oracles of God, but apply them in contexts that render them not only false, but anti-gospel. One example of this would be the proclamation of peace where there is no peace (Jer 6:14; cf. 4:10; 23:17; Ezek 13:10; Mic 3:5; John 14:27). Another might

---

[2] Russell D. Moore, "The Devil Is a Boring Preacher: The High Stakes of Dull Sermons," *Russell Moore* (blog), April 14, 2009, https://www.russell moore.com/2009/04/14/the-devil-is-a-boring-preacher-the-high-stakes-of -dull-sermons/.

be pointing the people to sacrifices and offerings when the Lord desired obedience (1 Sam 15:22; cf. Eccl 5:1; Hos 6:6; Matt 9:13). Some made appeal to dogmatic retribution (see Job 4:1–25:6) when what the Lord was revealing was a deeper mystery about Himself. In these types of instances, none of what was preached was patently false or unbiblical; it was simply not the message God wanted delivered to His people at those times.

Of course, the apex moment in this enterprise of misdirection appears in the earliest pages of the Gospels when Satan assaults the Son of God Himself with, of all things, the Word of God. He cites portions of Psalms that seemed to promise Jesus, in that moment: miraculous provision of food (even from stones, Matt 4:3); divine protection from disaster (even death, Matt 4:6), and considerable expansion of His boundaries/ territory ("all the kingdoms of the world and their glory," Matt 4:8). Here Satan literally lays out an expository argument as to why, biblically, Jesus should become a Satanist.

These instances seem absurd to us when they are enumerated on a page, and the Bible clearly points to them as such. But the question we must ask ourselves today is whether or not the church in Africa possesses an adequate hermeneutic to recognize such absurdities when they are presented in "sheep's clothing" (Matt 7:15). Could we discern, for instance, these same misleading questions or spins if posed by a "prophet" in a suit rather than by a snake in a garden? Could we recognize misapplications of the Bible if done by someone called "apostle" or "bishop" rather than someone called Bildad or Eliphaz? Could we hear the voice of the evil one as clearly if mouthed behind a clerical collar rather than by a devil in the wilderness?

There is certainly no shortage of biblical references and teaching in Sub-Saharan Africa. One must look no further than the nearest taxi vehicle to see Bible verses proudly emblazoned for all to see or the nearest street corner to hear loud and energetic preaching of what purports to be "Christian" messages. But if such men (or even angels, Gal 1:8) were actually preaching a contrary "gospel," could we even recognize it as such?

TOWARD A CHRISTOCENTRIC HERMENEUTIC IN AFRICA

The solution to this challenge is nothing new but is in fact something very old. We can learn from the example of our ancient African and Near Eastern church fathers that, whatever differences Christians may ultimately have in our approach to biblical interpretation, our guiding principle for exegesis must be to expose "in all the Scriptures the things concerning [Jesus Christ]" (Luke 24:27).

While entire volumes (indeed libraries!) have been and continue to be written on sound methodological principles for Christ-centered biblical interpretation, in the space allotted here it will suffice to propose two broad interpretive diagnostic questions.

Question 1: Who is this ultimately about? When approaching any biblical text, we must first ask the question, "Who is this about?" One of the great strengths of the African church is its emphasis on experiential faith. Africans, by and large, will not abide a faith that is merely cerebral and intellectual, but insist on a religious experience that is lived out in flesh and bone. A drawback to this positive emphasis, however, can be a rush in biblical exegesis to the question, "What does this passage mean for me?" To be clear, the drawback here is not the question itself, as certainly all Scripture has application and is "profitable" to us (2 Tim 3:16). The drawback, however, can be a *rush* to that question. In other words, is the Bible *first and foremost* supposed to be "about us"?

The apostle Paul refers to God's "will" as a mystery that has been "made known." This mystery was "not made known to the sons of men in other generations" (Eph 3:5) but has now been made known to Paul and others by "revelation" (v. 3). And Paul says the focus of this plan has always been in "the fullness of time, to unite all things in *him*, things in heaven and things on earth" (Eph 1:9–10, italics added). Although this is not a comprehensive treatment on the nature of Scripture, at least one thing we see here is that God's plan from "before the foundation of the world" (1:4) has been to architect a plan for uniting all things in Christ, "to the praise of his glorious grace" (1:6). So, if we want to know what is the "main point" of what God has "revealed," the answer is in short—it is all about Jesus, to the praise of God's glory.

Immediately with this idea, many good and valid interpretive questions will spring up. How can we see all Scripture as being about Jesus, even when most of it was written long before His incarnation and other parts seem to have little or no direct reference to His life or ministry? As mentioned above, countless volumes have been and will continue to be written addressing these types of questions, and good Christian exegetes can disagree on some of the specifics of how they are answered. However, if the church in Africa can begin (like the Alexandrians and Antiochenes) with the basic assumption that all of God's revelation is ultimately *first and foremost* about God's redemptive purposes in Christ, and then only *secondarily* applicable to believers, we will be on our way to developing a sound hermeneutic that can guard us against error.

Question 2: What time is it? World travelers must often be intentional to adapt their biological and actual clocks when traveling from one place to another. We refer to this phenomenon as changing time zones. In an analogous manner, we must grow in our understanding that different parts of the Bible were written across different redemptive-historical "time zones." Graeme Goldsworthy refers to these as "epochs" of redemptive-history.[3] Others may prefer to speak of "covenants" or "dispensations." Regardless of how we label these divisions or even how many we identify throughout the Bible, the guiding principle is that we recognize that not all Scripture may be understood or applied in the same way. We must learn to ask of any text, "What time is it here?"

To ask this question is to at least open the door to the task of biblical theology. This phrase does not simply refer to *theology* that is *biblical*, but rather to a discipline that "involves the quest for the big picture, or the overview, of biblical revelation. It is of the nature of biblical revelation that it tells a story rather than sets out timeless principles in abstract."[4] While the Bible does indeed give timeless principles, Goldsworthy points out, "They are given in an historical context of progressive revelation."[5] Seeking to understand the message and theology of the entire Bible enables us to relate any particular Bible passage or story to the message and story of the whole. We can truly understand each part of Scripture only in light of the unified canon, which conveys a single message.

In our pursuit of the whole Bible's message, we may fruitfully discuss and disagree regarding the themes and patterns it contains or the nuances of its unifying center (or even whether a singular center can be identified!).[6] But if we seek to organize our interpretive efforts around the Bible's own framework rather than immediate or personal application,

---

[3] Graeme Goldsworthy, *Preaching the Whole Bible As Christian Scripture: The Application of Biblical Theology to Expository Preaching* (Grand Rapids, MI: Eerdmans, 2000), 112–13.

[4] Goldsworthy, *Preaching the Whole Bible*, 22.

[5] Goldsworthy, 22.

[6] James M. Hamilton Jr., *God's Glory in Salvation through Judgment: A Biblical Theology* (Wheaton, IL: Crossway, 2010), chap. 1.

the church in Africa will inevitably grow toward a common understanding of the Bible's meaning and be less susceptible to erroneous interpretations when they are presented. Every part of Scripture is just that—part, of a whole. Only when we see a text in light of the broader storyline that has its crux in the gospel of Jesus Christ will we be able to soundly apply that text to our own lives within our particular "time zone" of the Bible's story.

Any scholar, interpreter, or even casual reader of the Bible will see these two diagnostic questions as basic and simplistic, perhaps overly so. But these two pillars form the foundation upon which any grander or more luxurious hermeneutical structure must be constructed. An approach to interpreting the Bible that is both: (1) Christ-centered (who is this ultimately about?); and (2) Biblical Theological (what time is it?), will serve as a hermeneutical North Star, guiding us through the foggy mist of the (mis)users and abusers of Scripture so prevalent on our continent.[7]

A PEOPLE OF THE BOOK

We are bombarded with statistics telling us of the vibrant movement of Christianity that is spreading throughout Africa.[8] To be sure, there is much to contemplate and celebrate in these numbers. But as we have seen throughout the present volume as well as in our own ministry contexts,

---

[7] For more on this approach, see Graeme Goldsworthy, *Christ-Centered Biblical Theology: Hermeneutical Foundations and Principles* (Downers Grove, IL: IVP Academic, 2012).

[8] See Jenkins, *The Next Christendom* (see intro., n. 5). See also Mark Noll, *The New Shape of World Christianity: How American Experience Reflects Global Faith*, repr. ed. (Downers Grove, IL: IVP Academic, 2013).

an abundance of churches, Bibles, and "Christians" does not always necessarily equate to a biblical expression of true, historic, orthodox Christianity. The best way for the African church to ensure the growth and vitality of true Christianity while guarding against counterfeits is for her to remain true to her roots—namely, the Bible. African Christians in general, and Baptists in particular, must vigilantly strive to be a "people of the Book."

In saying that, we must quickly reiterate that biblical reference and adulation alone will never build a true church. Sub-Saharan Africa may be second only to the Bible itself in its number of biblically named people, locations, and institutions. But an entity that merely appears "biblical" on the surface can never connect individuals to eternal life.

This is the message Jesus presented to the religious leaders in John 5. According to their hermeneutic, Sabbath keeping was the law of the day and in their estimation, Jesus (due to His displays of mercy and compassion) was on the wrong side of it. Interestingly, though, Jesus does not respond by rebuking their bibliolatry (honoring the Bible even above God Himself). Instead, He responds with a lesson in Christ-centered biblical theological hermeneutics. "You do not have his word abiding in you, for you do not believe the one whom he has sent. You search the Scriptures because you think that in them you have eternal life; and it is they that bear witness about *me*" (John 5:38–39, italics added).

The Bible is ultimately about Jesus, and no matter where we are reading in the Bible, the Scriptures are intended to point us to Him. These basic truths serve as the foundation stones of true, orthodox, historic Christianity. How we flesh out the implications of these truths may vary from tradition to tradition, church to church, even believer to believer. But those are discussions we must always be willing to have. Here in Africa, we have had them before.

CHAPTER 16

EMPHASIZE THE CHRIST OF SCRIPTURE

RONNIE DAVIS, PHD, SOUTH AFRICA

False teaching or heresy is not a new occurrence in the church; rather, one can find a number of references from the New Testament epistles in which an apostle is moved to challenge a teaching or encourage the church to set aside a false doctrine. In most cases, the false teaching centers on a misunderstanding of either the person or the work of Jesus. Either Jesus is seen as less than He is, as confronted by John in his first epistle, or the redemptive work of Christ is seen as needing some additional understanding, as Paul corrects in Galatians. In considering the movement of Neo-Pentecostalism and the prosperity gospel, great importance should be placed on the task of emphasizing the person, work, and position of Christ as found in the Scripture. Scripture must reveal for the

Unless otherwise noted, Scripture quotations in this chapter are taken from the New International Version.

Christian who Jesus is and what He has accomplished through His death and resurrection.

The early church demonstrated a clear focus on Jesus so that He affected every aspect of life. The Holy Spirit through the Gospel writers provide the Christian with Jesus's own words of the cost of following Him—that one must renounce self and radically follow (Matt 16:24; Mark 8:34; Luke 9:23). Throughout the epistles, Jesus is lifted up as the focal point of every believer. Believers are challenged to maintain a focus on Jesus so as to not grow weary or faint (Heb 12:1–3). Such reminders are particularly evident in the later New Testament writings when the church was experiencing persecution (see the prison letters of Paul, 1 and 2 Peter, Hebrews, Revelation), and the difficulty of circumstances provided a temptation to reject Jesus or to hide away. In response, the disciple is reminded that only in Christ is there truly hope and purpose in the journey.

In the face of a false gospel such as the current prosperity movement and Neo-Pentecostalism, one must seek to understand Jesus better, to ensure that the declarations from Scripture regarding the person, work, and position of Jesus are taught and that this Christ of Scripture is the center of the life of every believer and church. One could approach the task of providing an overview of the Christ of Scripture in various ways—from a systematic reading of the New Testament to an analysis of Jesus's self-revelation as recorded in the Gospels. In this chapter, however, the author will focus on a single passage of Scripture in which one finds a seven-fold Christological statement (Heb 1:1–3) and use those seven statements as a lens to examine Jesus in light of the larger testimony of Scripture. One might ask, "Why Hebrews?" Hebrews seems particularly relevant as the Holy Spirit moved the author to engage with followers of Jesus who were considering rejecting Jesus and the gospel that had been proclaimed to them in light of hardship and false teaching. The epistle to the Hebrews begins with a powerful declaration about Jesus and proceeds to expound on the person and work of Jesus relentlessly so that the reader is left with the overwhelming testimony that in Jesus, alone, is our life, hope, and identity found.

This chapter, then, will begin with an examination of Heb 1:1–3, highlighting the seven statements about the Son. Each of these statements will be explained considering the context of Hebrews, the larger New Testament, and Scripture as a whole. After these designations have been examined, the significance for the disciple of Christ and the church will be considered as a means of conclusion.

THE SEVEN-FOLD CHRISTOLOGICAL STATEMENT IN HEBREWS 1

The Holy Spirit through the author of Hebrews begins the epistle with the following words:

> In the past God spoke to our ancestors through the prophets at many times and in various ways, but in these last days he has spoken to us by his Son, whom he appointed heir of all things, and through whom also he made the universe. The Son is the radiance of God's glory and the exact representation of his being, sustaining all things by his powerful word. After he had provided purification for sins, he sat down at the right hand of the Majesty in heaven. (Heb 1:1–3)

The statement is validated immediately through the string of Old Testament passages in 1:5–13. While some momentary mystery is allowed around the identity of the Son, the author reveals the Son with the declaration, "But we do see Jesus . . ." (2:9). Throughout the epistle, Jesus is declared "more" than anything to which He can be compared. This understanding is crucial for the church today: no one stands above Christ. Consider the elements of this statement.

HEIR OF ALL THINGS

The first aspect of Jesus that is highlighted in the passage is one of position in relation to all that exists. Jesus is declared the heir of all that is. The concept of an heir reflects two particular elements: legitimacy and authority. Jesus is in His position because no one else deserves such a status. He alone is placed over all things. The aspect of dominion is emphasized in the use of Ps 8:6 ("you crowned him with glory and honor and put everything under his feet," paraphrased). This basic understanding of Jesus's position is echoed by the Lord Himself before the Great Commission when He declares, "All authority in heaven and on earth has been given to me" (Matt 28:18). For every follower of Jesus, the beginning of our confession about Jesus should be He, alone, has authority.

AGENT OF CREATION

Following from the declaration of Jesus's position, the Holy Spirit provides a statement of an initial aspect of the work of Christ—His role in creation. Contrary to any thought that would limit the role of Jesus to the period of incarnation, one is reminded of His eternal nature and role in creation itself. The author will quote Ps 102:25 as an illustration of this aspect of the work of Christ in Heb 1:10. The Holy Spirit led other

New Testament writers to include similar statements about Jesus's role in creation (e.g., John 1:3; Col 1:16).

RADIANCE OF GOD'S GLORY

The next two statements stand in compliment to each other. The first refers to Jesus as the one in whom the glory of God is seen. The emphasis is on a consequence of who Jesus is—because of who He is, the glory of God is seen in Him. The theme of God's glory runs throughout Scripture whether it is viewed as the overwhelming evidence of God's presence (such as the experience at Sinai) or the declaration of the work of God (Ps 19:1—heaven and earth declare His glory). It is uniquely connected to both the person and work of God—either His direct presence or the consequence of His actions. Thus, God's glory can be proclaimed and declared, it can fill the earth (Ps 72:19), and humanity can fall short of God's glory (Rom 3:23). Here, however, one is confronted with the reality that Jesus alone is the true radiance of God's glory. This declaration is similar to Jesus's own words in John 17:4–5 in which he states that He brought glory through the completion of work and also states that He had glory before the world began—Jesus reflects the glory of God both through His work and in His being.

EXACT REPRESENTATION OF HIS BEING

The follow-up statement to Jesus's reflection of God's glory is simply the explanation of why that is so—because He is God. In this short phrase, one encounters one of the strongest statements of the divinity of Jesus found in the New Testament. One should not think of the English word *representation* as if it is a picture of an original; rather, it reflects the concept of exactness. The image of the word is connected to the idea of the truest form or essence of anything. Here the Holy Spirit through the author is declaring that if one desires to know the truest form or most exact being of God, look to Jesus. Jesus radiates the glory of God, because He is God. Although this understanding is reflected throughout the New Testament, Jesus states it with clarity in John when He identifies Himself with God: "'Very truly I tell you,' Jesus answered, 'before Abraham was born, I am!'" (John 8:58). Further, Jesus demonstrates His divinity in actions such as the forgiveness of sins (Matt 9:2; Mark 2:5). This reality is the center of this seven-fold statement and is the climactic confession for any follower of Jesus.

SUSTAINING ALL THINGS

Having established the nature of Jesus as God, let us return to the focus of the work of Christ. While earlier the reader was made aware of Jesus's role in the creating of all things, one is now reminded that He is also the one in whom all things are sustained. The writer will recall the words of Ps 102:26 and Isa 51:6 in Heb 1:11–12, which state that the end of creation will be determined by the act of Jesus. Once again, this idea is not only found in Hebrews. Scripture declares that everything is sustained in Christ (Col 1:17) and that the end of creation is found in Him (2 Pet 3:10); this idea is seen most emphatically in the last chapters of Revelation.

PROVIDED PURIFICATION FOR SINS

Cradled between the initial work of Christ in creation and the continual work in sustaining creation, we are pointed to the critical work of Jesus as the atonement for sin. This aspect is the heartbeat of the work of Jesus throughout Scripture. The promise of true atonement and new covenant found in Jer 31:31–34 is fully realized in the work of Jesus— and is the focus of Jesus as our true High Priest in the book of Hebrews, climaxing in chapter 8. The writer of Hebrews rightly notes not only the unique work of Christ toward our salvation, but also the total efficacy of Jesus's purification of our sin—so that there is no other hope. Salvation, then, is clearly understood in the purifying work of Jesus, with no lack. Nearly every New Testament writer will engage this reality. Paul will offer the greatest examination of the salvific work of Christ in Romans, but the reality is found throughout the New Testament. One needs to connect the reality of the efficacy of the work of Jesus with His person. It is complete because He is God. Because of His nature, there is no lack. This reality is highlighted in Hebrews as the author points out that Jesus is the superlative priest (7:23–28) as well as the singularly perfect sacrifice (9:14–15).

SEATED AT THE RIGHT HAND

The final statement returns to the understanding of position. The seven-fold statement began with Jesus's position as heir, which reflected His dominion and authority, and finishes with Jesus's position "at the right hand of the Majesty in heaven." This statement is once again a picture of authority; however, the image also includes the understanding of power to complete the plans and actions of God. "Right hand" may also carry the understanding of ultimate justice or judgement. Hence, Jesus is the one in whom the authority to judge is placed. Note the overall chiastic structure of the seven-fold statement:

A: A declaration of the position of the Son (heir)

    B: A statement on the work of the Son (agent of creation)

        C: A statement on the nature/being of Jesus (radiance of glory of God)

        C': A statement on the nature/being of Jesus (exactness of God)

    B': Two statements on the work of the Son (sustains creation and purifies sin)

A': A declaration of the position of the Son (right hand of Majesty)

As a chiastic structure, two key points of emphasis are highlighted—the centerpiece (Jesus is God) and the final statement (Jesus is in the position of power). The particular role of judgement is a direct expression of His divine person. It is also a statement of the absolute certainty that such judgement will occur. Thus, the flow of the statement reveals that the Son who has been from the beginning and created all things and stands above all things is God, radiating His glory and reflecting His being. He sustains all of creation and gives life through the purification of sin and waits to welcome or judge all things.

CONCLUSION

The more fully the disciple of Jesus understands the nature, position, and work of Christ, the greater the ability to withstand and engage with any heresy or false teaching, such as Neo-Pentecostalism. As a means of conclusion, I will note the correctives presented by the biblical understanding of Jesus, specifically in light of Neo-Pentecostalism. Then I will suggest specific strategies that can be enacted to help disciples and church leaders in equipping other followers so they can avoid the deception of such false teaching.

A greater understanding of Christ moves the disciple to become more Christocentric in both theology and practice, which is critical in challenging Neo-Pentecostalism. The former aspect is important, as prosperity-focused theology is fundamentally anthropocentric as Jesus and the Holy Spirit are concerned in the well-being of humanity; thus, "people must see Jesus as much, much more than the solution to their problems and the means to achieve their aspirations."[1] Further, even when focused on God, Neo-Pentecostalism tends to place the Holy Spirit as the point of focus and the source of power, thus ignoring the primary role of the Spirit as bearing witness to Jesus. The focus of glory is to be God alone. With regard to practice, a more complete understanding of Jesus is critical for the Christian as Jesus alone has all authority and, thus, can order the steps of His followers. It is critical that Jesus's words on the life of discipleship—including suffering and self-denial—become the source of expectation for the believer. As Arnett notes, it is important to recognize that Jesus requires His followers to make adjustments in thinking, practice, and agendas.[2]

Finally, consider some practical actions that can be established to help equip the church to withstand the Neo-Pentecostal and prosperity movement in light of the Christ of Scripture. First, in preaching and teaching, give proper attention to the person of Jesus—His role, position, and nature—throughout Scripture. It is critical for the Christian to realize that Jesus is God eternally and pre-dates the incarnation. As a

---

[1] Arnett, *Pentecostalization*, 168 (see intro., n. 8).
[2] Arnett, 168.

result, there is testimony and evidence of Jesus in the full proclamation of Scripture (Old and New Testaments) and one must follow the example of the New Testament writers and engage with this full testimony of Scripture regarding Jesus.

Second, in preaching and teaching, give proper attention to the teachings of Jesus to His followers—especially regarding the certainty of their suffering. For example, Jesus uses the specific phrase "my disciples" in only a handful of passages. Those in John highlight qualities of His disciples (love one another, 13:35; obey Jesus's commands, 8:31) while those in Luke 14:25–33 highlight the cost of following Jesus—those actions without which one cannot be Jesus's disciple (priority of Jesus over all relationships; taking up a cross; giving up everything). Finally, in practice, Jesus's teaching and commands determine the actions of the church. As one preacher noted, the authority of Jesus for every church and disciple establishes priority, provides ability, and shapes identity.[3] Jesus is more than an "enabler of aspirations" or a celestial problem solver.[4] Instead, He establishes the agenda for His people.

In light of the desire to satisfy self that is an element in the seeking of comfort that is too common in the Neo-Pentecostal movement, the proper understanding of the nature, position, and work of Christ is critical not only for pastors, but for every follower of Jesus. Returning to the book of Hebrews:

> Therefore, since we are surrounded by such a great cloud of witnesses, let us throw off everything that hinders and the sin that

---

[3] C. Welton Gaddy, "Sermons on the Great Commission," in *The Minister's Manual: The 1994 Edition*, ed. James W. Cox (New York: HarperCollins, 1993).

[4] Arnett, *Pentecostalization*, 168.

so easily entangles. And let us run with perseverance the race marked out for us, fixing our eyes on Jesus, the pioneer and perfecter of faith. For the joy set before him he endured the cross, scorning its shame, and sat down at the right hand of the throne of God. Consider him who endured such opposition from sinners, so that you will not grow weary and lose heart. (12:1–3)

Chapter 17

Emphasize the Sin Nature

Rev. Jack Rantho, Botswana

My wife and I were watching news on local television, and that particular evening a clip showed thousands of people marching, lifting up banners, and shouting at the top of their voices. There was a call to end violence against women. It was so touching and heartbreaking. One speaker after another articulated emotionally the pain of women abused by men. The picture you could get was that Botswana men are bad and evil. The next episode of the news talked about cattle thieves; it showed people, both men and women, who had been caught that day. Later in the same news, the broadcaster talked about the problem of drug abuse in Botswana, of young men and women indulging in drugs. It suddenly struck us, and we said, "This is the sin nature." We concluded that all these things demonstrate the problem of the heart. This chapter aims to articulate the reality of the sin nature, its impact on people, and how it has been denied by many people who confess to be Christians.

Unless otherwise noted, Scripture quotations in this chapter are taken from the New American Standard Bible.

WHAT IS THE SIN NATURE?

Sin began with Adam and Eve. These two were the first people on earth. They were the beginning of all human races. God placed them in a beautiful place called the Garden of Eden with all they needed for life. He also gave them instructions on what to do and not do. He told them the outcome of failing to hold fast to His instructions. There was a penalty, and that penalty was spiritual death. However, Adam and Eve failed to obey God. They, therefore, received the penalty of disobedience, which is spiritual death (Gen 3:1–19). The Bible tells us that all people are born sinful because of Adam. Romans 5:12 said, "Therefore, just as through one man sin entered into the world, and death through sin, and so death spread to all men, because all sinned."

The sin nature is clearly set forth by King David in Ps 51:5. He has explicitly demonstrated that sin is now part of what we are. All people are infected and polluted by sin. This is clearly seen in people's behavior and inclinations. It is natural for people to do wrong of any kind. This is why the apostle Paul tells us in Romans that the law was put in place to show us that we are corrupted by sin (5:13). All the laws we have in our different countries are a clear testimony of sin. All the laws are trying to govern people from destroying themselves and each other. The law is not sin, and instead sin is illustrated by the law, exposing its hideous nature. Both Old and New Testaments use extensive vocabulary to describe sin; at the root of sin is the idea of missing the mark or failing to meet God's requirements. There is no exhaustive list of sins; rather, any act that misses God's perfect will is sin, separating the sinner from God.

Likewise, the people of the world produce little good from their tongues and mouths. The goodness of a sinful person is just like a grave. The Bible clearly states that the mouth or tongue speaks from the abundance of the heart (Matt 12:34–36; 15:18). The lying and the deception that go on in the world, whether in the political realm, the religious realm, the business realm, or the societal realm, are due to human depravity, or the sin nature. Neo-Pentecostals would attribute all of this to Satan and spiritual powers and forces. However, Paul attributes it all to sin, quoting Pss 14:1–3; 5:9; and 10:7.[1]

The innermost part of humans is dead. Though we are told that the law of God is written on our hearts (Rom 2:15), our sense of right and wrong in regard to this standard is skewed. The day Adam and Eve ate of the fruit of the knowledge of right and wrong, their inner person died. So Jeremiah says that the heart is deceitful and desperately wicked (17:9). He is talking about the sin nature. The heart is able to deceive its owner. In the Bible the heart is the central part of a person, where decisions are made. This is why Heb 4:12 speaks of the Word of God being the judge of the impulse of the heart. Without the Word of God, the heart kills its owner. Men and women have tried over the ages to do what is right. They tried to come up with procedures and processes that can keep people from doing wrong, but all of their efforts were empty and fruitless. Countries are filled with courts of law and prisons, just because of sin.

THE IMPACT OF THE SIN NATURE ON THE HUMAN RACE

The dilemma of the sin nature presents itself in two parts. First, it destroys the relationship with God. Second, it destroys relationships with each other. The dilemma of sin against God is clearly laid out for us in

---

[1] Rom 3:10–14.

Rom 3:9–23. Paul here makes it clear that human beings are unable to relate to God in their own terms because of our sin condition. He calls this spiritual death in Eph 2:1. According to Rom 3:23, all people are corrupted by sin. It is not the environment they live in nor their race or ethnicity. He makes it clear that because of sin there is no righteous person in the whole universe. All people have turned aside; they do not understand; they do not seek God. Therefore they can never reach out to God in their sinful condition. It is proper for us to say that sin separates people from God.

After the fall, Adam and Eve ran away from God. They hid themselves; they could no longer stand in His presence. This is clearly expressed throughout the Old Testament. We see the people that God brought out of Egypt turning to idols. People were bowing down before the works of their own hands. They did not regard their Creator as the One worthy of their worship. Paul says that people have exchanged the truth for a lie. The people who are made in the image of God are busy running after created things:

> For even though they knew God, they did not honor Him as God or give thanks, but they became futile in their speculations, and their foolish heart was darkened. Professing to be wise, they became fools, and exchanged the glory of the incorruptible God for an image in the form of corruptible man and of birds and four-footed animals and crawling creatures. (Rom 1:21–23)

In this passage Paul tells us that people are desperately sick. In a way, they are now seeking something to honor. Sometimes they honor other people or images of people. Yes, here in Africa, it is an open secret that our houses and mobiles [mobile phones] contain pictures of those whom people esteem to be supernatural—those who are thought of as having the ability to intervene in their circumstances. When reading the pages of the New Testament, you get a picture of people who made their own gods with their own hands. Men will put money on man-made gods and will give them their prayer and worship. They will offer sacrifices to them as if they are honouring a supreme being. What you read in this book is real in our communities. Sometimes people need to have religious tours so that they might grasp the separation that sin brings between humans and God. I once visited two religious temples, one Hindu and the other Sikh. I was shocked by their objects of worship. However, I want to appeal to you today that they are not alone; they are just a fraction of many who have turned away from God to idols.

At his root, his core, his heart, mankind is separated from and is hostile toward God. He prefers to satisfy his sinful cravings and desires more than to honour and worship God. The Bible tells us two things. First, human beings are spiritually dead, and, second, because of this they cannot relate to God. They have nothing that can connect them with God; they are totally separated from God and they are unable to connect with God. It is just like people whom we used to live with here on earth but who have died physically. These people are totally separated from us. They are deprived of the things that we experience and enjoy here on earth. They cannot bring themselves back.

Second, the sin nature has created enmity between people. Paul says, "All have turned aside; together they have become worthless; no one does good, not even one. Their throat is an open grave; they use their tongues to deceive. The venom of asps is under their lips. Their mouth is full of curses and bitterness. Their feet are swift to shed blood."[2] This is an image of hostility. It talks about how people view and treat each other.

---

[2] Rom 3:12–15 ESV.

It is easy for people to look at this and miss the centrality of human corruption. The sin nature, which has infected people of all races, brings killings, theft, and fraud into our world. This passage tells us that it is now natural for people to hate and look down upon each other. It paints a picture of the society that is unable to do any good to each other. By nature people are just like wild animals; it is a picture of the survival of the fittest. The current condition of humans is bad; it is evil. Mark 7:20–23 says that "what comes out of a person is what defiles him. For from within, out of the heart of man, come evil thoughts, sexual immorality, theft, murder, adultery, coveting, wickedness, deceit, sensuality, envy, slander, pride, foolishness. All these evil things come from within, and they defile a person" (ESV).

Paul quotes Isa 59:7–8 and Ps 36:1 to demonstrate that all the wars of the world are a clear testimony of human depravity (Rom 3:16–18). In the Neo-Pentecostal culture and theology, it is said that the essential cause of all that takes place at an individual and corporate level in terms of war and murder is Satanic in origin. However, the Bible states that every sin is a form of evil. The world will not know true peace and is incapable of realizing it because of human depravity. War is from the depravity of humanity. The world that we live in is filled with people without God, whereby people hate, deceive, cheat, lie, and kill each other. We must never fall into this trap of thinking that one can know God and His blessing outside the Lord Jesus Christ. The only way to find true peace is with a relationship with Jesus Christ our Lord and Saviour.

Now, because of the sin nature, people are the objects of God's wrath. Romans 1:18 (ESV) declares that the wrath of God is being revealed against people who do not honor God: "For the wrath of God is revealed from heaven against all ungodliness and unrighteousness of men, who by their unrighteousness suppress the truth." This is horrible news. People are not only separated from God, but they are also facing an angry God. The Bible talks about the enmity between people and God. There are disputes, and the Creator's wrath is being displayed. The Bible takes sin seriously. We likewise must do the same. If Christians and the lost world are to know the Creator God, all must understand His standards against sin.

CHAPTER 18

PRESENT SALVATION AS RECONCILIATION

MOSES AUDI, PHD, NIGERIA

Salvation is one of the central themes of the Christian faith, indeed of every religion. The Christian definition of salvation has been variously challenged. These challenges are global, and they come from various religions, as well as from new trends within and outside the church. Some such trends within the church include movements like Neo-Pentecostalism, independent church movements, and liberation movements. The challenges from without include scientific and philosophical movements such as secularism, humanism, socialism, anthropology, and psychology. While some of the views of salvation may overlap among the perspectives identified above, they are different and often opposed to the biblical view. The views cast a shadow of distrust or doubt on the

Unless otherwise noted, Scripture quotations in this chapter are taken from the New International Version.

biblical perspective or consider it inadequate. Some of these views are identified below.

African Traditional Religion includes in its view of salvation deliverance from spiritual forces and spirits of the ancestors. One who is saved will live a comfortable life. Spiritual forces will not confront them and ancestral spirits will not make demands of them, and they will rest in peace.

The Islamic view of salvation is similar to that of Judaism, which emphasizes works and obedience to the law. The saved will live a prosperous life as a result of following the law and doing good works. Although in Islam there may not be a clear-cut view of salvation, observing the "five pillars" brings one to a point of being considered for God's mercy since "God saves only those he wills" (Surah al-Qasas 28:56, paraphrased).

Views associated with global trends within the church draw inspiration from members' historic religions. Neo-Pentecostal and independent church movements in Africa, for instance, have been said to borrow their perspectives from African religions, relating salvation to deliverance from the spirit world, ancestral curses, or even evil people.[1] The power encounter is informative of their several perspectives of the experience of the saved. This will be discussed further in this chapter.

The socio-economic and political situation, on the other hand, informs the perspective of salvation for the liberationists. For them, freedom from oppression, suffering, and economic suppression constitutes their definition of salvation.

---

[1] Asamoah-Gyadu, *African Charismatics*, 233 (see chap. 2, n. 4). See also Jacob Oladipupo, "African Wildfires, Yoruba Tradition, Neo-Pentecostal Power and Baptists, from 1990 to 2015" (PhD diss., Southwestern Baptist Theological Seminary, 2017).

The scientific or secular view of salvation is defined by the level of independence from God.[2] Human knowledge, ability, and capacity enable self-actualization, which to them is salvation. Various shades of this view are expressed by the philosophical perspectives as stated below.

Humanism, socialism, anthropology, and psychology share a similar view, which defines salvation in terms of all forms of comfort that appeal to human desires and nature. When human beings are able to pursue and achieve comfort and satisfaction of their perceived need, then they are saved. This informs the concept of success couched in the wealth and health gospel.

All of the views presented above provide a perception of "present salvation," the aspect of salvation expressed in physical life on earth—the here and now. They seek to answer the questions, If I am saved, what will be the condition of my life now? What evidences should I look for to tell if I am saved or not?

An attempt to answer these questions justifies the definitions of salvation as indicated above. The ground for the justification is not far-fetched. Each one coming to faith in Christ held to one of these views over time. Unless one's discipleship has consciously raised the question of defining salvation as present at conversion, the historic view is subsumed into the newfound faith.

PERSPECTIVES OF NEW CHURCH MOVEMENTS

J. Kwabena Asamoah-Gyadu, discussing the concept of salvation among the Charismatics in Africa, noted three broad categories as expressed in

---

[2] Millard J. Erickson, *Introducing Christian Doctrine*, 2nd ed., ed. L. Arnold Hustad (Grand Rapids, MI: Baker Book House, 2001), 293–94.

this section.[3] Though his discussion grows from the context in Ghana, it is representative of the development in Africa.

First, salvation means becoming more spiritual as an individual. It supports pious platitudes, promoting self-centeredness. Salvation makes the individual powerful spiritually to stand up to forces, live a victorious life, and command control over spiritual forces.[4] Becoming "born again" makes one a new person.

It is also focused on living a comfortable life as a person, not community. The concern for living in wealth defines salvation. It rejects poverty, even in expression. Human destiny is attributed to their spirituality, mindset, and what they say rather than to God. It has given birth to the doctrine and practice of "positive confession" and the "claiming of promises."

The prevalent view of salvation also focuses on deliverance from spiritual forces and ancestral curses, as well as physical healing. Some of this emphasis results in spiritual clinics, prayer houses, deliverance services, and so on. Salvation implies living a problem-free life. Failure to grow as a Christian as defined by the Bible could be from holding to a definition of salvation as expressed in this sub-section rather than as reconciliation with God through Christ.

THE CHALLENGE OF THE PREVALENT VIEWS OF PRESENT SALVATION

Christians of evangelical persuasion could easily become attracted to the Neo-Pentecostal, Charismatic perspectives because they fall within similar

---

[3] Asamoah-Gyadu, *African Charismatics*,132–232.

[4] See Moses Audi, "Power and the Manifestation of the Supernatural: Who's in Charge?," *Nigerian Baptist Pastors' Magazine*, April 2012, 4–6.

purviews as their historic religions. Randy Arnett vividly demonstrated how the Pentecostal perspectives influenced the Baptists in Africa.[5]

The prevalent views of salvation focus on the individual, posing many challenges to the individual Christian, the church, and the church's ministry. They ignore the concern for others by solely promoting individual spirituality. They deny the communal dimension of the church. The views of salvation above ignore relationships, which are very central to the image of God in humans and central to salvation in the Bible.

Seeing salvation in these ways ignores the impact that transformation brings to humans both at individual and corporate levels. Although the views affirm the change caused by being "born again," the corresponding evidence to the observer is lost. The change that occurs turns the convert into a self-made hero rather than a God-made servant to the community. The impact on the community and the ministry-driven focus that comes as a result of salvation are replaced by self-gratifying desire. Consciousness of others is replaced by the desire for greater pleasure. This overturns the goals of Christian ministry.

Such perspectives lead to rejection of suffering and any appearance of it. Suffering is perceived as a result of divine chastisement for one's sin(s). This complicates ministry by raising many questions such as: Why is this happening to me? What wrong have I done or what good have I failed to do? Do I deserve this from God? And so on. The ministry providers, on the other hand, leave the needy feeling they are not spiritual enough; they need deliverance; there must be something following them. Instead of being comforted, the people are accused of being responsible for what happens to them. It becomes difficult to interpret God's love in suffering, peace in the face of suffering, and so on.

---

[5] Arnett, *Pentecostalization* (see intro., n. 8).

The prevalent view perverts authentic biblical hermeneutics. Faulty hermeneutics are responsible for the rise of corruption and the widening gap between faith claims and practical living. One of the crucial herme- neutical defects is the damage to relationships in the Christian life and the materialistic, mundane, here-and-now drive over against God's will and heaven consciousness that the church is expected to see in the Bible.

The views ignore the centre of salvation, which is reconciliation. This development necessitates constant re-appraisal of the biblical view of present salvation as presented below.

UNDERSTANDING PRESENT SALVATION AND RECONCILIATION

For evangelicals, present salvation is reconciliation. At the point of being saved through repentance and faith, one is reconciled with God, self, and others, as well as with God's creation. This is explicitly and implicitly implied in the biblical expressions regarding salvation.

God initiated the process of reconciliation and commits those He reconciles to continue it (2 Cor 5:18–19). The process of reconciliation restores relationship in many facets. The salvation God offers the world is described as follows.

> For he himself is our peace, who has made the two groups one and has destroyed the barrier, the dividing wall of hostility, by setting aside in his flesh the law with its commands and regula- tions. His purpose was to create in himself one new humanity out of the two, thus making peace, and in one body to reconcile both of them to God through the cross, by which he put to death

their hostility. He came and preached peace to you who were far away and peace to those who were near. For through him we both have access to the Father by one Spirit. (Eph 2:14–18)

First, salvation as reconciliation is reconciliation with God. The primary damage sin caused was to disrupt God's relationship with human beings. God therefore seeks for human beings by providing an avenue to restore them to the original state intended at creation (2 Cor 5:18a). When the first human beings sinned, it was God who sought them out (Genesis 3). Sin created enmity between God and humans; but, out of love, God restored the lost relationship through the death of Christ Jesus (Rom 5:9–11).

Second, salvation reconciles an individual with others. The call to love makes sense and is possible only for someone who has experienced salvation as transformation (1 John 4:7–8). The teaching in the Gospels affirmed that godly relationships are fundamental indicators of pleasing God and receiving salvation. One who does not forgive others cannot receive divine forgiveness (Matt 6:14–15; 18:21–35). One who goes to worship but harbours resentment against someone in his heart will not be accepted by God (Matt 5:23–24). One who is saved is required to love his enemies and feed them and pray for them (Matt 5:43–48; Rom 12:17–21).

Third, salvation reconciles the individual with self. "If anyone is in Christ, the new creation has come: The old has gone, the new is here!" (2 Cor 5:17). This defines the expected transformation. In a similar manner, Paul said: "Do not conform to the pattern of this world, but be transformed by the renewing of your mind" (Rom 12:2). He further affirmed this in Gal 2:20. Because of this, the believer overcomes the pressure of doing what the flesh desires (Rom 7:15–20).

Fourth, salvation reconciles beliefs and practices. One of the greatest banes of the African society is the widening gap between faith claims and practical living. The faith claim and life of the church in Antioch led to the impact the church made in its generation (Acts 11:26). This informs some songs we sing: "The things I used to do, I do them no more . . . there's a great change since I've born again." This is what the Bible means when it says: "You are the light of the world . . ." (Matt 5:14). "Walk by the Spirit, and you will not gratify the desires of the flesh" (Gal 5:16).

Fifth, salvation brings about harmonious management of God's creation. The saved person sees the need for humans to live responsibly toward all that God created for the use of humans. The first assignment God gave humans was to take care of the creation (Gen 2:15). This original state of the world, which human sin has damaged, can only be restored by the regenerated who, through God, reconcile humans to their environment. The natural environment proclaims the glory of God, and those who are in Christ understand this. One who is saved will live a responsible life of caring for God's creation as a way of worshiping God.

The experience of salvation as reconciliation does not only reconcile humans with God, self, others, creation, and beliefs and practices; it also entrusts a ministry to reconcile others to God, alongside all the other dimensions noted above (2 Cor 5:17–18). Failure to see salvation this way either perverts the message of salvation or de-motivates one from engaging in missions at all. This may account for the practice of evangelism among those in other churches by those who hold these perspectives, rather than targeting those who are from other religions. Salvation as reconciliation is therefore further justified below.

JUSTIFICATION OF PRESENT SALVATION AS RECONCILIATION

The first justification of present salvation as reconciliation is the affirmation of the Bible. The Bible's perspective seems unrealistic; but the ground of its workability is in God who instructs the church and is sovereign over all. The early church upheld the biblical perspective, and the church grew tremendously. It accounts for their resilience through persecution and perseverance to the end. The perspective of salvation as reconciliation turns the believer into a lover for the lost, one who has a burden for them and sees them as "harassed and helpless, like sheep without a shepherd" (Matt 9:36), or as acting out of ignorance and needing to be pitied and sought after (Acts 3:17).

Historically, the Middle Ages held similar prevalent views of salvation, which encouraged self-centred spirituality like what is seen today. During this period the church grew numerically but died spiritually. The church turned violent both within and without with the inquisitions and crusades. The Reformation called for a return to the Bible, upon which the discovery of salvation as reconciliation led to the birth of modern missions. People once considered enemies and good only as slaves or for the sword received the gospel, resulting in mutual reconciliation. This is a second justification.

Third, the prevailing perspectives in Neo-Pentecostalism discussed above have not only failed the church, but they have also damaged the image of the church, put to death the church's missional responsibility, destroyed spirituality in the church, and made the church a stench to the perishing world. Note the discussion on the challenges posed by the prevalent views discussed above. These pose a threat to the future of the church.

CONCLUSION

At this point, it is pertinent to ask: Is salvation presented as reconciliation unconcerned with the issues expressed by the prevalent views? The answer is, it is very concerned, but the content of the concern is very different. Salvation as reconciliation responds holistically to the concerns expressed by the prevalent views. The prevalent views of Neo-Pentecostalism are concerned with here and the temporal, but salvation as reconciliation is concerned with the ultimate, the eternal.

Failure to see salvation as reconciliation makes the church irrelevant and a stench to the world. It hinders transformation of the individual and society, thereby replacing the message of salvation with messages of bondage and instilling unnecessary fear in the people. It nurtures hatred and murderous disposition toward enemies, expressed in prayers of deliverance and warfare against enemies rather than for them.

Salvation as reconciliation brings to life a divine attribute in humans, as expressed in the Bible: "Dear friends, let us love one another, for love comes from God. Everyone who loves has been born of God and knows God. Whoever does not love does not know God, because God is love" (1 John 4:7–8). This love is self-giving after the love God has for us. The act of loving is itself a sign of being God's children (1 John 4:9–12).

CHAPTER 19

INSTILL THE VICTORY OF THE CROSS

RODNEY MASONA, PHD, ZAMBIA

The title of this chapter suggests that the message of the victory of the cross is in flux, a trend that has negative consequences on those that are so misled. The message of the victory of the cross as communicated by Neo-Pentecostals and health-and-wealth-gospel adherents waters down the clear teaching of Scripture regarding the atoning work of Christ on the cross. The message of the victory of the cross needs to be communicated clearly in order for people to be saved from the deception posed by our Neo-Pentecostal and health-and-wealth-gospel friends.

COMMUNICATING THE BIBLICAL THEOLOGY OF THE CROSS

Granted that many audiences to which ministers of the gospel communicate the Word are oral rather than non-oral people, the communicator

Unless otherwise noted, Scripture quotations in this chapter are taken from the New American Standard Bible.

will do well to share the truth according to what God has communicated in His written Word.[1] Scripture is God's authoritative Word and is God's revelation of Himself and His will.[2] It follows that we understand God's revelation by studying Scripture. Our engagement in ministry tasks is dependent on our obedience to the instruction of the written Word. The importance attached to Scripture is clearly seen in the apostles, who would not neglect the ministry of the Word. They stepped aside from serving tables so that the work of ministry could be done without hindrances (Acts 6). Paul pointed out to Timothy that "all Scripture is inspired by God and profitable for teaching, for reproof, for correction, for training in righteousness; so that the man of God may be adequate, equipped for every good work" (2 Tim 3:16–17).

By communicating the victory of the cross, the believer is engaging in the ministry of the Word. The prophets and the apostles are the foundation upon which the church is built, and Christ is the Chief Cornerstone (Eph 2:20). The message of the cross is a key doctrine of the apostolic teaching that the church cannot ignore. Paul wrote, "For the word of the cross is foolishness to those who are perishing, but to us who are being saved it is the power of God" (1 Cor 1:18). God has given the speaking or communication of the rational content of the cross supernatural

---

[1] See Ned L. Mathews's excellent chapter, "The Disciplines of a Text-Driven Preacher," in *Text-Driven Preaching: God's Word at the Heart of Every Sermon*, ed. Daniel L. Akin, David L. Allen, and Ned L. Mathews (Nashville, TN: B&H Academic, 2010), 75–98, in which personal discipline in the communicator is linked to Christlikeness and teaching sound doctrine.

[2] See for example Exod 24:4; Isa 40:8; Matt 5:17–18; John 5:39; Heb 1:1–2; 4:12; 1 Pet 1:25; 2 Pet 1:19–21. For a comprehensive list of texts, see The Southern Baptist Convention's *The Baptist Faith and Message 2000* at http://www.hsbchurch.com/Misc_Images/Hsbchurch.com_misc_image49318.pdf.

power. Addressing the Galatians, the apostle Paul emphatically stated: "But may it never be that I would boast, except in the cross of our Lord Jesus Christ, through which the world has been crucified to me, and I to the world" (Gal 6:14). Peter wrote, "Grace and peace be multiplied to you in the knowledge of God and of Jesus our Lord; seeing that His divine power has granted to us everything pertaining to life and godliness, through the true knowledge of Him who called us by His own glory and excellence" (2 Pet 1:2–3). It follows therefore that right and faithful communication of Scripture is important if believers are to live lives that are true to its teaching. In other words, text-driven proclamation and teaching of Scripture leads to text-driven application of the message.[3]

To be sure, our Neo-Pentecostal and health-and-wealth-gospel friends use Scripture to back what they communicate and practice. The question is, do they handle the Word in a way that points to the authority of Scripture? The contention in this chapter is that, in general, there is some subtlety employed by Neo-Pentecostals and health-and-wealth-gospel adherents in the handling of Scripture. Those who indulge in this practice do it so as not to alarm their listeners. The very fact that Scripture is referenced at all is meant to present a common ground from which the preachers and teachers attract their audiences. This approach of communication is tantamount to the "carrot" being dangled before the consumer as bait so that their improperly interpreted message may be taken in. Proper exegetical and hermeneutical tools are not really considered or employed by those who indulge this subtlety in communicating the message of the cross.[4]

---

[3] For an excellent article on text-driven application, see Daniel Akin, "Applying a Text-Driven Sermon," in *Text-Driven Preaching*, 269–93.

[4] See for example Abraham Kuruvilla, *Privilege the Text!: A Theological Hermeneutic for Preaching* (Chicago: Moody, 2013), 23–24, 54–65, 132;

Several passages are commonly referenced when communicating the victory of the cross. Some texts would fall under the clear category. The Passion Narratives (Matt 26:36–27:66; Mark 14:32–15:47; Luke 22:39–23:56) are usually referenced in local churches, especially during Easter services. It may be noted that the theme of suffering resonates with many in the African context, perhaps as identification with suffering that has been witnessed and experienced in many communities. The wide attraction to the Passion Narratives is commendable as it gives a positive picture regarding the numerical growth of the church. However, the attraction seems to be driven by a theology that portends to be genuine when in fact it is not. This theology strongly advocates the theme of liberation, hence the title given to it of "liberation theology." True or genuine liberation, however, does not consist in release from physical bondages, as important as those are. The Lord's atoning work on the cross primarily addresses man's depravity or corruption due to sin.

One of the texts that clearly reveals truth on the impact of Christ's work of atonement is Romans 6. Paul argues that one who experiences the new life in Christ will not habitually indulge in sin since the power of sin has been broken by the cross (v. 6). Enslavement to sin is rendered null and void for the believer (v. 9). Christ Jesus is the Master who takes over the reins of the surrendered life (v. 11). The victory of Christ's death results in the displacement of reign of the old master as Christ now rules the life of the believer.

---

and David Alan Black, "Exegesis for the Text-Driven Sermon," in *Text-Driven Preaching*, 135–62.

Some texts present difficulties in interpretation in Neo-Pentecostal circles. One that is often quoted for healing is 1 Pet 2:24. It is not uncommon for the preacher or teacher to claim that the physical healing of the afflicted subject(s) depends on the "stripes" of Jesus as the text says (KJV). What is not communicated well by those who misinterpret this text is that it is a quotation of Isa 53:5. One has to properly deal with both texts if justice is to be done to the meaning of the texts. Isaiah was used by God to prophesy concerning the coming Messiah, that is, the Christ. Not only is He presented as the Suffering Servant but also as the Conquering King. Isaiah communicated that though God's judgment upon the nation of Judah was coming, there would also be His comfort and redemption. Isaiah 53 reveals God's redemption through His Servant, the Messiah. The Messiah was utterly polluted because of our transgressions. He experienced crushing because of our iniquities. The chastening or correction that brought our completeness or peace was placed upon the Servant of God, the Messiah. It is by means of His stripes or blows that we are healed.

The apostle Peter quoted Isaiah to point to the effects of the atoning work on the cross for the believers who were to exhibit God's salvation in the diaspora (1 Pet 1:1–11). In addressing how employees were to conduct themselves before their masters, Peter made reference to what Christ had done to set an example for them to follow. The servant was to remember the grace of Christ, who died to free us from the bondage to sin and to enable all beneficiaries to live righteous lives. In this case, the apostle Peter was laying emphasis on proper Christian behaviour that was expected of the servant who had experienced the saving grace of Christ. The healing from sin, effected through the atoning sacrifice of the Suffering Servant, results in proper Christian conduct.

TRUE OR FALSE TEACHERS OF THE CROSS

Other texts that Neo-Pentecostals misinterpret are 1 John 2:20, 27. First John 2:18–27 points to distinctions between false and genuine teachers of the Word. The apostle John communicated about the negative activity of the Antichrist in the last days, which he called the "last hour." Those holding to true teaching will continue to hold to truth and not abandon it like the false teachers, since they belong to the faith (vv. 18–19). The believers have the God-given ability or enablement to know and to hold the truth, which John calls the anointing (vv. 20, 27). The one who gives the anointing is the Holy One, which refers to both Jesus and the Holy Spirit. Those who oppose the truth concerning the incarnation of Christ are clearly incompatible with the apostolic message and therefore liars (vv. 21–22). The issue that our Neo-Pentecostal friends seem to emphasize is the anointing of the believer. Sadly, the teaching is taken out of context. It is not uncommon to hear that the anointing is seen in the believer who is overcome by a divine influence, resulting in things like speaking in tongues, holy laughter, spiritual insight, and so on. The text under consideration is not making reference to any such activities.

In John 14:16, the Lord Jesus made it clear to His disciples that the Holy Spirit would teach believers all things that He had taught. Believers get the ability to "know" all things through the Spirit of God as indicated in 1 John 4:2. It follows, therefore, that the anointing that believers experience concerns the ability to discern truth from error involving the person and work of Jesus Christ. Those who hold to true teaching are to be wary of those who profess to possess the "anointing" and seek to impress unsuspecting followers with miraculous powers, signs, and wonders. Time and time again, an "anointed" personality has been alleged to do things like walking on thin air, transferring funds to some individual bank accounts, raising someone from the dead, and so on—all in the name of an anointed ministry! Nothing could be further from the truth. The teaching of Scripture is clear on this matter as has been explained above.

From these few examples cited, it is clear that many so-called men of God mishandle Scripture in their purported endeavours to instill the victory of the cross of Christ. Scores of adherents to their kind of teaching and preaching are taken in "hook, line, and sinker," and their error goes on undetected until, by God's grace, the distortions of the practice are exposed. The question that goes begging is, What has "bewitched" the ears and eyes of the multitudes who follow such erroneous teachings? This question leaves one astounded when people fall victim to false teachers even though the truth about them is being made clear by God's faithful servants every day of the year. One cannot help but recall the extreme consternation the apostle Paul experienced upon learning the reality of the spiritual declension among the Christians at Galatia. The apostle laid a charge against the Galatians for deserting Christ and distorting the gospel for one that was different from the genuine one they had received (Gal 1:6–8). What are usually erroneously considered victories of the cross invariably carry a tinge of the "different gospel" in our times.

Scripture adequately gives warnings to the faithful reader concerning false teachers and their messages that have gone out into the world. The Lord Jesus pointed to such a future reality in Matt 24:4, 11. The disciples were to be wary of being misled as many will be taken in by those claiming to be Christ. Jesus indicated in Matthew 7 that faithful believers would recognize false teaching from the fruits of the false teachers. The fate of false teachers is sealed, for God will reject them and their works at the second coming of Jesus (vv. 15–23).

The apostle Paul pointed out to the Ephesian church leaders that many would come among them to teach false doctrines with the intent of drawing them away from the truth of the gospel (Acts 20:29–30). The context of this warning clearly reveals that Paul had labored among the Ephesians, nurturing them in the truth of the gospel (vv. 17–35). He could therefore declare with a clear conscience that he was innocent as far as what would befall any soul that would be misled by the false teaching among them, since they knew the truth well. This points to the importance of discipleship of the flock (the church) by the pastor with intent to ground them in the whole counsel of God (v. 27). Knowledge of sound doctrine is the biblical instruction for pastoral leaders and the flock under their care (Titus 2:1).

In 1 John 4:1–6, the apostle John gave a compound command concerning how to deal with communicators of the gospel who abuse the ministry of the Word. The first command in verse 1a prohibits the believers from believing the spirits that have gone out in the world with a false gospel. Believers who invest their lives listening to erroneous teaching end up having spiritual ill health. The second command (v. 1b) is that the believers are to test the spirits, that is, to subject teachers to scrutiny so as to ascertain whether they and their message are genuine or false. Believers are commanded to scrutinize the teachers' confession (vv. 2–3), their teaching regarding eternal life (v. 4), and their teaching regarding truth (vv. 5–6). The test is meant to either affirm the teachers and their teachings or to reject them on the basis of whom they represent.

CONCLUSION

It is clear that those who seek to be faithful to the teaching of Scripture on the cross are to be wary of doctrines that emphasize what the texts do not mean. The goal should be to arrive at the meaning of the text regarding the cross and its victory for the individual Christian and the body of believers. The faithful communicator of truth will point to what false teaching is and what the Scriptures have revealed as to how to handle those who have gone out into our communities with such teaching.

CHAPTER 20

INSTILL AN EVANGELICAL
DNA IN THE CHURCH

REUBEN ISHAYA CHUGA, PHD, NIGERIA

The term "evangelical" is derived from the Greek term *euangélion*, which means "the good news." An evangelical therefore should mean one who brings the good news of Jesus Christ, yet the term means more than that in its modern usage. Evangelicalism today is linked historically to the reform movements in Christian history, especially the sixteenth-century Reformation and the eighteenth-century Great Awakenings.

Evangelicals are thought of as those Christians who hold to the historic doctrines of the faith and, sometimes, are conservative in practice and outlook. Evangelicals are also sometimes described as Christians who are opposed to liberal Christianity. Correctly understood, evangelicals are Christians who are conservative in questions of belief and basically hold distinctive theological beliefs.

THE EVANGELICAL DNA

BIBLICAL AUTHORITY

Generally, evangelicals hold to the historical doctrines of the Christian church, especially as defined by the Protestant Reformation. Foundationally, all evangelicals hold to the authority of Scripture as the only sufficient guide in matters of faith (i.e., beliefs) and practice. This seems to be the one doctrine that determines whether one is evangelical or not. Biblical authority is ingrained in the DNA of evangelicals. The Bible is the inspired Word of God. Some evangelicals will add that it is absolutely inerrant in all respects, while others prefer the limited inerrancy view. The Scriptures, as the Word of God, must be rightly interpreted using proper theological, historical, and contextual methods. The Scriptures contain the plan of God for the salvation of fallen humanity.

THE KNOWLEDGE OF GOD

The knowledge of God is foundational to all other Christian doctrines. In fact, it is fundamental to salvation. Evangelicals follow the historic confessions of traditional orthodoxy on the doctrine of God. In view of the biblical teaching in its entirety, they hold to the Trinitarian view of God as Father, Son, and Holy Spirit, and each fully God. Each exists as a separate person with individual responsibilities within the Godhead.

Evangelicals generally believe that God has revealed Himself in two ways: through general revelation in nature and through special revelation in the Scripture and ultimately in Jesus Christ. General revelation prepares the way for special revelation, creating an awareness of God in the human mind, but is itself not salvific.

THE DOCTRINE OF CREATION

Evangelicals are united in their belief that God is Creator of all that exists and that man is His unique creation in His own image. They affirm that man was originally created innocent (Col 3:10) but through the disobedience of Adam, sin entered into the human race and is passed on to succeeding generations (Rom 5:12). Man is therefore totally depraved and corrupted, requiring God's grace for his redemption. The death of Jesus Christ on the cross was a sufficient substitute for the redemption of the entire human race (Matt 20:28; 2 Cor 5:21; 1 Tim 2:6). The atoning death of Jesus satisfied the justice of God and thereby reconciled man to God (2 Cor 5:19). The bodily resurrection of Jesus Christ affirmed His redemptive death and brought good news to all believers that they will follow in the same way (1 Cor 15:20–23). Christ ascended bodily into heaven (Acts 1:9) and will return in the same manner (Acts 1:11).

SALVATION BY GRACE

Evangelicals believe that only a personal relationship with Jesus Christ through conversion, after repentance and acceptance of Christ's atoning death, can bring salvation. Salvation comes through faith in the finished work of Jesus Christ. No human works can satisfy God's demand for salvation; it is by grace through faith in Jesus Christ alone.

Evangelicals teach strongly that salvation is by grace through faith and not works (Eph 2:8–9). The believer in Christ is declared righteous through faith alone (Rom 5:1) and reconciled to God (2 Cor 5:19). God answers the prayers of believers according to His sovereign will and plans and not according to the whims and caprices of individual worshipers.

THE CHRISTIAN LIFE

Evangelicals emphasize a life of personal discipline in conformity with the New Testament pattern. A life of simplicity, humility, and self-control is encouraged. Personal piety, love for others, prayers, study of the Bible, and fellowship with other believers in a local congregation are considered basic to New Testament Christianity.

EVANGELISM

Evangelicals have always emphasized the importance of the preaching of the Word of God to the lost world in order to win people to faith in Jesus. The preaching of the good news of salvation through faith in Jesus has been a core belief and practice of evangelicals. World evangelization, discipleship, and mission are three principal reasons for the existence of the church. The preaching and teaching of the Word of God, planting of churches, and sending of missionaries to different parts of the world have been the preoccupation of evangelicals since the beginning of the modern missionary movement.

ESCHATOLOGY

Evangelicals come with a wide range of views on eschatology. They insist that strong emphasis must be placed on the facts of Christ's return. Other details of eschatology are biblically vague and theologically peripheral.

The evangelical distinctives seen above constitute theological perspectives that are biblically rooted and seek to remain consistent with apostolic or primitive Christianity. At every historical epoch, evangelicalism seeks to find its bearing from the Scripture, the person of God as revealed in Jesus, and the fundamental practices of the primitive church. Evangelicals have always believed that the gospel of Jesus can transform people in every situation and therefore they have always placed a central stress on applying the Bible to correct social situations. They have prayed together simply and freely and teach that every believer has access to God through Jesus Christ. These define the DNA of evangelicals.

INSTILLING THE EVANGELICAL DNA

Our pluralistic world preaches tolerance and mutual respect for all shades of beliefs and practices. It also rejects dogmatism and particularity of truth and prefers relativism to anything absolute. How can evangelicals instill their DNA into members of the church?

First and foremost, we must begin by saying that the Christian faith is essentially fixed and absolute because it is truth revealed from God. God has spoken through the prophets and in these last days through his Son (Heb 1:1–2)—it is foolish not to believe this as absolute truth. God's truth is absolute truth, although our understanding of it may be limited. On matters that the Bible is clear about, we must teach strongly and hold strong views, but where the Bible is not very clear, we should teach with humility and opened minds, but with focus on principles that can be learned from the Scriptures. Truth must always be taught patiently and continuously as it is also practiced daily and consistently.

CHAPTER 21

DEVELOP BALANCED LEADERS

PROF. ELIZABETH MBURU, PHD, KENYA

The current wave of new churches in Africa has brought with it numerous problems of leadership. While the need to indigenize churches is valid, the leadership that it is creating is cause for concern. This chapter will address the issue of leadership in these largely Neo-Pentecostal churches, focusing particularly on traits that promote unbalanced, toxic leadership. Because many of these traits can be traced back to African culture and worldview, this aspect will also be discussed. However, it should be noted that not all is doom and gloom. There are many biblically sound churches in Africa.

CHARACTERISTICS OF LEADERS IN NEO-PENTECOSTAL CHURCHES

POSITIVE CHARACTERISTICS

Leaders in Neo-Pentecostal churches in Africa have several positive characteristics.[1] (1) They tend to be very missional, even establishing churches abroad in a bid to re-evangelize the world (e.g., several pastors from Nigeria and Ghana have gone global). This reverse missionary impetus is positive. (2) They emphasize the Holy Spirit and the accompanying gifts. (3) They often include women in various leadership positions. (4) They encourage the use of cultural resources in worship. (5) They emphasize experiential faith.

NEGATIVE CHARACTERISTICS

Although leaders are to be commended for these positive aspects, a number of emphases are detrimental to biblical Christianity. (1) They promote a "health and wealth," "word-faith" or even "name it and claim it" theology, which results in a wrong view of suffering and the accumulation of excessive wealth. (2) They overemphasize the miraculous gifts including healings, tongues, prophecies, and miracles with other gifts being ignored, thus impeding the healthy growth of the church. (3) They use and sell "anointed" items such as holy water, holy oil, and even clothing, believed to have power in themselves to heal, deliver, or answer

---

[1] See also J. Kwabena Asamoah-Gyadu, "Pentecostalism and the Transformation of the African Christian Landscape," in *Pentecostalism in Africa: Presence and Impact of Pneumatic Christianity in Postcolonial Societies,* ed. Martin Lindhardt (Leiden, NL: Brill, 2014), 104–5.

prayer. (4) They overemphasize spiritual warfare, which leads to a lack of genuine repentance and personal accountability for sin. (5) There is a hunger for power and an exalted reverence for their own status, resulting in the "big chief" or "great man of God" syndrome. (6) They fail to interrogate the African culture and worldview, resulting in syncretistic and/or heretical teaching.

THE WAY FORWARD

How can this trend of leadership be reversed so that balanced leaders become the norm rather than the exception? The following characteristics must be emphasized and nurtured.

SERVANT MENTALITY VERSUS "THE GREAT MAN OF GOD" SYNDROME

Issues of status, power, and position are integral to the African worldview. Those with senior positions often get recognition, and those who are "nothing" in society often struggle to get even what is theirs by right. Neglecting to refer to someone by his or her title, even in unofficial contexts, is considered disrespectful. Africans place a high value on guarding horizontal relationships with other people, and even more so with leaders. This worldview is so ingrained in the society that it is little wonder that pastors have taken on the label "great men of God."

This is not unique to Africa, as we see from an incident in the Gospel of Mark. As the disciples are headed to Capernaum, they are arguing about who among them is the greatest (Mark 9:34). This argument reveals two things. (1) They have failed to understand Jesus's identity and mission. (2) They are ignorant of the values that are the foundation of the kingdom of God. In the worldview of the kingdom, greatness has nothing to do with status, power, or position. The disciples have been participants and firsthand witnesses of Jesus's power in teaching, healings, and exorcisms, and undoubtedly assume that this is what matters. By taking a child as His model, Jesus emphasizes that the kingdom entails a reversal of expectations and often contradicts cultural expectations. Those who wish to be first must be last and the servants of all (Mark 9:34–37; cf. 10:45). Indeed, Jesus Himself demonstrated this when He washed His disciples' feet (John 13). When we realize that this task was too demeaning even for Jewish slaves, then we begin to understand what a servant mentality truly entails. This lesson seems almost counter-intuitive for most African cultures, where humility is seen as cowardice and therefore a weakness.[2] However, a true leader is one who demonstrates a servant mentality.

INTEGRITY AND ACCOUNTABILITY VERSUS UNBRIDLED POWER

Unbridled power leads to the false impression that some leaders are exempt from God's moral laws. Unfortunately, the African worldview propagates this. Although the chief was accountable to a council of elders, accountability to the ordinary people was a foreign concept. Indeed, as one scholar has noted, the word *accountability* does not exist in most African languages.[3] Most churches have no accountability structures, and

---

[2] Richard Gehman, *Learning to Lead: The Making of a Christian Leader in Africa* (Wheaton, IL: Oasis International, 2008), 88.

[3] Dwight Mutonono, *Stewards of Power: Restoring Africa's Dignity* (Carlisle, UK: HippoBooks, 2018), xi.

church splits are often because of power struggles rather than doctrinal differences. This is further exacerbated by the inherited, strong hierarchical system that generally characterizes church structure.

This worldview influences how texts that appear to protect those in authority are interpreted. For instance, 1 Sam 24:3–7 is usually used to protect the positions of men and women in authority, who are considered the "Lord's anointed."[4] Leaders demand unquestioned loyalty and any opposition is viewed as rebellion against God Himself. Followers may also fall into the trap of sycophancy, afraid to confront the leader for fear of reprisal or loss of benefits.[5] They argue that if David himself did not dare touch the Lord's anointed, who are we to question what church leaders are doing, no matter how bad? However, such an interpretation promotes abuse of power, oppression, and poor leadership. David was simply recognizing that God Himself had appointed Saul as king over Israel, and David had not received any directions from God allowing him to do whatever he liked with Saul.

Power must be handled with integrity and leaders must exercise accountability to God and to their followers. Daniel was one such leader. He was a well-educated young man from a noble family, who was taken into exile after Jerusalem was destroyed by King Nebuchadnezzar in 586/7 BC. There, he learned the language and literature of the Babylonians and eventually became the third highest ruler in Babylon (Dan 2:48; 5:29). He had tremendous power. Despite this, he exercised integrity in all he did (see for example Dan 6:6–10). As a leader, he committed himself not

---

[4] For this example see Elizabeth Mburu, *African Hermeneutics* (Carlisle, UK: HippoBooks, 2019), 42.

[5] Mutonono, *Stewards,* 99–100.

to lord it over his people, but to pray for them. He was accountable both to God and to his followers.

SELF-SACRIFICE VS. GREED

The acquisition and accumulation of wealth has become a priority for many in Africa. Whereas accumulation of wealth for personal gain was unheard of in the past, modern Africa tells a different story. The Kenyan proverb "Wisdom is better than wealth" no longer holds true in practice. Lavish homes, fancy cars, designer clothes, and so forth are avidly sought after, even at the cost of impoverishing church members. Gimmicks to generate money include prophetic "gifts," healings, and even secret knowledge about the congregants. Spiritual and physical prosperity are emphasized and the exercising of dominion over spiritual and physical territories is encouraged.[6] These leaders use religion as a tool "where *faith-power* or faith in Christ, has become a means to success that largely gets measured in terms of material gain."[7] This can also be partly attributed to the inheritance of the ATR transactional understanding of our relationship with the Supreme Being.[8]

The Gospel of Luke tells the story of a rich young ruler who intercepts Jesus with the aim of finding out how to inherit eternal life (18:18–23). The man refers to Jesus as "good teacher," which Jesus immediately refutes. Jesus's definition of good is very different from what the man

---

[6] Asamoah-Gyadu, "Pentecostalism," 110.

[7] Joseph Galgalo, *African Christianity: The Stranger Within* (Limuru, Kenya: Zapf Chancery, 2012), 87.

[8] Mburu, *African Hermeneutics,* 31.

expects. It entails sacrifice. Although the young ruler had been faithful in keeping the law, his heart and his priorities were tied to his material possessions. He could not see that giving his wealth to the poor was an act of sacrifice that would bring him closer to understanding the kingdom of God.

This lesson is a valuable one for spiritual leaders. As in our African culture, it was expected that the rich would have easy access to many places. This is not so for the kingdom of God. The love of money is a hindrance to true faith (Matt 6:19–20; 1 Tim 6:9–10; Heb 13:5–6). Moreover, when money becomes a motivation for ministry, and wealth is promoted above the message of the gospel, it makes Christ a means to the end we really want—health, wealth, and prosperity (1 Cor 9:9–12; 1 Thess 2:5; Acts 20:33–35).[9]

GOD'S PURPOSE VERSUS NEEDLESS SUFFERING

Poverty, conflict, displacement, disease, oppression—this kind of suffering is familiar to modern Africans. In the traditional African context, illnesses and accidents were generally believed to have a spiritual and not a physical cause. They were seen as punishments for moral offences. Natural disasters were also regarded as direct punishment by the Supreme Being.[10] Many still believe that suffering is a punishment for displeasing God, and retribution theology continues to define our responses to it.

---

[9] See Michael Maura et al., *Prosperity? Seeking the True Gospel* (Nairobi, Kenya: Africa Christian Textbooks, 2015), 118.

[10] John S. Mbiti, *African Religions and Philosophy*, rev. ed. (1969; repr., Nairobi, Kenya: East African Educational Publishers, 1992), 44.

However, not all African societies have the same understanding of suffering. For some, suffering is attributed to divinities, spirits, and witches or sorcerers. The health and wealth theology teaches that believers should not expect suffering in this life. Even more damaging is the teaching that suffering is either an indication that one is being punished for sin or that witchcraft is involved. This is where some pastors take advantage of their congregants. They may even use objects in the physical world with which to "protect" their congregants.

The Bible makes it clear that suffering is not always a consequence of sin and that while Satan may initiate it, God is always in control. The story of Job and of the man born blind (John 9) illustrate this truth. John Piper suggests six reasons that God allows suffering. (1) Suffering serves to deepen faith and holiness. (2) It makes our cup increase. (3) It awakens boldness in others. (4) It fills up what is lacking in Christ's afflictions. (5) It enforces the missionary command to go. (6) It magnifies the supremacy of Christ.[11] Christ Himself endured suffering (John 15:20; Matt 10:25; Acts 14:22; 1 Pet 4:12–14; 2 Tim 3:12) and told His disciples that they should consider themselves blessed when they faced persecution (Matt 5:11; Luke 6:22). God's reward also comes with suffering in the present. While we cannot always explain suffering, we can know that suffering is part of His greater purpose. This is a truth that must be taught if the health and wealth gospel is to be confronted.

---

[11] John Piper, *Let the Nations be Glad! The Supremacy of God in Missions,* 2nd ed. (Grand Rapids, MI: Baker Academic, 2003), 86–101.

BALANCED SPIRITUALITY VERSUS SYNCRETISM

Africans believe in the worldview of holism, which teaches that there is no separation of spiritual and physical reality—there is only one reality.[12] Holism is associated with the law of harmony, which encourages living at peace with the physical and spirit world. Despite the intrusion of globalization, this worldview remains very real for most Africans today. They assume that life's questions, particularly in times of crisis, generally have a spiritual answer. The activity of angels and demons is a reality, and many still believe in the power of witchcraft over their lives. Establishing communication with the spirit world and even vying for power to control this unseen realm is common.[13]

The focus on power offers a substantive explanation for the blossoming of the more Charismatic African Instituted Churches. Some leaders not only take advantage of this worldview, they integrate it into their ministries such that what results is a syncretistic blend of Christianity and ATR, with the pastor serving as a mediator to the spiritual realm where God resides. The leaders of these churches encourage believers to exercise power over the demonic realm through exorcisms and other rituals. This has led to an avoidance of personal responsibility for sin since almost everything can be blamed on the spiritual realm.

The Bible presents us with a different reality. While the spiritual realm is indeed real, not everything can be blamed on the devil. All people have personal responsibility for their sin. In his first letter, John

---

[12] Yusufu Turaki, *Foundations of African Traditional Religion and Worldview* (Nairobi: WordAlive, 2006), 32.

[13] Turaki, 35.

admonished his readers about denying their sinfulness. He labels this tendency self-deception. The correct response to sin is acknowledgement and repentance (1 John 1:8–9).

Right Teaching vs. Heresy

The misinterpretation of Scriptures is a major characteristic of Neo-Pentecostal leaders. Biblical truth is often distorted. The simplicity of this distorted gospel is attractive, for it promises relief in the *here and now* to many who are financially, socially, and physically disadvantaged. The Western concept of time as linear, with an indefinite past, a present, and an indefinite future does not exist in traditional African thought. Time is either two-dimensional (with a long past and a present, but no future) or the future is merely a continuation of the present (the potential present).[14] Rewards in the here and now are therefore a greater motivation. Little wonder that the prosperity gospel has taken Africa by such storm. For these preachers, God is a small god and Jesus is merely a means to get to material prosperity and health. They misdiagnose our greatest needs as physical, financial, and relational rather than spiritual. They empty the gospel of its power by claiming that Christ's death was primarily for our healing and prosperity in this life. They rob God of His glory by obscuring our understanding of sin, the gospel, and the sufficiency of Christ.[15] Much of this wrong preaching stems from a desire to make the Scriptures fit their theology.[16]

---

[14] J. N. K. Mugambi, *African Heritage and Contemporary Christianity* (Nairobi: Longman Kenya, 1989), 83.

[15] Maura et. al., *Prosperity?*, 3–12.

[16] See Maura et. al., 17, 19, 22, 25, 31.

In his letter, James cautions his fellow believers that not many of them should desire to hold the office of teacher since these would be subject to a stricter judgement (Jas 3:1). Since they were responsible for teaching God's Word to His people, they had a greater responsibility to uphold it (3:2). It was therefore an important role with great responsibilities. James was warning those aspiring to hold a teaching office, and even those already in such an office, against the dangers of harming the body of Christ with damaging and destructive speech, and perhaps even propagating false teaching. As Matthew points out, the consequence for falsely representing Christ is eternal rejection (Matt 7:15–23). Rather than indulging in false teaching, biblical leaders must be a prophetic voice, advocating for spiritual and moral renewal through the preaching of the right doctrine.

CONCLUSION

When Jesus called His twelve disciples, His purpose was twofold: (1) To be with Him. (2) To be co-participants with Him in His mission (Mark 3:14–15). Being with Jesus takes priority over preaching and spectacular miracles. This is the difference between "being" and "doing." Richard Gehman rightly asserts, "Ministry grows out of character, not vice versa; and character grows out of a deep and personal relationship with God."[17]

Life in traditional Africa is very relational. Indeed, the oft-repeated maxim "I am because you are, and because you are, I am" reflects this. An African understands that building relationships is a crucial part of life. This is the emphasis that Jesus makes. Unfortunately, while traditional Africa emphasizes relationships, many spiritual leaders in modern Africa

---

[17] Gehman, *Learning to Lead*, 47.

focus more on "doing" rather than "being." The emphasis in this call narrative reveals that we need to redefine leadership if the characteristics discussed above are to take root. It is not how much one does, how powerful or wealthy one is, how many followers one has, or even how spectacular one's ministry is, but rather how closely one walks with Jesus. Godly, mature, and balanced biblical leadership is about relationship and not works.

Chapter 22

Create a Vibrant Church Body

Rev. Roberto Carlos Carmona, Botswana

Instead of giving much attention to Pentecostalization, this chapter will give more importance to the main subject, "the abandoned gospel." This is because Pentecostalization is a consequence of abandoning sound doctrines in historical churches. The lack of a solid foundation was the problem for churches, and the Pentecostal view had its opportunity to take place and grow as has been seen. Therefore, since the Pentecostal movement is a result of the weaknesses of previous institutions before its upsurge, church history should be looked at as a whole to enable thoughts on the abandoning of the gospel.

Teachings about church history have always kept in mind the institutional actions that were taken under leaders of each period, often with more attention focused on their personal views, or visions, than on their obedience to the Scripture itself. No doubt these leaders' works were

Unless otherwise noted, Scripture quotations in this chapter are taken from the English Standard Version.

important and crucial to keep the gospel spreading wherever they were through their calling and love for the Word of God. However, it is clear that because of the desires of each generation, people demanded that Scripture be taught in a way that approved their own thinking rather than nurturing them. The works of some of these leaders started to match people's demands, and the truth about what the Scripture calls the body of Christ became replaced with men's thoughts instead.

History also shows that there were some revivals of the church, meaning a great movement of people toward the Lord by repentance. However, many of these converts were not guided toward others; hence, the work of those leaders of the revivals just came to an end once their hearers did not disciple others. Writers of the Bible, especially Paul, teach that a disciple must make disciples by example (1 Cor 11:1). The problem is that most people lack the desire to make disciples once it requires hard work and a living example. Another problem is that many leaders make disciples of men instead of Christ. Those who make disciples of themselves produce groups of privileged leaders who boast in their actions, have crowds under their control, and do not serve people. These kinds of groups (known by the society as churches) are anything but the body of Christ, so they tend to die or to grow without the Lord. This is the growth of dead bodies. It is found in Rev 3:1: "I know your works. You have the reputation of being alive, but you are dead." Some huge congregations, with tons of activities, shows, publicity, and a high social status, are today's Sardis churches. They seem to be vibrant, but they are not.

A CHURCH THAT IS ALIVE

Here comes the point of this work: "A Vibrant Church Body." We need to get the meaning of *vibrant*: full of life, alive. If a group of people is really full of life, then we have vibrant people. They are alive people, meaning born again people, committed to the Lord's will. The core understanding of "being born again" must fit Scripture in various texts, of which I want to share only one, John 12:24: "Truly, truly, I say to you, unless a grain of wheat falls into the earth and dies, it remains alone; but if it dies, it bears much fruit." For me this verse synthetizes the idea of the vibrant body. It is paradoxical that in order to have life, death must precede. This happens to individuals but leads to the community level: from "a grain" to "much fruit." Individuals, by His work, are collectively known as His body: "Now you are the body of Christ and individually members of it" (1 Cor 12:27). This verse clearly shows how the individual is an important part of the whole, the body of Christ.

As a result of abandoning the gospel, the current meaning of the terms "church body" and "vibrant" among Neo-Pentecostals in Africa differs deeply from what they mean biblically. Even though there were some revivals in times past, as said before, there was more regression than there were advances. We have seen churches closing their congregations and selling buildings all around the world. Another thing that happens is the moving from sound doctrinal leadership to others that match people's demands. When leaders struggle to keep members, they tend to use friendly, politically correct language; as a result, miraculous models come to life. Unbiblical strategies and actions are put in place, and the gospel is gone.

The Scriptures address the matter of leadership with clear comparison between the world and Jesus's words. Matthew 20:25–28 says:

> But Jesus called them to him and said, "You know that the rulers
> of the Gentiles lord it over them, and their great ones exercise
> authority over them. It shall not be so among you. But whoever

would be great among you must be your servant, and whoever
would be first among you must be your slave, even as the Son of
Man came not to be served but to serve, and to give his life as a
ransom for many."

Based on these words of our Master, one of the main problems of
churches in history has been the way their leadership and membership
roles are structured. Many churches are structured based on a secular
mindset of leadership, and leaders end up not being able to understand
biblically their part of the ministry. Those who are called to "equip the
saints" (Eph 4:12) for the ministry have become CEOs of institutions
and are being held accountable in terms of management results rather
than the spiritual health of the flock. Hence, church members became
clients. As customers, they have the right to make demands for their individual and community lives, and the individual is prioritized despite the
needs of others. Churches of today valorise individuals more than they
do the whole community.

DISCIPLESHIP AND A LIVING CHURCH

What can be done to prevent such things from happening? How do we
keep people in churches without the efficient strategies and models? That
is where I believe we fail. Churches have drifted far away in terms of biblical guidance about leadership and fellowship. The first step should be
to review how leadership was established and its roles defined throughout history, as well as how membership has been understood. For sure
we can find some things that will stay valuable in the restoring process,
but a sincere evaluation should be put in place in order to find the gaps
in the wall that allow escapes. The relationships between people that are

added to church membership by all means have to be guided by the Scripture. Each member has to be discipled biblically. Discipleship cannot be understood as a classroom where new believers will learn institutional principles of living.

Another of Jesus's words show an example of true discipleship:

> And Jesus came and said to them, "All authority in heaven and on earth has been given to me. Go therefore and make disciples of all nations, baptizing them in the name of the Father and of the Son and of the Holy Spirit, teaching them to observe all that I have commanded you. And behold, I am with you always, to the end of the age." (Matt 28:18–20)

Known as the Great Commission, this text brings to us some basics about the ministry itself. The nature of Jesus's commands is spiritual. Through a relationship with people as recipients of the gospel and its consequences on their new lives as believers, we build up the body of Christ. It is a spiritual work and not a social/community development work. Even though this has been part of missional work, and there is no problem with that in itself, it is not what Jesus wants His disciples to do based on the proposed Scripture. Through clear understanding of the gospel and the transformation it imposes on their lives, new believers will be led to serve the community. An effort to make them do so through institutional work will perhaps not be necessary.

How then can disciples create a vibrant church body? What should be done in order to reach this goal? The answer is to not depend on human efforts and return to the gospel. At the beginning this action will lead some people to leave the congregation, and others will get a bit lost if their mindset is built on a long-term religious system, but it will be possible to see how great our Lord is through it. The current mindset might lead us to ask: Is reducing the number of members a sign of a vibrant church body? Yes, sometimes it is, when we understand what we stated above as the meaning of a vibrant church body. The worldly mindset of church leaders says that a vibrant church is a frenetic, spirited, effervescent, fiery, sparkling movement of people in modern buildings with sumptuous stages. The Bible says that the church is a body and is alive, full of life spiritually.

> Now you are the body of Christ and individually members of it.
> (1 Cor 12:27)

> For as in Adam all die, so also in Christ shall all be made alive.
> (1 Cor 15:22)

Try to get rid of earthly desires that lead people to individuality and self-righteousness. Instead seek the will of God for His people on this matter.

Abe Huber in one of his writings says that in the church of Christ unity can be compared to a bowl of mashed potatoes.[1] One is not able to count how many potatoes were mashed unless he knows it before the action. Three kinds of churches can be found in the world: the raw potatoes church, the cooked potatoes church, and the mashed potatoes church.

The first group comprises thousands of raw potatoes, people gathered in a place that is known institutionally as a church. They are enrolled as members of this group and the leaders have great skills in administration and entertainment, so they are able to build big temples and set up very

---

[1] Abe Huber, *O Purê de Batatas* (São Paulo, Brazil: MDA Publications, 2016).

modern sound systems and all the other stuff needed to keep the show on. They hire famous preachers, singers, musicians, and efficient staff to manage everything with excellence to achieve their goal of being the biggest church in their region. Hence the world should accept it as a vibrant church of Christ. However, their growth is made by human effort instead of transformation by the gospel. Their pots (buildings) are full of potatoes (people), but they are raw and hard inside their skins. Individually they can be healthy, but they are not able to be one as Jesus said they should be. It is easy to separate one potato from the pot and keep it alone.

The second group is composed of thousands of cooked potatoes. These are the ones who gather as churches formed by people who understand the gospel but are not really following the commandments of Jesus and tend to still be individualists. They are one step toward being vibrant, but they stumble in their boasting of being like the raw-potato churches, efficient in their skilled management by professionals and having satisfied clients. They prefer to show their oneness as individuals. Even though the pot holds cooked potatoes, because of their way of working, the raw potatoes also come to join them and refuse to be cooked, and thus are unable to be mashed. They also can be separated from the pot as individuals and be kept alone. Therefore, they cannot experience the biblical sense of being a vibrant church body.

Finally, the third group is the mashed potatoes church. This group is made of people who understand the truth of being born again and the transformation they can experience by allowing the Holy Spirit to work through their lives. To be mashed they were cooked, and they did not deny going forward in the spiritual process. They allowed the cook to take their skin and to smash them into a beautiful bowl of mashed potatoes. One will not be able to see individual potatoes. They are really united in one vibrant body. They might not have famous people or highly skilled professionals to manage their community lives, but they do not fall out of the pot. They are able to know each other and work for each other, not viewing their own lives as higher so that all will experience the unity. This is what we can call a vibrant church body. It is full of spiritual life, abundant life that is shared with all. How beautiful is this church body fully united! It clearly shows the difference between union and unity.

In conclusion, there is no need to create a church body based on human efforts; what is needed is to let God make it happen. Scriptural verses that support this mashed-potatoes view of the church of Christ are as follows:

> I in them and you in me, that they may become perfectly one, so that the world may know that you sent me and loved them even as you loved me. (John 17:23)

> And they devoted themselves to the apostles' teaching and the fellowship, to the breaking of bread and the prayers. And awe came upon every soul, and many wonders and signs were being done through the apostles. And all who believed were together and had all things in common. And they were selling their possessions and belongings and distributing the proceeds to all, as any had need. And day by day, attending the temple together and breaking bread in their homes, they received their food with glad and generous hearts, praising God and having favor with all the people. And the Lord added to their number day by day those who were being saved. (Acts 2:42–47)

Jesus's prayer in John 17 was answered through the early church's actions reported in Acts 2. It is clear that the church allowed God to smash them, transforming thousands of raw potatoes into one big and beautiful pot of mashed potatoes, united by the Holy Spirit showing the power of the gospel through their new lives, leading them into a new spiritual united mindset. All because they devoted themselves to the teachings of the apostles, who were faithful to Jesus's teachings. They did not abandon the gospel. Instead, they lived it totally in its essence.

CHAPTER 23

CONSTRUCT AN APPROPRIATE CHURCH POLITY

REV. EBBY MUSIKA, ZAMBIA

The church is living in times when people experience physical and spiritual oppression that calls for redemption from the bondage and pain. The victims desperately seek answers to remedy or mitigate the pain caused by such misfortunes. On the other hand, some people have taken advantage of the desperation, and they pretend to provide solutions to the suffering masses. Most people believe in the existence of God and seek divine intervention in their afflictions, including some who look to Neo-Pentecostalism for their physical and spiritual answers.

Neo-Pentecostalism mostly offers physical elements to provide spiritual and physical healing to different life challenges, deceiving those who desperately seek immediate solutions. There is an increase in ministers of

Unless otherwise noted, Scripture quotations in this chapter are taken from the English Standard Version.

Neo-Pentecostalism taking advantage of the desperate need for help and offering false hopes to victims.

Christian churches agree that God is the ultimate authority on all matters of doctrine and faith, but there are different opinions on how and through whom God exercises authority. In this chapter, I will discuss the influence of Neo-Pentecostalism on different types of governance systems. I will not discuss which polity is better for our time in encountering the effects and influence of Neo-Pentecostalism, because I appreciate the power of unity in diversity in helping people.

The church today is faced with great challenges of Neo-Pentecostal practices and beliefs that raise many questions when compared to the biblical teaching. In Africa, it is clear that these practices and beliefs point to the influence of African Traditional Religion and mystical groups. The similarities between ministers of Neo-Pentecostalism and African Traditional Religion are clear in that they both promise to provide answers to human challenges and they supposedly derive their powers from higher spiritual authorities. On the other hand, the afflicted people are desperately looking for solutions to life challenges and move from one faith healer to another.

The influence of Neo-Pentecostalism has changed the contemporary understanding of church for many, supposing that it is a gathering where spiritual leaders perform miracles and wonders, with resistance from perceived demonic forces—power encounters. Focus has been shifted from the actual meaning: that it is a spiritual body redeemed by the blood of Jesus Christ from bondage and slavery of sin. The problem is worsened by Neo-Pentecostal misconceptions that new converts to Christianity must experience external signs to show that they have received the Holy Spirit. Attention is given to the external acts and practices of mystical powers of African Traditional Religion, which has negatively affected the church.

Over time, the church has developed several forms of governance systems or church polity. While church polity is good for administrative purposes, the debates about the influence of Neo-Pentecostal practices and beliefs have divided believers and robbed the church of its opportunity to accomplish the Great Commission given by Jesus Christ (Matt 28:18–20). Arguments and competition about believers' spiritual powers have robbed the church of the much-needed unity of purpose by the body of Christ and resulted in denominational fragments.

In this chapter I will discuss the effects and influence of Neo-Pentecostalism to help believers understand how it has affected the different forms of governance systems. The goal is to empower believers to actively participate in the extension of the kingdom of God on earth. Our study will deal with the influence of Neo-Pentecostalism on several common forms of church government.

INFLUENCE ON CHURCH POLITY

Although Neo-Pentecostalism affects all governance systems, our observation is that it has less influence upon the structures and authority of the highly structured Episcopal polity. Bishops in highly structured Episcopal polities make decisions that cannot be questioned by the flock. Meanwhile the decisions of bishops in less structured Episcopal polities can be questioned, and often result in punishment and breakaways.

The episcopal supremacy of authority to regulate the practices of Neo-Pentecostalism in highly structured episcopal churches is established at different levels of hierarchy, ranging from priests through bishops.

METHODIST

The effects of Neo-Pentecostalism on the Methodist Church has been visible because bishops have no authority of pastoral placements. As a result, the ability to monitor practices and beliefs of individual pastors and church leaders is reduced. This reduction opens doors to the negative practices of Neo–Pentecostalism, and results in breakaways by those who resist change.

ANGLICAN

The effects and influence of Neo-Pentecostalism in the Anglican Church are minimal because the archbishop of Canterbury, who is appointed by the king or queen of England, has the authority of pastoral placements. This structure guarantees supervisory powers over the structures and hierarchy of the clergy. Therefore, Neo-Pentecostalism has less influence because bishops monitor and guide the practices of the clergy, which reduces breakaways.

ROMAN CATHOLIC

The Roman Catholic Church has managed to keep Neo-Pentecostalism under control because of the authority vested in the hierarchy of superiors and bishops, who have pastoral placements and power to discipline erring clergy. The pope and his cardinals exercise unlimited authority in governing the church, such that when the pope speaks in his official capacity on matters of faith and practice, he is considered to be infallible (never wrong).

The Roman Catholic Church has managed to control the spread of Neo-Pentecostalism by allowing Charismatic movement practices similar to Pentecostalism within the confines of mainline church practices. The decision to allow Charismatic practices has reduced the negative effects of Neo-Pentecostalism and breakaways because bishops guide and closely monitor the clergy.

ORTHODOX

The Orthodox Church is one of the least affected by the influence of Neo-Pentecostalism because Orthodox churches are not highly spread in Africa. This helps bishops to easily monitor the practices of priests in the midst of African Traditional Religion and Charismatic movements.

PRESBYTERIAN

The effect of Neo-Pentecostalism upon Presbyterian polity in Africa is high. One of the reasons is the multiplicity of leaders (elders), who do not possess unquestionable authority. Presbyterian churches in Africa allow believers in local churches to exercise freedom of expression through divine guidance of the Holy Spirit in matters of doctrine and faith. Despite the presence of presbyteries and other external structures, such as historic confessions of faith, most members of local churches make decisions on how they govern themselves, without a great deal of external influence from denominational leaders. As a result, it can be difficult to control Neo–Pentecostal activities in different local churches.

CONGREGATIONAL

The effects and influences of Neo-Pentecostalism are gradually becoming high in congregational churches. The practice of soul competency allows believers in local churches to exercise freedom of expression under the divine guidance of the Holy Spirit in matters of doctrine and faith. This freedom is balanced through being interrelated to churches of like faith. The pastors exercise oversight over their congregations, and sometimes become influential. Taking advantage of local church autonomy, they can adopt Neo-Pentecostal practices due to lack of denominational hierarchy.

A closer look at a number of Baptist churches revealed that they include documentation on pure doctrinal outlines and guidance in matters of church administration. However, they say nothing about how the rising influence of Neo-Pentecostalism should be handled or regulated in order to protect believers from deception.

NON-GOVERNMENTAL

The effects of Neo-Pentecostalism are very high in churches that eliminate all forms of governance systems; they open doors to unbiblical practices and less accountability. Non-governmental churches have no consistent order of worship because they believe that the Holy Spirit guides believers in aspects of worship.

Non-governmental polity stresses inner working of the Holy Spirit, who directly exerts influence upon believers, rather than human guidance through organizations and institutional rules. The effects of Neo-Pentecostalism are worsened by the belief that the church exists on earth primarily in its invisible form, which is made up of true believers who are led by the Holy Spirit. The emphasis on personal encounters with the Holy Spirit makes it difficult for the evaluation of spirituality and takes away control measures over Neo-Pentecostal beliefs and practices.

EVALUATION OF THE INFLUENCE
ON CHURCH POLITY

Although human beings cannot control the ministry and influence of the Holy Spirit upon believers, I believe that this belief has been stretched to extremes. The most unfortunate part is the emphasis that the power of God is mostly imparted through physical elements such as anointing oil and holy water. Neo-Pentecostalism claims that anointing oil and holy water smeared or sprinkled upon afflicted body parts and possessions such as houses, motor vehicles, utensils, and anything else that a person uses will heal, restore, and protect the victim have caused unnecessary deception. There is unnecessary emphasis on these two elements administered by privileged few who claim to have a monopoly on access to God's divine power as anointed men and women of God. The claim of divine authority causes abuse by ministers who exploit unsuspecting, desperate victims of circumstances seeking physical and spiritual healing. This kind of myth is not only found among Pentecostal believers; it cuts across denominations in Africa because of extended family connections. The victims are charged high amounts of money to buy anointing oils and water, which cost far less in stores and groceries.

The other myth is that people can protect themselves from effects of demonic forces by buying anointed staffs, ranging from brooms to handkerchiefs and various types of clothing from anointed men and women of God. Unsuspecting victims are blinded to accept such myths and spend their hard-earned money buying those elements at unacceptably high prices.

These kinds of doctrinal practices are unbiblical. The apostle Paul warned against such practices, saying, "Now the Spirit expressly says that in later times some will depart from the faith by devoting themselves to deceitful spirits and teachings of demons" (1 Tim 4:1). These practices are grounded in the beliefs and practices of African Traditional Religion, which attributes every calamity to spiritual or human causes, and can only be mitigated by appeasing ancestral spirits using physical elements. This belief grows the deepest roots in African nations, which only God uproots when people genuinely accept Jesus Christ as the Lord and Saviour of their lives.

REGULATING ABUSES IN ZAMBIA

The negative influence of Neo-Pentecostalism caught the attention of the Zambian government through the Ministry of National Guidance and Religious Affairs, which has taken steps to correct such vices. The ministry has been consulting with denominational bodies to try to regulate Neo-Pentecostal practices because the government upholds the doctrine of separation between the state and the church. The ministry has been working with denominational bodies to find ways of developing a document that will guide churches and religious bodies to regulate themselves rather than being regulated by the government.

However, the influence of Neo-Pentecostalism has become so strong that some church leaders, hiding in the doctrine of "freedom of worship," are resisting the proposal to regulate unbiblical practices of Neo-Pentecostalism. Resistance against regulation is also seen in congregational churches, which believe in the autonomy of local churches, because they think that accepting regulations will infringe the freedom of worship for the church.

The belief that regulating Neo-Pentecostalism will result in infringement of believers' freedom of worship must be seriously evaluated on both sides. On one hand, it may be true that if there came another national leader, who is not aware of the process and consultations made before the regulations were completed, that may result in heavy-handed approaches and the total control of the church by the state. On the other hand, the call for self-regulation is necessary considering that most of the churches that are deeply rooted in such exploitative practices do not belong to any denominational bodies that monitor certain practices.

The question that requires our attention is, "How will self-regulation be monitored?" The duty of monitoring these practices would not be difficult for churches that are members of denominational bodies, but it will be difficult for churches that are independent. This situation may force the government to monitor and punish offenders. The church will do well to accept that there is a problem that demands its immediate response.

If we think that the churches do not need self-regulation rules, we all will be guilty of indifference. We will be pretending that there is nothing wrong with Neo-Pentecostalism, when there is evidence of abusive conduct reported by the victims in the name of church.

My conviction is that the body of Christ needs to realize that we are living during difficult times when the spiritual battle has taken a different twist. There is no physical torture and shedding of blood as seen in the first century by forces against the kingdom of God, but there is severe spiritual abuse and spiritual and psychological enslavement of both believers and unbelievers through the dictates and practices of Neo-Pentecostalism that must be reduced or brought to an end. The deception of Neo-Pentecostalism should be stopped, and innocent victims assisted to direct their attention to God, for whom nothing is impossible.[1]

---

[1] Matt 19:26; Luke 1:37.

CONCLUSION

Neo-Pentecostalism has found fertile ground in contemporary churches due to the emphasis upon individual encounters and external expressions as visible signs of Holy Spirit manifestation, which are sometimes difficult to evaluate. Some practices reveal similarities between Neo-Pentecostalism and African Traditional Religion. The practices include the expectation of followers to prophesy (especially foretelling), and making people fall down after laying hands on them. These are considered to be signs of anointing. Neo-Pentecostalism opens doors to manipulations by the demonic forces, whose acts may appear like signs of the indwelling of the Holy Spirit in the believer's life, and yet they are acts of the agents of the dark kingdom.

In this chapter, I have studied different church polities to see whether there are rules that help protect believers from the negative influence of Neo-Pentecostalism. My conclusion is that there are almost no explicitly written documents among denominations that forbid or regulate practices and beliefs of Neo-Pentecostalism.

The effects and influence of Neo-Pentecostalism have negatively impacted the Great Commission of the church (Matt 28:18–20). Believers must watch their activities and avoid all forms of confusion (1 Cor 14:33). My conviction is that Neo-Pentecostalism is a new form of African Traditional Religion, in which demonic forces disguise as angels of light while manifesting magical powers. In order to avoid the deception of Neo-Pentecostalism, believers must understand the characteristics and effects of Neo-Pentecostalism and how they influence the churches in all the different types of polity or governance systems. Therefore, we propose that churches regulate themselves according to an agreed document of self–regulation.

Chapter 24

Sensitize the Church to Neo-Pentecostalism

Jeff Singerman, PhD, DRC

Counterfeit currency and products are everywhere. Banks and businesses often display bogus bank notes in prominent areas of their establishments to reveal that they are aware of this common practice and to warn customers of counterfeits and the penalties for their use. How do we detect what is counterfeit? Authorities never thoroughly examine something that is counterfeit but instead spend their time studying and knowing in great detail the aspects of real currency. Intimately knowing real printed currency allows an agent to spot a counterfeit at a glance. The same applies to biblical truths. Studying the true biblical gospel enables us to immediately identify an aberrant or fake gospel.

Instead of overemphasizing the content of this false gospel, sensitizing the church to Neo-Pentecostalism should focus on clearly presenting biblical truths in a way that emphasizes the kingdom of God, communicates through oral methodologies, and seeks to disciple church members' worldview. As an agent studying real currency must be able to handle and examine a true-printed bill to know it, we must present the gospel in a way that allows people to effectively "hear" God's Word. In this way churches will be equipped with a clear standard that exposes deviant Neo-Pentecostal thought and practice.

PROCLAIM A KINGDOM FOCUS

When Jesus began His ministry and taught His disciples, He mentioned the kingdom of God more than one hundred times and yet only mentioned the church twice. Jesus's first sermon announced the kingdom (Mark 1:15–17), the need to repent and believe, and the invitation to follow Christ and to become fishers of men. Jesus's words set the DNA for disciples today. This DNA is to follow Christ and to fish for men. To follow Christ honors His lordship. Following and fishing are to be our identity in Christ. Following and fishing are kingdom activities.

Christ's priority is to usher in God's kingdom on earth. His teachings point people to the kingdom and kingdom living. Through the Sermon on the Mount (Matthew 5–7) Christ emphasizes principles for kingdom living. In the kingdom parables (Matthew 13) Jesus communicates the nature of the kingdom. His teachings on the Father's heart (Matthew 5–7; Mark 1) illustrate God's desire to see His kingdom established among the nations. Christ's description of and model prayer (Matt 6:5–15) characterize the lives of those living by kingdom principles as those who seek God, worship, live in anticipation of God's kingdom rule, rely on God, forgive, and desire purity.

When you place God's kingdom, which includes the activities and attributes of the kingdom, as the primary focus of your life, your thinking is changed. Kingdom principles transform your priorities. You strive to live out the "one anothers" of Scripture, putting God and others before yourself and your desires. With kingdom thinking you make the kingdom of God, and thus, the mission of God, the most important life value (Matt 6:33). Your lifestyle changes. Your spending and living habits change. Your priorities reflect God's priorities. Your passionate desire becomes pointing people to God and seeing the kingdom of God expand and grow. Further, when the kingdom takes priority in our lives we truly do for others what Christ did for us. We seek to glorify God in all we do and say. We emphasize and practice living the kingdom of God over self and self-interest, in joy, suffering, and persecution, even if it costs us our lives.

To enhance kingdom understanding, the metanarrative of the Bible must be taught in a way that hearers can receive the truths.[1] The biblical metanarrative includes creation, the fall, the life of Abraham, the establishment of Israel, the prophets, and the coming of Christ as the Messiah who is the King of the coming kingdom that will be consummated in Christ's return. In a thorough kingdom understanding we must know the King and the principles by which He lived on this earth. We must know Jesus is coming to restore His creation and establish His eternal kingdom. We must have kingdom-centered thinking to communicate kingdom practice and principles. That which is perfect needs to be well taught, well known, and well lived so that which is counterfeit can be exposed.

---

[1] The metanarrative of Scripture is also known as the grand narrative. It includes four delineations, Creation, Fall, Redemption, and Restoration. These four themes set the foundation necessary for understanding the Bible.

EMPLOY ORAL METHODOLOGIES

Evangelicals have long discussed the shallowness of Christianity on the African continent. A common remark about the African faith is that Christianity is a mile (or kilometer) wide, but only an inch (or centimeter) deep.[2] Many who claim to believe in Christ live a syncretistic faith or revert to African Traditional Religion (ATR) in difficulties and are susceptible to Neo-Pentecostal influences because of a lack of biblically grounded faith. This may be blamed, in part, on the literate methods of evangelism and discipleship used with oral preference peoples (OPP). Grant Lovejoy brings to light the type of discipleship, teaching, and preaching that needs to take place among OPP, suggesting:

> Literate missionaries need to reformulate our presentations to reflect the realities of oral communication. Some representative suggestions include learning to teach narratively instead of expositionally and learning to present the gospel narratively instead of propositionally. We need to develop discipleship approaches based on storytelling and dialog and to develop theological education and leadership training for oral communicators.[3]

Discipleship among OPP is effective when oral presentations of biblical stories are accompanied by participative Bible studies. Testimonies

---

[2] Gideon Para-Mallam, "Theological Trends in Africa: Implications for Missions and Evangelism," Lausanne World Pulse, March 2008, https://www.lausanneworldpulse.com/lausannereports/920/03-2008.

[3] Grant Lovejoy, "Chronological Bible Storying: Description, Rationale and Implications," Southwestern Baptist Theological Seminary, accessed July 16, 2017, http://reachingandteaching.org/wpcontent/uploads/sites/8/2014/06/CBS.pdf. No longer accessible.

show that church members, through participative Bible studies, have an in-depth understanding of the stories, the gospel, salvation, and their kingdom responsibility to share Christ.

Consider the effect if the world's four billion OPP are evangelized and discipled in culturally appropriate, worldview-transforming methods that enable them truly to understand God's Word, to "hear" (Rom 10:17).[4] If faith comes through hearing God's Word, and not just listening, we need to employ the presentation methodologies that best enable the hearers to hear. The literate evangelical community needs to reconsider evangelizing and discipling as they were evangelized and consider how the receptors "hear." Evangelicals need to adjust their presentations and teachings to be reproducible, contextualized, and oral for OPP.

OPP possess multi-faceted ways of communicating and receiving messages. Therefore, sharing the truths of the gospel requires an understanding of each particular OPP communication style. Effective communication results in the receptors having the ability to reproduce the message. James Slack explains, "Primary oral communicators do not understand the gospel when it is presented to them by means of expository outlines, principles, precepts, steps, and logically developed discourses. Even if they do understand, they are helpless when faced with the need to remember and reproduce what they heard."[5] Pastors and church leaders who plan to engage effectively, communicate appropriately, and disciple OPP adequately will desire the disciples to be able to

---

[4] Grant Lovejoy, "The Extent of Orality: 2012 Update," *Orality Journal* 1, no. 1 (2012): 28–29.

[5] James B. Slack Jr., J. O. Terry, and Grant Lovejoy, "Chronological Bible Storying: A Methodology for Presenting the Gospel to Oral Communicators," *Chronological Bible Storying Southwestern Baptist Theological Seminary Edition* 1 (2001): 2–33.

reproduce what they have learned to realize an evangelical movement among the target people.

A vast number of communicators center on the message to be communicated and do not spend enough time considering the receptor and his culturally prescribed methods of communicating and receiving information. The receptor's view of communication should direct the communicator's methods of evangelism, discipleship, church planting, and theological education.

Tom Steffen asserts that communicators should ask the following all-important question: What is the receptors' preferred delivery method that will enable them to understand and more importantly reproduce and share what they have been told? Steffen relates, "Messengers communicating cross-culturally often use modes of communication familiar and comfortable to them. The only problem is that these are often not familiar or comfortable for the host audience. Because we tend to teach as we were taught, our pedagogical preferences just may make the Bible one of the most poorly taught books in the world."[6] The communication model should be receptor driven. When it is not, people may not be able to internalize the gospel message and may be susceptible to aberrant beliefs because they have no firm foundation in a biblical gospel.

The use of narrative guides and generates responses among OPP. Oral people "live" the story or narrative as it is told. For narrative-oriented people, cultural beliefs are embedded in those narratives. Daniel Sheard continues this thought, stating:

Without narrative, values cannot be transmitted. In the same way that theology in the Old Testament is, for the most part,

---

[6] Tom A. Steffen, *Reconnecting God's Story to Ministry: Cross-cultural Storytelling at Home and Abroad* (La Habra, CA: Center for Organizational and Ministry Development, 1996), 122.

transmitted in the historical books through narrative, oral cultures transmit their cultural belief systems through narrative. Narrative contains theology. A missionary uses his stories to replace and displace earlier stories to re-create a theology that is biblical.[7]

Using biblical stories through narrative transmission provides OPP with a new reference, a basis for life, and allows for culture to be transformed.

Gospel communicators should bear in mind, however, that the grand narrative of the Bible, the gospel, "is not just another explanation of reality. Instead, it is the story by which all other stories are to be evaluated."[8] Narrative beings need the metanarrative of Scripture as the guide to life, beliefs, and cultural values. Christian communicators need to consider employing narrative methodologies that provide a basis for culturally appropriate communication.

Stories provide the mnemonic device upon which to attach wisdom and allow for recall even over an extended time period and will help lead people in their interaction with others.[9] OPP will often clothe a valuable "truth, teaching, or concept . . . in a story which can easily be remembered. Stories are powerful carriers and disseminators of information among literates, but more so among illiterates."[10] Stories, then, provide a key for the successful transmission of truth.

---

[7] Daniel Sheard, *An Orality Primer for Missionaries* (self-published, 2007), loc. 951, Kindle.

[8] Bruce Riley Ashford, ed., *Theology and Practice of Mission: God, the Church, and the Nation* (Nashville, TN: B&H Publishing Group, 2011), loc. 2226, Kindle.

[9] W. Jay Moon, "Understanding Oral Learners," *Teaching Theology and Religion* 15, no. 1 (January 2012): 34.

[10] Slack, Terry, and Lovejoy, "Chronological Bible Storying," 12.

DISCIPLE THE WORLDVIEW

One of the keys for discipleship, according to Randy Arnett, is to emphasize the narratives of biblical characters. Teaching biographical stories and discussing the character qualities found in these stories provides a way for group-oriented hearers to digest and internalize the story. Together, they analyze the negative and positive traits and evaluate the current practice of Christian living in light of these stories. One may also identify a current practice within a church and then discover biblical stories that may correct the aberrant practice. It is imperative that pastors, leaders, and teachers model biblical Christianity consistent with kingdom purposes. Leading disciples to know and understand the grand biblical narrative and key stories will provide church members with appropriate responses to Neo-Pentecostal practice and belief.

Discipleship that uses the participative Observation, Interpretation, and Application (OIA) Bible study format after teaching stories brings significant change and understanding to the congregants. Donald Smith insists, "Discussion produces greater change in beliefs, preferences, and attitudes than do lectures, documentary presentations, or any other passive exposure to information. Questioning to stimulate discussion develops active participation, the key to attitude change."[11] Discussing the biblical story affords the participants an opportunity to share how the story affects them. Furthermore, discussion, not a monologue, is the traditional way that oral learners resolve issues.

---

[11] Donald K. Smith, *Creating Understanding: A Handbook for Christian Communication across Cultural Landscapes* (Grand Rapids, MI: Zondervan, 1992), 139.

A pastors' institution of participative Bible studies, or OIA, in collaboration with the telling of biblical stories transforms lives and cultures. Congregants discover biblical truths through the story-study process. Pastors and teachers encourage personal application of truths encountered. Finally, the Bible study leaders require each participant to retell the story in the community as part of the accountability process. The pastors' and leaders' use of the participative Bible story process calls church members into obedience to Christ and holds them accountable to share the stories with family and community members.

Oral methodologies equip pastors with an OPP communication tool that can transform worldview. Research reveals that worldview change engenders life change. Life change affects families, church members, and the community. As this impact grows, biblical stories overtake traditional stories in the lives of the church and community. God's stories become the center upon which a kingdom life is lived, the source of wisdom, and the answer to community problems. Traditional cultural stories lose their exclusivity among the people. Individual worldview transformation can lead to community worldview transformation and provides a framework to interpret and to reject aberrant gospels that are proclaimed.

Steffen's words support the research findings. He believes that worldview change "requires the hearing and/or seeing of competing symbols and stories. To change a people group's worldview so that Christ becomes central in life requires the hearing and/or seeing of rival symbols and stories from Scripture."[12] Worldview change in OPP is possible with contextualized communication.

---

[12] Steffen, *Reconnecting God's Story*, 67.

N. T. Wright relates that the use of stories provides a way to challenge culture in a non-confrontational way. He discloses:

> Stories are, actually, peculiarly good at modifying or subverting other stories and their worldview. Where head-on attack would certainly fail, the parable hides the wisdom of the serpent behind the innocence of the dove, gaining entrance and favor which can then be used to change assumptions which the hearer would otherwise keep hidden away for safety.[13]

Church members, empowered to share the Bible through rival, non-confrontational stories, witness to people believing and turning to Christ.

Stories are particularly important as they can influence, modify, or even undermine other stories and thus, a person's worldview. Stories are a key ingredient in the development of worldview whether it is secular or biblical. Steffen relates, "Our worldviews are developed through symbol-based stories that provide meaning and memory; they are deconstructed and reconstructed through rival symbol-based stories."[14] These stories provide a window into an OPP world and allow an outsider to better understand the belief system of a particular people. Rival stories, for example, biblical stories, can then be told that can influence currently held beliefs. When a worldview is story-centered, the person needs to hear rival stories that can overtake the traditional worldview stories. Biblical stories transform worldview, and OPP need a complete transformation.

---

[13] N. T. Wright, *The New Testament and the People of God* (Minneapolis, MN: Augsburg Fortress Publishers, 1992), 40.

[14] Tom Steffen, "Story in Life, Ministry, and Academics" (paper presented at the Faculty Luncheon, Biola University, La Mirada, CA, April 9, 2014), 4, https://www.academia.edu/8401732/Story_in_Life_Ministry_and_Academics.

The various bridges and barriers of a worldview should be addressed and appropriate biblical stories chosen that speak to the belief system of the target people. In certain instances, a story or a parable told will subtly challenge and, if embraced, ultimately transform a closely held worldview. Stories and parables provide an acceptable, non-combative, and effective means to influence people's worldview and give a foundation for filtering Neo-Pentecostal practice.

CONCLUSION

Neo-Pentecostalism is a real threat to the church in Africa and beyond. Counteracting this menace requires the proclamation and lifestyle of a kingdom focus, communicating a biblical gospel with oral methodologies, and intentional discipleship of the deep worldview of believers. Consider the faith-empowerment that OPP believers acquire if they study and retain simply one Scripture story a week with its theological applications. Consider the global effect of adults, youth, and children sharing God's Word through stories with their family, friends, communities, countries, continents, and beyond. Consider the impact this would make on building the kingdom.

A Fon proverb from Benin voices, "A child that does not know his father's story is worthless and insults his father." How can one know the Word of God without knowing the Father's story? Our Father God's story must be made known in a way that communicates the biblical gospel and not a counterfeit, superficial, and ungodly Neo-Pentecostal substitute.

Conclusion

Historical Comparison Between Pre-Reformation Europe and Modern-Day Africa

Matthews Ojo, PhD, Philip W. Barnes, PhD, and R. I. Chuga, PhD

The Beginnings of Christianity in Africa

In this concluding chapter, it is necessary to take an overview of Christianity in Africa, a faith whose astonishing demographic growth has been noted since the 1970s, first by Andrew F. Walls, the famous Scottish church historian.[1] This growth has partly contributed to the challenge of maintaining

---

[1] A. F. Walls, "Africa in Christian History: Retrospect and Prospect," *Journal of African Christian Thought* 1, no. 1 (June 1998): 2–16; A. F. Walls, *The Cross-Cultural Process in Christian History* (Maryknoll, NY: Orbis Books, 2002). Also consulted for this chapter was David Peterson, ed., *The Word Became Flesh: Evangelicals and the Incarnation* (Cumbria, UK: Paternoster Press, 2003).

Unless otherwise noted, Scripture quotations in this chapter are taken from the English Standard Version.

doctrinal integrity and spiritual fervency largely because many converts lacked discipleship and could not maintain a lifestyle of holiness. Consequently, various doctrinal emphases and religious practices that in certain respects have deviated from a scriptural foundation have been propagated.

Christianity in pre-colonial Africa was largely restricted to Egypt, where the Coptic Church, with millions of members, has existed since the first century; and to Ethiopia, where the Ethiopian Orthodox Church, with a state-church status and with millions of members, traces its history to the acceptance of Christianity by the king of the ancient kingdom of Aksum in the early fourth century. Its first bishop, Frumentius, was ordained by the patriarch of Alexandria, and this provided a continuous ecclesiastical relationship between the patriarchate of Alexandria and the church in the Aksum kingdom until the modern era. From the fifteenth century to the eighteenth century, Portuguese trade voyages offered the platform for the introduction of Roman Catholicism among African groups on the coastal regions in Ghana, Nigeria, São Tomé and Príncipe, Angola and Mozambique.

Protestant Christianity was introduced in the late eighteenth century first in the colony of Freetown, Sierra Leone, and from the early nineteenth century through the activities of mission agencies from Europe and North America. The intensification of evangelicalism and social concerns in Europe throughout the eighteenth and nineteenth centuries provided the inspiration for Protestant missions in the arduous task of evangelisation of the uncharted African world. Colonialism, which was introduced by the European powers for various altruistic and commercial motives, had much impact on the growth of Christianity in many regions of Africa in the nineteenth and early twentieth centuries.

Although in certain places colonialism safeguarded the interests of Christianity by allowing missionaries to evangelize unmolested in hostile regions, in other places, such as in Northern Nigeria, it restricted the advance of Christian missions. Moreover, in southern Africa, it caused racial divisions in the church and society with lasting legacies. Indeed, in some places there were conflicts between Christian missionaries and colonial administrators over policy issues and denominational allegiances, which impacted the evangelization of indigenous peoples.[2]

GROWTH AND ITS ATTENDANT CHALLENGES

The explosive growth of Christianity in Africa occurred from the late nineteenth century to mid-twentieth century when millions of Africans shifted their religious allegiance from the various traditional religions to the Christian faith. Direct proclamation of the gospel, the establishment of Western education to nurture a future generation of Africans with new worldviews, the establishment of healthcare institutions to provide relief from the ravaging diseases of the continent, the provision of vocational training to empower converts economically and provide life-sustaining skills, the creation of literacy and translation of the Bible into indigenous languages, and the development of indigenous leadership initially by apprenticeship to Western missionaries and later by training in formal theological institutions, and so on, were some of the strategies that were used to convince Africans to leave their traditional gods and embrace a new faith and the superior material culture that accompanied it.

---

[2] For fuller details see Bengt Sundkler and Christopher Steed, *A History of the Church in Africa* (Cambridge: Cambridge University Press, 2000) and Adrian Hastings, *The Church in Africa 1450-1950* (Oxford: Oxford University Press, 1994).

Beyond the socio-economic and political reasons that aided the spread of the Christian faith in Africa, the gospel of Jesus has its own inherent power, which was amazing as it broke down cultural and religious barriers and transformed cultures and worldviews. Certainly, the ministry of Jesus Christ was accompanied with the demonstration of power to the amazement of fellow Jews (Mark 1:21–27; Luke 4:36), and this same power was demonstrated in many places in Africa as the Christian faith confronted other spiritual realities, and led to the deliverance from bondages of millions of people who eventually became Christians.

Nineteenth-century missions in Africa have largely been considered a civilizing and a humanitarian enterprise, substantially serving as stimulus of change to the nations and peoples among whom the missionaries and mission societies worked. Missionaries, as change agents, were the bearers of a whole civilization, a new religious culture, and a new social order. Of particular interest are the legacies of literacy, a product of Western education, which stimulated many social, cultural, and political transformations in Africa. In this regard, according to some scholars, missions were a substantial ally of colonization and European imperialism of the nineteenth and early twentieth centuries. In contrast, a recent discourse by Brian Stanley and others argues that Christian missions in the twentieth century have been linked to the dynamics of anticolonial nationalism and decolonization in the non-Western world.[3]

In the massive growth of Christianity, a number of stimuli in the form of indigenous revivalist movements emerged in response to the

---

[3] Brian Stanley, ed. *Missions, Nationalism, and the End of Empire* (Grand Rapids, MI: Eerdmans, 2003). See also B. Stanley, *The Bible and the Flag: Protestant Missions and British Imperialism in the Nineteenth and Twentieth Centuries* (Leicester, UK: Apollos, 1990), 85–90, 98–101.

particular socio-political milieu of the regions from the late nineteenth century. One such lasting stimulus that cuts through all the regions was Ethiopianism, a movement that brought together the agitation that promoted African cultural ideals and indigenous leadership in the Christian churches in Africa. It began in the early 1880s first in South Africa when indigenous workers among the Tembu formed their own African-led churches. Similar agitations were recorded in Nigeria and in East Africa in the same period.

African Christianity has recorded some significant revivalist movements, and each of them indirectly has expanded the frontiers of religion, resulting in numerical growth and some territorial acquisition; expanded the social influence of Christianity; and in some places eventually led Christianity to become a grassroots religion. The Aladura movements from 1918 into the 1950s was a revival that rejected nominalism, focusing on the power of God, and promoted a fervent reliance on prayers to overcome all problems of life. The Balokole revival beginning in Uganda in the 1930s spread to other parts of East Africa, where its vibrancy challenged any association with traditional religious practices, affirmed confession of sins and the new birth as radical religious experiences needed to become genuine Christians, and lastly created a new moral culture for Christians. In addition to the promotion of the centrality of the Scriptures, some revivals produced results not initially envisaged. The emphases on healing, for example, soon produced itinerant faith-healers who were establishing congregations but lacking the depth of the Scriptures.

Since the 1970s, as noted in chapter 3, the Pentecostal and Charismatic movements that initially arose as renewal movements produced a plethora of independent churches and Bible study groups. Dissatisfied with the nominalism in the existing Christian churches, they emphasized the new birth as the defining mark of a Christian. The revivalists also gave a contextualized understanding of Christian faith with emphasis on healing of diseases, and further sought to provide practical means to address some felt needs of the people.

By the middle of the twentieth century, the trajectory of the growth of the Christian faith in Africa had taken shape and one could predict the future. The national independent movement in the 1960s and 1970s further enhanced the status of Christianity, as in many countries those who were in the forefront of the independence movements had received education in mission schools and sought to enhance their political freedom with the Christian ideals of freedom and justice. However, in the massive growth of evangelical Christianity in Africa, the centre could no longer contain the bursting enthusiasm of millions of converts to Christianity. The more the number of conversions, the more the cultural baggage that was carried over into the Christian churches. This was the beginning of some of the doctrinal errors and practices that later surfaced.

From this brief historical background, it is clear that Christianity in Africa faced its greatest challenge to the integrity of the gospel in the massive growth witnessed in the twentieth century. Just like in the pre-Reformation era in sixteenth-century Europe, nominalism and superstition crept into the church as more people became Christians, largely as products of social change rather than from genuine conversion. Second, the search for healing, which became a preoccupation of some African Christian revivalist movements, led many to become victims in the hands of false prophets who exploited the ignorance of the people. Third, the credibility and integrity of the church and its leaders declined as materialism overtook genuine spirituality. Fourth, the Scriptures were interpreted to suit every kind of unwholesome doctrinal emphasis and practice largely because the scriptural foundation of the Christian faith had been eroded. Fifth, the lifestyles of many church leaders have not demonstrated righteousness and holiness; rather, the contemporary African church was promoting a lifestyle of celebrity and successful business executives for its pastors—hence, the church was being turned into an entertainment arena.

No wonder that in many African countries with majority Christian population, corruption and predatory governance overtook selfless service and democratic ideals. These are some symptoms of the ailing church in Africa, which this book partly addresses. Definitely, some leading figures of Neo-Pentecostalism have not shown much concern about the false gospel being broadcast. They are more interested in protecting their status and fame rather than responding creatively to the problems and challenges of misinterpretation of the Scriptures, which their teachings have brought about.

It is not far-fetched to make a comparison of the state of spirituality in the church in Africa from the late twentieth century with the church in sixteenth-century Europe. In the early sixteenth century, the church in Europe was afflicted by abuses and corruption as various exploitative practices were institutionalized. Indeed, the clergy were too concerned with secular pursuits, and many clerical appointments were made not on religious considerations alone.

More important, the purchase of indulgences, a practice that yielded much money for the pope, could not be defended from Scripture. The institutionalization of the sale of indulgences brought much abuse and led the church to focus more on money and material gains rather than promoting true spirituality. Consequently, the challenge of the reformers was that the root of corruption in the church was caused by doctrinal deviations, which in turn weakened the moral conscience of the church. Hence, Martin Luther, using his conversion experience that the sinner receives forgiveness by grace from God, searched the Scriptures to vehemently attack this-worldly concern.

The church in Africa is on the same trajectories of the sixteenth-century pre-Reformation church. Just as the papacy and the clergy gave false assurances of salvation on the purchase of indulgences, contemporary Neo-Pentecostal clergy have been offering a gospel that is this-worldly, that denies the sacrificial death of Christ on the cross, denies a lifestyle of holiness, and presents a "gospel" that what matters most in the life of a believer is to be successful materially. Gary S. Maxey and Peter Ozodo have argued that the church in Africa has been seduced by Satan as its attention was diverted from its scriptural foundation and fundamental purpose of transforming the society to building religious empires for self-styled apostles, bishops, and archbishops.[4] They further argued that since the late twentieth century, Neo-Pentecostalism has presented faith as the means of achieving all things in life. Hence people began seeking this-worldly concerns and jettisoning holiness as outdated.

THEOLOGICAL CONTRAST BETWEEN PROTESTANT THEOLOGY AND NP THEOLOGY: AN AFFIRMATION OF THE CENTRALITY OF THE SCRIPTURES

The prosperity "gospel" and Neo-Pentecostalism are contrary to historic orthodox Protestant theology.[5] The teaching of each of these groups represents a profound departure from the teachings of Luther, Calvin, Zwingli,

---

[4] Gary S. Maxey and Peter Ozodo, *The Seduction of the Nigerian Church* (Lagos: West Africa Theological Seminary, 2017).

[5] For the remainder of this chapter, we will use the term Neo-Pentecostalism, or NP, to refer to and represent the teachings of both of these overlapping groups.

the Anabaptists, the English Puritans, the Wesleys, and others. We will demonstrate this sharp divergence by proving that Neo-Pentecostalism (NP) teaching contradicts all of the major points of the Protestant Reformation commonly summarized under the heading known as the Five *Solas*. The Five *Solas* were a collection of teachings intended to specifically combat the false theology being promoted by the Roman Catholic Church in the sixteenth century. This body of teaching still represents orthodox biblical teaching that can be helpfully contrasted with NP teaching.

SOLA SCRIPTURA

The first of the *solas* is *sola scriptura*. *Sola scriptura* contends that the Scriptures of the Old and New Testaments alone are sufficient for mankind to know God and His plan of salvation.[6] The Bible alone is the ultimate authority for the church. Neither the pope, nor church counsels, nor creeds, nor any additional teaching from any human source holds the same authority as Scripture. Many historical and modern-day statements of faith—including the confessions held by Baptist denominations around the world—affirm that the Bible is the sole authority for doctrine and for practice.

The Reformation itself bears testimony that we must affirm not only that Scripture alone is sufficient; we must also assert that Scripture must be read, interpreted, and applied in a way that is consistent with

---

[6] There is no definitive order of the Five Solas. We believe that it is helpful to list *sola scriptura* as the first one in order to establish that all doctrine (including the other *solas*) flow out of Scripture's authority. The order that we are using here comes from Fred Zaspel, "The Five Solas: An Overview of the Reformation Solas," The Gospel Coalition, accessed 13 February 2020, www.thegospelcoalition.org/course/the-five-solas/.

how Scripture interprets and presents itself and not allow Scripture to be twisted or abused. For instance, when Luther was confronted with the idea that the pope was above the Bible he responded, "His Holiness abuses Scripture."[7] Just because someone teaches or preaches *from* the Bible does not mean that he is teaching biblically.

Nearly five hundred years later, Pastor Ken Mbugua notes, "The word of God has been twisted, both unintentionally and intentionally, and the result is a deceptive man-made message."[8] Elsewhere Pastor Costi Hinn grieves his time in the prosperity gospel movement by saying that they "twisted Scripture" and "misrepresented" Jesus.[9] Similarly, scholar Femi Adeleye writes, "In reading the Bible, our goal must be to seek what God intends us to know and understand from the text, not what we intend to find."[10] NP teachers consistently and regularly twist Scripture to fit their unbiblical teachings. In his important book *A Different Gospel,* D. R. McConnell demonstrates that NP teaching is in fact a modern-day Gnosticism, and this teaching subverts the Protestant teaching that Scripture alone is our authority for all doctrine.[11]

NP teachers violate *sola scriptura* by twisting and misreading Scripture. NP teachers also violate *sola scriptura* when they teach that

---

[7] Erwin W. Lutzer, *Rescuing the Gospel: The Story and Significance of the Reformation* (Grand Rapids, MI: Baker Book House, 2016), 51.

[8] Kenneth Mbugua, "Misunderstanding the Bible," in *Prosperity? Seeking the True Gospel* (Nairobi, Kenya: African Christian Textbooks, 2015), 15.

[9] Costi W. Hinn, *God, Greed, and the (Prosperity) Gospel* (Grand Rapids, MI: Zondervan, 2019), 142.

[10] Femi Bitrus Adeleye, *Preachers of a Different Gospel: A Pilgrim's Reflections on Contemporary Trends in Christianity* (Nairobi, Kenya: Hippo-Books, 2011), 131.

[11] D. R. McConnell, *A Different Gospel: A Historical and Biblical Analysis of the Modern Faith Movement* (Peabody, MA: Hendrickson, 1988), 103–15.

new revelation is happening all the time and that this new revelation is needed for individuals to know God and His plan—sometimes referred to as "present truth" or "new truths."[12] These new revelations are theoretically subservient to Scripture, but Doug Geivett and Holly Pivec conclude that "NAR leaders allow for new revelation that is treated on par with Scripture."[13] Geivett and Pivec's conclusion concurs with Arnett's evaluation of Neo-Pentecostalism's tacit denial of *sola scriptura*: "In practice, a word from a prophet today holds more power and appeal than an antiquated word from God in the Bible."[14]

SOLUS CHRISTUS

Jesus Christ alone is the foundation, source, and assurance of grace and salvation. The doctrine of *solus Christus* asserts that grace is not mediated by the church, nor by the sacraments, nor by any representative of the church, such as the pope. Christ alone mediates salvation to individuals.[15]

---

[12] R. Douglas Geivett and Holly Pivec, *A New Apostolic Reformation? A Biblical Response to a Worldwide Movement* (Bellingham, WA: Lexham Press, 2014), 38. Although the NAR movement is separate from the history of Pentecostalism and the prosperity gospel, we believe that the NAR movement represents one of the historical streams that has helped to create NP teaching and teachers.

[13] Geivett and Pivec, *A New Apostolic Reformation?,* 50.

[14] Arnett, *Pentecostalization,* 38 (see intro., n. 8). The word *antiquated* here does not represent Arnett's view of the Bible but rather the implicit view of the Bible held by NP teachers.

[15] Ulrich Zwingli and others helped to bring clarity to the *biblical* teaching of the Lord's Supper by showing that the Lord's Supper is a symbol and does not act outside of the faith of the participant.

NP teachers will likely not directly contradict the truth that Christ is the sole mediator between God and man. However, many NP teachers clearly imply that so-called apostles, prophets, and "men of God" have special access to God that ordinary Christians do not have.[16] One manifestation of this elevation of men to the level of Christ is the movement's prohibition against "touching the Lord's anointed."[17]

Another way that NP teaching violates the spirit of *solus Christus* is by following the false Arian teaching that Jesus was "similar" but not "the same" as God.[18] This undercutting of the biblical view of Jesus as fully God often coincides with the heretical view that men and women can become "little gods" or "little Christs" through the so-called doctrine of identification.[19] This false doctrine is deeply at odds with the Reformation truth of *solus Christus*.

SOLA GRATIA

God saves by grace alone. Nothing outside of God's free will compels Him to act in a gracious way toward sinful humanity. The truth of *sola*

---

[16] Geivett and Pivec's critique of the New Apostolic Reformation, including the assertion that the offices of apostle and prophet continue to today, clearly demonstrates that the foundation on which much of NP teaching is built is faulty and ultimately false. Geivett and Pivec, *A New Apostolic Reformation?*

[17] Hinn, *God, Greed, and the (Prosperity) Gospel,* 50.

[18] Costi W. Hinn and Anthony G. Wood, *Defining Deception* (El Cajon, CA: Southern California Seminary Press, 2018), 94. While this aspect of NP teaching is not inherently connected to the concept that Christ is the sole mediator between God and man, Arian teaching that Jesus is something less than 100% God is clearly a departure from orthodox Christianity.

[19] McConnell, *A Different Gospel,* 122.

gratia was not a new teaching brought by Luther in the sixteenth century. Rather it was a reassertion of what the Bible taught and what Augustine saw many centuries before.[20] God's free act of grace is central not just to a recovery of Reformation teaching but also to protecting the core of the gospel itself.

Neo-Pentecostalism speaks about God as being duty-bound to act in certain situations. Neo-Pentecostal preachers often say that they can manipulate situations in such a way that God *must* act in a way that accords with their wishes and whims. Some preachers in Africa will say that "God has the power, but I have the authority." They teach that God's power cannot be unleashed unless "the man of God" unlocks that power by inviting God to act. Charles Farah reports an incident in which a word of faith teacher told him, "In the Old Testament God was sovereign, but in the New Testament He committed His sovereignty to the Church. We are now in charge; His sovereignty has been entrusted to us."[21] These kinds of claims are clearly contrary to God's free act of grace. Anything (and anyone) who claims that God is compelled to act because of the actions of His creation does not understand the gospel.

SOLA FIDE

The Protestant Reformation correctly demonstrated that God acts out of His grace to save sinful humanity. The Reformation also faithfully presented the truth that the salvation process is by grace alone *through* faith alone. This teaching, of course, is merely a recovery of the New Testament

---

[20] Lutzer, *Rescuing the Gospel*, 50.

[21] Charles Farah Jr., *From the Pinnacle of the Temple: Faith or Presumption?* (Plainfield, NJ: Logos International, 1979), 148.

truth that we are saved by grace and not by works.[22] The Reformation's reemphasis on faith over works was a response to the false teaching of the Roman Catholic Church that people are saved by faith and works.

Neo-Pentecostalism also teaches that we must add to faith with our works. Unlike the biblical teaching that good works always follow saving faith, according to Neo-Pentecostal teaching, these works (which are often in the form of giving, but they can also be in the form of prayers and fasting) are a foundational part of salvation: "Like ATR, Neo-Pentecostalism promotes human efforts as an essential element in the search for well-being."[23] The practice of so-called strategic level spiritual warfare is one expression of the underlying belief that our works play a role in either our salvation or in the salvation of others.[24]

SOLI DEO GLORIA

Finally, the doctrine of *soli Deo gloria* provides a capstone for the first four *solas*: "Only if all these things are true, the sinner contributing nothing to his own salvation, can all the glory go to God."[25] The Protestant Reformation and all orthodox Christians down to today proclaim that God alone is worthy to receive glory. John Piper has influenced an entire

---

[22] Eph 2:8–9.

[23] Arnett, *Pentecostalization*, 135.

[24] See Geivett and Pivec, *A New Apostolic Reformation?*, 150–73. Strategic-level spiritual warfare is the practice of attempting to find out the name of the demon or demons charged with demonizing a given geographic area, group, or institution and then praying specifically against its demonic work. This practice is considered essential by those who promote it as an approach to missions and evangelism.

[25] Michael Reeves, *The Unquenchable Flame: Discovering the Heart of the Reformation* (Nashville, TN: B&H Academic, 2009), 106.

generation of pastors and missionaries by reminding us that God is most glorified when we are most satisfied in Him.

NP teachers often seek to rob God of His glory by seeking it for themselves. This attempt to steal God's glory is seen in many different aspects of NP preachers' lives and ministry events. For instance, when NP preachers and teachers walk onto a stage to hymns like "How Great Thou Art," they are attempting to draw attention to themselves as being "great." This attempt to steal God's glory is also seen whenever NP preachers build kingdoms for themselves by spending lavish amounts of money on cars, planes, and accommodations.[26]

A survey of the Five *Solas* has demonstrated that NP preachers and NP theology and practice are at odds with historic Protestant theology, which is rooted in Scripture and was recovered by the Reformers. There is no sense in which we can call NP theology Protestant. In fact, NP theology is not even truly Christian. It is anti-gospel and anti-truth. Nigerian author Femi Adeleye is surely correct when he wrote "that the very heart of the gospel is being corrupted."[27] So, what is to be done? The true church must rise up in Africa and call all those who bear the name of Christ to a Reformation—to a return to the faith delivered once for all time to the saints (Jude 3)!

A Call for Reformation

It is true that in the last fifty years Christianity has grown exponentially in Africa in terms of number of converts and churches, yet like the pre-Reformation decades, these are dark days for the church in Africa.

---

[26] See Costi Hinn's various accounts of this kind of lavish spending by his uncle Benny Hinn in Costi's book, *God, Greed, and the (Prosperity) Gospel.*

[27] Adeleye, *Preachers of a Different Gospel,* 2.

Anyone who desires the restoration of the church to its apostolic tradition will weep over her unfaithfulness to biblical truth, lack of theological depth, and shameful lifestyle of some preachers. The light of the church has become dimmer as its numbers increased, and this reminds one of the prophet's lament: "How the gold has grown dim, how the pure gold is changed!" (Lam 4:1). In the same way, Paul makes the exclamation: "I am astonished that you are so quickly deserting him who called you in the grace of Christ and are turning to a different gospel" (Gal 1:6).

Indeed, the situation of the church in Africa today requires a reformation. It appears as if the force of the sixteenth-century Reformation is spent and the errors that prompted the reforms have resurfaced in the church in Africa. One may say five hundred years are long enough for a strong movement to lose momentum, yet the abiding principle laid down by the Reformation remains valid and instructive for any genuine subsequent reformation. This underlying principle is that whenever the church finds itself adrift from its course, it should return to the primitive gospel of Jesus Christ as proclaimed by the apostles. The template for a genuine reformation of the church is to return to the Scriptures (one of the five *solas* of the Reformation).

Though these may be dark days for the church in Africa, these are not hopeless days because the Lord has never left Himself without a witness. In this confidence, we must all resolve to be instruments of God in reforming the church today by earnestly contending "for the faith that was once for all delivered to the saints" (Jude 3). This is possible through a threefold commitment:

a. knowing and standing firm in the gospel,
b. proclaiming the gospel faithfully, and
c. living out the gospel.

KNOWING AND STANDING FIRM IN THE GOSPEL

What is the gospel? The apostle Paul answers this question in the first letter to the Corinthian church:

> When I came to you, I did not come with eloquence or human wisdom as I proclaimed to you the testimony about God. For I resolved to know nothing while I was with you except Jesus Christ and him crucified. I came to you in weakness with great fear and trembling. My message and my preaching were not with wise and persuasive words, but with a demonstration of the Spirit's power, so that your faith might not rest on human wisdom, but on God's power. (1 Cor 2:1–5 NIV)

Here Paul identifies the gospel as revealed truth from God. It appears as foolishness and weakness in the eyes of men, but it is actually the power and wisdom of Jesus Christ.

Paul wrote to the Corinthians knowing that the city of Corinth, like the contemporary African continent, was made up of inhabitants that were proud, materialistic, immoral, corrupt, intellectually arrogant, and self-indulgent and that the gospel, which called for humility, contentment, repentance, and self-denial, was naturally repugnant to such people. Nevertheless, he resolved to preach it anyway. Towards the end of the same letter, Paul returns to the theme of the gospel:

> Now, brothers and sisters, I want to remind you of the gospel I preached to you, which you received and on which you have taken your stand. By this gospel you are saved, if you hold firmly to the word I preached to you. Otherwise, you have believed in vain. For what I received I passed on to you as of first importance: that Christ died for our sins according to the Scriptures,

that he was buried, that he was raised on the third day according to the Scriptures, and that he appeared to Cephas, and then to the Twelve. (1 Cor 15:1–5 NIV)

From these words, John Stott has gleaned six noteworthy aspects of the gospel:[28]

1. The gospel is centred on Christ. The thrust of the gospel is that "Christ died for our sins . . . (and) that he was raised." If Christ is not preached, the gospel has not been preached, and the authentic Christ is the Christ who was crucified, died, and was raised from death.

2. The gospel is biblical. The gospel that the church proclaims must be the one presented in the Scriptures of both the Old and New Testaments.

3. The gospel is historical. The events of Jesus Christ are real historical events: His birth, ministry, death, resurrection, and ascension were datable.

4. The gospel is theological. The Christ event is more than a mere historical event; His birth, life, death, and resurrection have meanings beyond any physical observations of these events. His birth for example was the incarnation of God as man; His death was for the remission of sins of the world. In other words, the gospel of Jesus must be understood or interpreted theologically.

---

[28] The following works by Stott were consulted for this chapter: John Stott, *Evangelical Truth*, 2nd ed. (Downers Grove, IL: InterVarsity Press, 2003) and John Stott, *Christ in Conflict*, rev. ed. (Downers Grove, IL: InterVarsity Press, 2013).

5. The gospel is apostolic. The gospel to be proclaimed must be that which was received and transmitted by the apostles. It should belong to the apostolic tradition to be authentic.

6. The gospel is personal. The gospel is God's way of providing salvation to all individuals who accept it by faith. Every person has to respond personally to the gospel and hold firmly to it in order to be saved.

Christianity is old and depends on the historical incarnation, life, ministry, death, and resurrection of Jesus Christ. What Jesus did and taught was unique and final. God's self-revelation was climaxed in Him. This truth has been preserved for all generations in the apostolic tradition. Our world today is suspicious of tradition and anything old and inherited; it prefers to generate its own truth and loves anything new and trending. The modern mindset hates institutionalism and anything that has a semblance of *status quo*. A new kind of gospel is being invented with a new form of entertainment church with the pastors as performing artists and entertainment celebrities. Knowing and standing firm in the old, original, and apostolic tradition is one key to reforming the church today.

PROCLAIMING THE GOSPEL FAITHFULLY

Christianity is a revealed faith. God has spoken through the prophets and in these last days through His Son (Heb 1:1–2). It is what God has revealed that the church proclaims and urges people to believe and be saved. Faithfulness in proclaiming the gospel means that the church must proclaim only what God has revealed and have the humility to admit ignorance of some truth not clearly revealed or not revealed at all.

The Scriptures teach that there are truths that God reserves to Himself and some He reveals to humanity. For example: "the secret things belong to the LORD our God, but the things that are revealed belong to us and to our children forever" (Deut 29:29); and "it is not for you to know times or seasons that the Father has fixed by his own authority" (Acts 1:7). In these verses the sum total of truth is divided into two parts: those things that belong to God and those things that God has revealed to us. The preoccupation of the church must be the proper understanding and proclamation of the revealed truth.

The church should proclaim revealed truth with conviction and confidence because it is the truth from God. Christians do not need to be doubtful or apologetic about what is clearly revealed in the Bible. The New Testament is replete with clear affirmations like "we are confident" (see the first letter of John, for example).

LIVING THE GOSPEL LIFE

Reformation cannot happen only with the church knowing and proclaiming the gospel; the church and Christians must live a life worthy of the gospel. Paul, writing to the Philippian church, said, "Only let your manner of life be worthy of the gospel of Christ, so that whether I come and see you or am absent, I may hear of you that you are standing firm in one spirit, with one mind striving side by side for the faith of the gospel" (Phil 1:27–28).

Paul's main concern here is the integrity of the gospel as it is lived in the lives of the Philippian believers. Christians today, in the same way, must conduct themselves in a manner worthy of the gospel of Jesus Christ. Their conduct must be in keeping with their calling both as citizens of their respective countries and as citizens of heaven. There should not be any dichotomy between what we profess and what we practice. In other words, what we profess and what we practice should be consistent. The Gospel that we preach must be confirmed by our conduct in society.

The reformation of the church in Africa is not only an urgent task, it is a feasible one because it is in the purpose of God. God has already made His power available. What remains is for the church to show commitment to theological truth and depth, faithfulness in proclaiming the gospel, and living a life worthy of the gospel.

Name and Subject Index

Scripture Index

Made in the USA
Columbia, SC
18 July 2021

42042362R00176